access

Civil Rights in the USA 1865–1992 for OCR

NICHOLAS FELLOWS AND MIKE WELLS

HODDER EDUCATION
AN HACHETTE UK COMPANY

Caution: several of the historical extracts and quotations in this book contain words that are vulgar and offensive.

The Publishers would like to thank the following for permission to reproduce copyright material:

Photo credits: p16 Library of Congress, LC-USZ62-15984; **p18** The Granger Collection/TopFoto; **p19** Library of Congress, LC-DIG-cwpbh-03751; **p34** World History Archive/TopFoto; **p37** TopFoto.co.uk; **p41** Kean Collection/Getty Images; **p51** Library of Congress, LC-DIG-ppmsc-01277; **p55** The Granger Collection/TopFoto; **p70** Library of Congress, LC-USZ62-119495; **p71** The Granger Collection/TopFoto; **p75** Creative Commons Attribution 3.0 Unported via Wikimedia Commons; **p86** TopFoto/ImageWorks; **p92** Paul Thompson/Topical Press Agency/Getty Images; **p92** Niday Picture Library/Alamy Stock Photo; **p117*t*** John N. Choate/MPI/Getty Images; **p117*b*** John N. Choate/MPI/Getty Images; **p127** Library of Congress, LC-DIG-hec-28781; **p132** National Anthropological Archives, Smithsonian Institution, NAA Photo Lot 75-33; **p135** https://commons.wikimedia.org/wiki/File:Bia-sit-in.jpg; **p137** GGNRA, Park Archives, GOGA-2316 77-c-353; **p138** Ralph Crane/The LIFE Picture Collection/Getty Images; **p163** The Granger Collection/TopFoto; **p173** World History Archive/TopFoto; **p175** Everett Collection Historical/Alamy Stock Photo; **p178** Library of Congress, LC-U9-23069-20; **p187** Library of Congress, LC-USZ62-99103.

Acknowledgements: Bantam, *A History of Women in America* by Carol Hymowitz and Michaela Weissman, 1978. Cambridge University Press, *The Great Depression and the Americas 1929–39* by Nick Fellows and Mike Wells, 2013. Collins, *United States 1776–1992* by Derrick Murphy, Kathryn Cooper and Mark Waldron, 2001. Heinemann, *Civil Rights in the USA 1865–1992* by David Paterson, Doug Willoughby and Susan Willoughby, 2009. Hodder Education, *Prosperity, Depression and the New Deal: The USA 1890–1954* by Peter Clements, 2008. Johns Hopkins University Press, *Black Power: Radical Politics and African American Identity* by Jeffrey O.G. Ogbar, 2005. Jonathan Cape, *The American Century* by Harold Evans, 1998. Macmillan, *New Perspectives in American History* by Wallace E. Davies, 1964. Palgrave Macmillan, *Women in the United States 1830–1945* by S.J. Kleinberg, 1999. Penguin Books, *Before the Mayflower: A History of Black America* by Lerone Bennett, 1969. Random House, *FDR's Folly: How Roosevelt and His New Deal Prolonged the Great Depression* by Jim Powell, 2003. Routledge, *Black Civil Rights in America* by Kevern Verney, 2000. Sentinel, *A Patriot's History of the United States by* Larry Scheikart and Michael Allen, 2004. W.W. Norton, *America: A Narrative History* by G.B. Tindall and David Shi, 1996; *The Feminine Mystique by* Betty Friedan, 1963.

Orders: please contact Bookpoint Ltd, 130 Milton Park, Abingdon, Oxon OX14 4SB. Telephone: +44 (0)1235 827720.
Fax: +44 (0)1235 400454. Lines are open 9.00a.m.–5.00p.m., Monday to Saturday, with a 24-hour message answering service.
Visit our website at www.hoddereducation.co.uk

First published in 2008 by
Hodder Education
An Hachette UK Company
Carmelite House, 50 Victoria Embankment
London EC4Y 0DZ

Impression number	10	9	8	7	6	5	4	3	2	1
Year	2020		2019		2018		2017		2016	

Cover photo © MPI/Hulton Archive/Getty Images
Produced, illustrated and typeset in Palatino LT Std by Gray Publishing, Tunbridge Wells
Printed and bound by CPI Group (UK) Ltd, Croydon CR0 4YY

A catalogue record for this title is available from the British Library

ISBN 978 1471867880

Contents

Dedication

Keith Randell (1943–2002)

The *Access to History* series was conceived and developed by Keith, who created a series to 'cater for students as they are, not as we might wish them to be'. He leaves a living legacy of a series that for over 20 years has provided a trusted, stimulating and well-loved accompaniment to post-16 study. Our aim with these new editions is to continue to offer students the best possible support for their studies.

Introduction

This introduction gives you an overview of the following:

★ The OCR A level course

★ How you will be assessed on this unit

★ The different features of this book and how they will aid your learning

The OCR A level course

This study will form part of your overall History course for the OCR specification, of which there are three unit groups and a topic-based essay. The unit groups comprise:

- British period study and enquiry (unit group 1)
- Non-British period study (unit group 2)
- Thematic study and historical interpretations (unit group 3).

This book has been written to support your study of the thematic study and historical interpretations unit Y319, Civil Rights in the USA 1865–1992.

This unit considers the factors that helped and hindered the development of civil rights in the USA for African Americans, trade unions, Native Americans and women. It will consider how far these groups obtained civil rights in their political, social and economic spheres, and how and why progress varied over time. In particular, it will assess the roles of the groups and the federal government in bringing about changes, as well as considering who opposed the changes and why. There is also an in-depth analysis of the three interpretation depth studies:

- Civil rights in the Gilded Age
- The New Deal and civil rights
- Malcolm X and Black Power.

How you will be assessed on this unit

Each of the three unit groups has an examination paper, whereas the topic-based essay is marked internally but externally moderated.

Unit group 1	Unit group 2	Unit group 3
The British period study is assessed through two essays from which you answer one, and the enquiry is assessed through a source-based question. This counts for 25 per cent of your overall marks	The non-British period study is assessed through a short essay and one longer essay. This counts for fifteen per cent of your overall marks	The thematic and historical interpretations are assessed through two essays which cover at least 100 years, and one in-depth question based on two interpretations of a key event, individual or issue that forms a major part of the theme. This counts for 40 per cent of your overall marks

For the topic-based essay you will complete a 3000–4000-word essay on a topic of your choice. This counts for twenty per cent of your overall marks.

Examination questions for unit group 3

You will be entered for a specific unit for your A level, and your examination paper will contain only the questions relating to that unit. There will be two sections in the examination paper. Section A is the historical interpretations and Section B is the thematic essay.

In Section A there will be two interpretations about one of the depth studies, and one question. The question will be worth 30 marks.

In Section B there will be three thematic essay questions, each worth 25 marks, and you will have to answer two of them. As this is a thematic paper the questions may be drawn from more than one key topic.

Section A questions

Section A questions will be worded as follows:

> Evaluate the interpretations in both of the passages and explain which you think is more convincing as an explanation of Y. [30]

For example:

> Evaluate the interpretations in both of the passages and explain which you think is more convincing as an explanation of the problems facing African Americans in the Gilded Age. [30]

Section B questions

Examples of questions using some of the more common command terms, and specific requirements for answering each term, can be found at the end of each chapter. The command terms are important. A key to success is understanding what these terms mean and what you have to do.

Command term	Description
Assess	Weigh up the relative importance of a range of themes and reach a supported judgement as to which is the most important across the whole period
To what extent/ how far	Consider the relative importance of the named issue or theme and weigh up its role by comparing it (comparative evaluation) with other issues or themes and reach a balanced judgement as to its relative importance across the whole period
How successful	Consider a range of issues or themes and make a judgement as to how successful each was before reaching an overall judgement about success by comparing each issue or theme

Answering the questions

The A level examination is two and half hours long. Section A carries slightly more marks than each question in Section B and, therefore, particularly as you will need time to read the interpretations, it would be sensible to spend about one hour on Section A and 45 minutes on each essay in Section B. Before you start any of the questions, make a brief plan. Advice on planning both the historical interpretations question and the thematic essay is given on pages 58 and 61.

The answers you write will be marked against the relevant mark scheme. It would be useful to familiarise yourself with these before the examination so that you are aware of the criteria against which your work will be marked. Mark schemes offer guidance, but they cannot cover everything. If you write something that is relevant and accurate, but not in the mark scheme, you will gain credit for it. You will be rewarded for well-argued and supported responses that show evidence of synthesis across the period (see page 103). Marks will not be deducted for information that is incorrect, but you should remember that incorrect knowledge may undermine your argument.

The different features of this book and how they will aid your learning

The book starts with a chronological overview of the period of history in the USA which will be explored throughout the main thematic chapters in the book. This is intended to act as a reference point that can be referred to throughout your study of the main themes.

Each main thematic chapter in the book covers one of the key topics listed in the OCR specification.

Each chapter also has a section on the three named depth studies and provides more detail and, where relevant, discussion of any historical debates about that study in relation to the theme of the chapter. The first chapter will look at the position of African Americans, the second will focus on trade unions, the third will examine the position of Native Americans, and the final chapter will look at the position of women.

At the end of the book is a timeline of the major events (pages 202–3) and suggestions for further reading.

The headings below outline the main features of each main thematic chapter.

Chapter overviews

Chapters start with a brief overview of the theme and a series of bullet points which list the main issues discussed. The structure of the chapter is outlined and a timeline lists the key dates for the events discussed in the chapter.

Chapter sections

The chapters are divided into sections, each addressing one of the bullet points listed in the overview. The section addresses a key question or questions, and is further broken down into a series of sub-headings to help your understanding of the topic. By the end of each section you should be able to answer the key question. Your understanding will be reinforced by a summary diagram for each section.

Profiles

These are brief sections detailing the life and key dates of important people in relation to the topic studied.

Key figures

Concise summaries are given of important people in relation to certain events to do with the topic studied.

Key terms

The key terms that you need to understand in order to grasp the important concepts and issues surrounding the topic are emboldened in the chapter the first time they are used in the book, and are defined in the margin and the glossary at the end of the book.

Key debates

Historians often disagree about the causes or significance of historical events and the role and impact of individuals. Key debates are listed at the start of the chapter and are discussed in the historical interpretations section at the end. Not only will this introduce you to some of the key historical debates about the period you are studying, but by using your historical knowledge and the information in the chapter you will be able to test the views of the historians, which will help you to prepare for the Section A examination question.

Chapter summaries

At the end of each chapter there is a summary of the key points covered in the chapter, which will help with revision.

Refresher questions

There will be a series of refresher questions at the end of each chapter. These will not be examination-style questions, but will be designed to ensure that you have a clear understanding of the main points and issues raised in the chapter.

Study skills

Each chapter has a study skills section. In each section one part will develop the skills needed for the thematic essay and the other part will develop the skills needed for the historical interpretations question. There will often be examples of strong and weak paragraphs and the opportunity for you to practise the skills on relevant questions and interpretations.

A chronological overview of the main periods in the USA

The era of Reconstruction 1865–77

The period after the Civil War saw a rapid growth of civil rights for African Americans as a result of the actions of Congress and in the face of opposition from the Southern states. Constitutional amendments indicated that change would be permanent. However, the problems of enforcing political rights were considerable, as the South resorted to violent opposition. By the 1870s, African American rights were being eroded by intimidation, and undermined by poor economic conditions.

Despite their contribution to the war effort on both sides, women did not receive any reward in terms of support for demands for political equality. The war increased divisions within the women's movement, and the post-war period saw a diffusion of energy into other public causes, particularly temperance.

The economy began to become more industrialised, and factories developed, but the rights of workers were limited to what they could negotiate with their employers.

For Native Americans, this period began as it would continue, with attempts by the US government to destroy their culture and lifestyle. They were increasingly driven from their lands by white westward expansion, aided by the development of the railways which cut across the Great Plains.

The Gilded Age 1875–96

This was a period of economic growth when both the state and federal governments were concerned with the social and economic impact of industrialisation and the high level of immigration. The impetus turned from reform to expansion. The South was too important as a market and as a source of raw materials for US governments to alienate, and was allowed to impose its own racial policies and restrictions on African American voting rights. Segregation was officially approved by the Supreme Court in 1896. The political gains of the post-war period were largely wiped out as African Americans' participation in political life was severely reduced.

Women continued to take an active role in public activities but there was little progress in achieving the right to vote nationally. The economic diversification and expansion did offer more opportunities in terms of jobs, and an expanding economy needed an educated workforce, so women made progress in education.

Despite the growing economy, the position of workers did not improve much, and this was not helped by the violent actions of some strikers.

The position of Native Americans continued to decline as the reservations on which the US government had forced them to live were gradually reduced in size, and then replaced by allotments, as a further attempt to assimilate them into American society. This continued to destroy their culture and communal way of life.

Empire, reform and war 1896–1920

This period is also known as the Progressive Era and reflected the response to growing industrialisation. Governments were more willing to contemplate both social and political reform. This had a particular impact on the position of women, who were given the vote nationally in 1919. The growth of temperance campaigns during the First World War helped women to be prominent in public affairs. Following increasing numbers of state decisions to give women the vote, the Nineteenth Amendment of 1920 enfranchised women. This was a huge step, but was not accompanied by changes to bring about social and economic equality.

However, very little was done for the civil rights of African Americans. The period did see the first major organisation to promote civil rights – the National Association for the Advancement of Colored People (NAACP) – although initially this was largely led by white people. Although industrial opportunities led African American workers to migrate northwards, and there were some opportunities in the armed forces, white workers and soldiers resented this progress. The revival of the white supremacist Ku Klux Klan in 1915, growing racial tensions and the policies of an avowedly segregationist president, Woodrow Wilson, culminated in the racial unrest of Red Summer in 1919.

The period saw a rapid growth in union membership but there were still industries which did not have unions.

The Native Americans had mostly lost their lands, but continued to resist assimilation, even if some were to fight on the side of American forces in the First World War.

The Roaring Twenties 1920–9

As the name suggests, this was a time of economic boom and prosperity following the First World War. Women seemed to be enjoying a greater freedom, in the form of less restricted dress, more sexual freedom and greater participation in political life. However, given the continuation of double standards, the lack of equal pay and the problems that women faced in rural communities, which did not share the prosperity, there were limitations. In many areas, birth control was frowned on and many gains made by working women in the war were lost in the return to 'normalcy'.

The social changes of the war meant that African American rights became more of a national issue than one that was purely Southern. The persistence of a high level of social repression (at its most extreme in the form of lynching) in the South showed a reluctance to accept change.

Workers gained from rising real wages, and companies often set up their own unions and introduced welfare schemes, but did not allow strikes.

In 1924, the government granted Native Americans citizenship, but this was not what they all wanted; their main concern was still to resist assimilation and preserve their traditional rights and lifestyle.

The Depression and the New Deal 1929–41

The collapse of the world's economy and the ensuing Great Depression ushered in a period of change. Under the leadership of the Democrat President Roosevelt, American women and labour unions saw their position improve, and the government showed an increased willingness to tackle social and economic problems. The lowest paid groups, including African Americans, felt the impact of the Depression most harshly. Although African Americans gained from aspects of the New Deal, there was little political interest in extending their civil rights.

Women often played a role in the New Deal administration, and the first female cabinet minister was appointed, but, in general, women workers lost out when there was greater competition for jobs. Increasingly, it was becoming clear that having the vote in itself did not mean that women were treated as equals in a social or sexual sense, or that there was economic equality.

Native Americans did benefit from some of the legislation, with some suggesting that there was a New Deal for Native Americans. However, the government still aimed to pursue a policy of assimilation. This meant that much of the legislation did not make a substantial difference.

Although this period saw high unemployment and conflict between workers and employees, significant legislation was passed that helped to improve the position of workers as their rights were increasingly recognised.

The Second World War and the Cold War 1941–60

This period witnessed considerable changes. The government's initial concern in the early 1940s was victory in the Second World War, which required it to mobilise its domestic resources. This helped to revitalise industry, which had not recovered from the Depression, and increased affluence. However, US forces remained segregated throughout the war. Black troops gained new experience and confidence in the armed forces, and a war against Nazi racism and for democracy over fascism raised issues of the need for change at home.

Civil rights groups grew; there was more mobility between South and North, and greater economic opportunity. The South, however, remained opposed to change. The 1950s, with greater prosperity and a more critical outlook, was a key time for change and the conflicts over civil rights became more acute than at any time since the 1860s and 1870s.

In terms of greater rights for women, the suburbanisation of the USA and the fear of change during the Cold War may have led to a period of reaction after the changes and opportunities of the war. The influx of women into traditionally male occupations, including the armed forces, did not lead to a sustained period of change after 1945, and women were often forced into the stereotypical role of homemaker.

Generally, the period after the war saw some significant reversals, particularly in the rights of workers, as US governments thought they had gained too much power.

The Second World War meant that there were fewer funds to help the Native Americans, and their conditions continued to decline on the reservations, to which some had returned. Although the government encouraged them to move to urban areas, conditions were little better for them there, as they were not welcome in the workforce. The government, more determined than ever to bring about total assimilation, began the policy of termination.

Reform and reaction: Kennedy, Johnson and Nixon 1960–74

Some 35 million Americans were still living below the poverty line in 1960. Improving the lives of these people became the biggest challenge for the USA, and was part of President Kennedy's 'New Frontier' and President Johnson's 'Great Society'. As a result, this period was one of significant change, with ambitious programmes of social reform. These improvements impacted on the position of workers and labour unions, so that while prosperity increased, changes in technology resulted in a decline in union power and influence.

The Republican era of the 1950s had been one of social and political conservatism, but Kennedy's election marked a change of mood. This was seen in an intensification of mass civil rights activities led by stronger organisations and new leaders such as Martin Luther King Jr. This was also seen in the development of a new form of feminism which challenged fundamental assumptions about the nature and role of women. The shock of Kennedy's assassination led to support for Civil Rights Acts passed by Johnson, which harked back to the post-Civil War period in ending segregation and protecting African American voting rights. However, by then, new demands had arisen from more radical African American leaders and a new radicalism emerged with the Black Power movement.

This was a period of great change for African Americans, and the same was true for Native Americans. The policy of termination was abandoned and government policy changed so that Native Americans gained more control over their own futures as a reform programme was begun.

Ford, Carter, Reagan and Bush 1974–92

The fall of President Nixon following the Watergate scandal created a period of uncertainty in America. The economy was depressed and, under President Reagan, the position of labour unions declined even further.

Ongoing inequality for women, African Americans and Native Americans was still evident and many issues were unresolved by 1992.

African Americans had achieved the political aims that they had been campaigning for, but a new generation found that the more fundamental problems of social and economic inequality had not been tackled. Instead of greater harmony, there was still tension with the continuing agitation by radical groups. The police brutality towards African Americans which had seemed part of an earlier era resurfaced in 1992, and is still a major problem.

The shift away from demands for change being purely political was also seen in the ongoing disputes about women's issues such as abortion, sexism and discrimination in society in general. The number of women in high-earning positions or in leadership roles in politics seemed disappointingly low given the amount of political activity and the degree of social change since 1865.

The start of the period saw previous gains made by the Native Americans continue to grow. However, a declining economic situation in the latter part of the period meant that funds for them were reduced, but at least there was finally recognition of their right to live according to their tribal culture.

How is the USA governed?

The United States of America is a republic which has a federal system of government. This means that power is shared between the central government and the governments of each of the individual states. The federal government is situated in Washington DC. The head of state is the president, who heads the executive branch. This branch is separate from the legislature, which discusses laws and has to agree to the people chosen by the president to help him rule. The third branch is the judiciary, the courts for the whole of the USA. Each state has its own executive called a governor. There are state legislatures and state courts.

There is a written constitution (a set of rules by which the country is governed). This dates from 1787 but with amendments passed since then. This sets out the role of the three branches of government.

The executive

This is headed by the president, who is elected every four years. The president is responsible for domestic policy affecting the USA as a whole and is also the commander-in-chief and responsible for defence and foreign policy. Usually, presidents have asked Congress to draft laws, but Congress can introduce laws.

A cabinet, appointed by the president and approved by Congress, but not elected directly, helps the president to govern.

The legislature

Congress is the legislature, made up of two houses:

- The House of Representatives consists of members who are directly elected. The number of congressmen or congresswomen for each state depends on the size of the state's population.
- The Senate is made up of two elected senators from each state.
- The judiciary is the courts and judges. The Supreme Court, made up of nine senior judges, is the highest court. Its judgments on cases referred to it are final. Its role is to ensure that neither the president nor Congress exceeds the powers given to them by the constitution. If the Supreme Court declares a law unconstitutional, it cannot be passed. There are federal courts throughout the country.

Political parties

The USA is now dominated by two political parties: the Republicans and the Democrats. This was not always the case, as in the nineteenth century the Populist Party emerged. However, for much of the period covered by this book you will need only to be aware of the major two parties:

- *Republicans*. They are now associated with conservative policies, a belief in big business and reduced government. However, at the start of the period they were the party of reform that freed the slaves, and its radical members aimed at promoting the rights of African Americans.

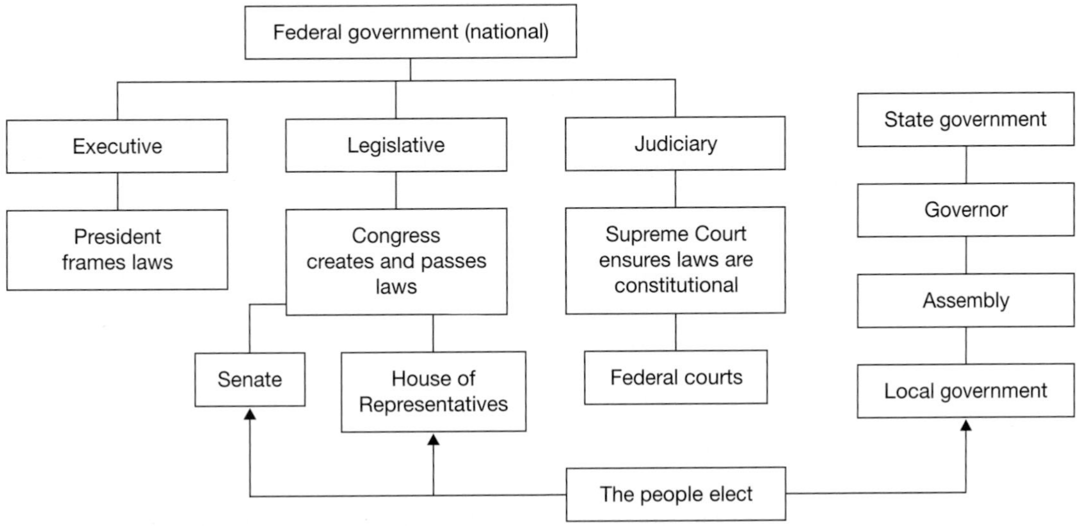

Figure 0.1 How the USA is governed.

- *Democrats*. For most of the period they were associated with progressive reform in the North, but segregation and restriction of African American rights in the South. From the 1930s, they won more support from African Americans and minorities. The major Civil Rights Acts were passed by a Republican Congress in the 1860s but by Democrat presidents in the 1960s.

Problems arise for the presidents when there is a majority from the opposing party in either of the houses in Congress. They can find it hard to pass the laws they want. Presidents can veto laws but if both houses agree with a two-thirds majority, the veto is overridden. The Supreme Court can also block laws by declaring that they are unconstitutional.

CHAPTER 1

African Americans and civil rights

After the Civil War ended in 1865, Congress took the lead in passing measures to give African Americans political rights, and several amendments to the constitution enshrined these in law. However, Southern states restricted the voting and civil rights of African Americans. Individuals worked for educational, economic and political progress, and the first major organisation to promote civil rights was founded in 1909, but segregation and discrimination were entrenched in the South. Despite changes brought about by two world wars and the New Deal of the 1930s, significant change did not emerge until the 1950s. Reforms of the 1960s restored political rights and brought legal desegregation, but social and economic inequalities persisted. This chapter will analyse the developments under the following headings:

★ The position of African Americans in 1865
★ The role of the US government in the development of civil rights
★ The role of African American individuals in the development of civil rights
★ The opposition to civil rights
★ The importance of organisations in the development of civil rights

It also considers the debates surrounding the three in-depth topics:

★ Should the Gilded Age simply be seen as a period of reaction and lack of progress in African American civil rights?
★ How much did African Americans benefit from the New Deal?
★ How far did Black Power promote the cause of African American civil rights?

Key dates

1865	Civil War ended
	Black Codes passed by interim governments in the South
1866	Civil Rights Act
1867	Congressional Reconstruction
1877	Hayes–Tilden Compromise
1890s	Increase in Jim Crow laws
1896	*Plessy* v. *Ferguson*: Supreme Court accepted 'separate but equal'
1909	National Association for the Advancement of Colored People (NAACP) founded
1933	New Deal
1942	Congress of Racial Equality (CORE) founded
1948	Desegregation of armed forces
1954	*Brown* v. *Topeka Board of Education*
1957	Montgomery Bus Boycott
1964	Civil Rights Act
1966	Black Panthers formed
1984	Jesse Jackson stood as Democratic presidential candidate
1988	Jackson's second campaign as Democratic presidential candidate

1 The position of African Americans in 1865

▶ *What was the position of African Americans in 1865?*

KEY TERMS

Amendment The USA has a fixed constitution, or set of rules, but Article 5 allows for some amendments for matters so important they cannot be dealt with by usual laws.

Freedmen People released from enslavement.

Abolitionist Member of the movement, largely in the Northern states, which saw slavery as a moral evil and socially and economically backward.

There were 4 million African American slaves in the USA at the outbreak of the Civil War in 1861. The Thirteenth **Amendment** to the constitution, signed in February 1865, a few months before the end of the Civil War, stated: 'Neither slavery nor involuntary servitude … shall exist within the United States, or any place subject to their jurisdiction'. In April 1865, with the surrender of the Confederate states, the entire South came within the Union's jurisdiction and, therefore, slaves became free. However, their new status as **freedmen** did not mean that they immediately gained the same rights as their former white owners. The war left unresolved what the position of African Americans in the US would be:

- One suggestion was that all former slaves should leave the USA, but President Lincoln had ruled this out as impracticable.
- Another idea would be to ensure that African Americans had the same rights and status as whites. This would meet formidable problems in the South, given the resentment by a defeated white population accustomed to considering African Americans in terms of being more akin to property than citizens. Even in the North, a minority of Americans saw total political and social equality between the races as undesirable.

Thus, former slaves were caught between being legally free and yet not being seen as equal. There was also the issue of quite what they were free to do, given that many had no means of making a living.

The American Civil War

The Confederate states was the name given to the Southern states which broke away from the Union in 1861 (see the map on page 15) after the election of the Republican Abraham Lincoln (see his profile on page 16). Lincoln was opposed to the further expansion of slavery and was considered a threat to slavery itself. A civil war was fought from 1861 to 1865 between the North (the Union) and the South (the Confederacy). **Abolitionists** fought hard to end slavery, eventually succeeding in 1865.

The practical solution was 'sharecropping'. Under this system, white landowners allowed former slaves to work their land in return for a considerable share of what was produced. In many cases this was not very different from slavery. While it was true that former slaves were now allowed freedom to move, to enjoy personal liberty and to no longer be separated from partners and children, they still faced considerable limitations to their liberty. African Americans suffered

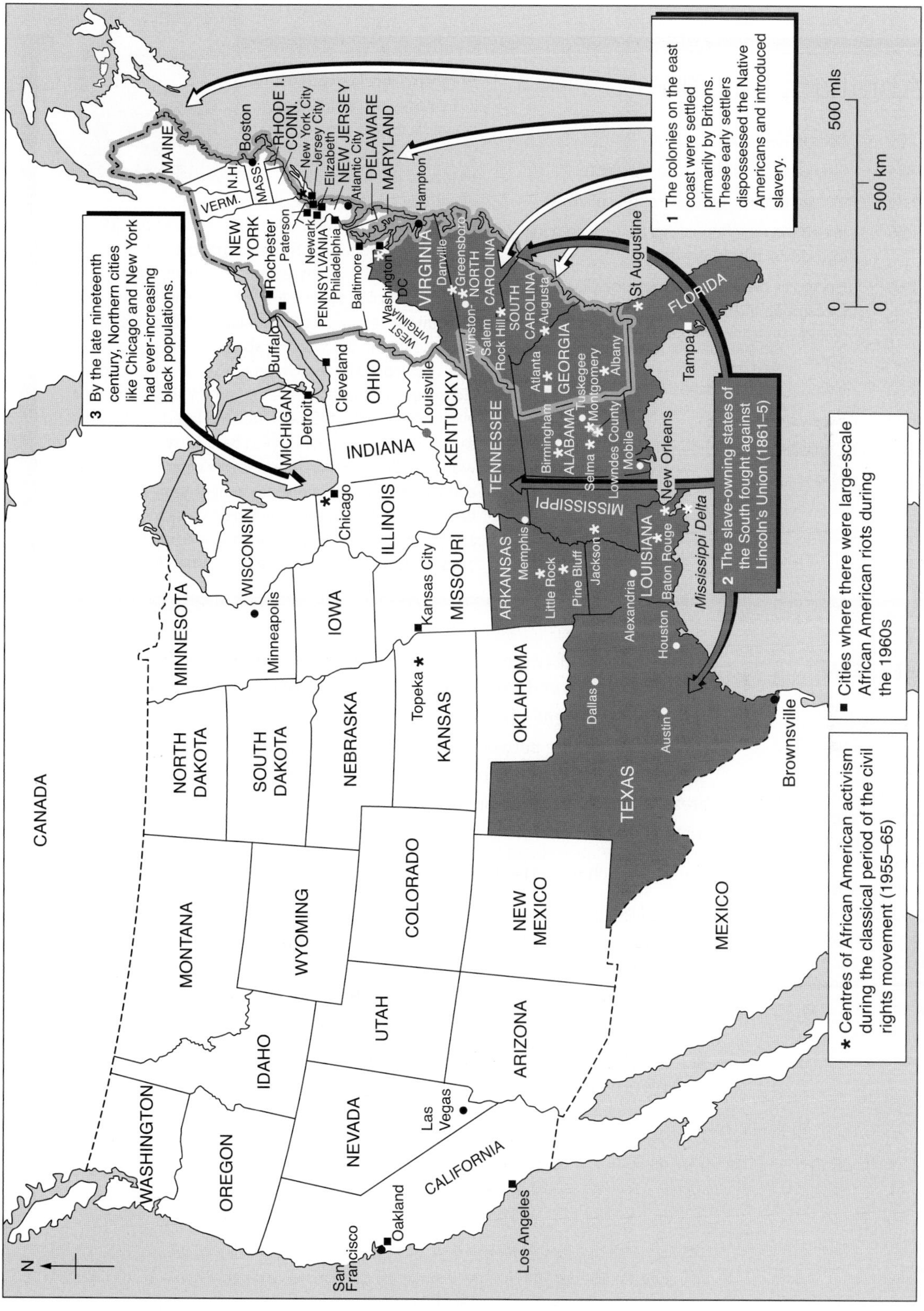

Figure 1.1 A map of African American history.

Abraham Lincoln

1809	Born in Kentucky
1834	Elected to the Illinois state legislature
1846	Elected to the House of Representatives
1856	Joined the new Republican Party. Increasingly focused on the slavery issue
1860	Elected as president in November. In December, the first Southern state seceded (withdrew) from the Union of the United States
1863	Issued the Emancipation Proclamation
1864	Re-elected president
1865	Confederacy surrendered
	Assassinated

Abraham Lincoln was born in Kentucky and worked as a lawyer in Illinois. He entered politics and served in the House of Representatives, eventually campaigning against the extension of slavery. He was elected as president in 1860 with no Southern states supporting him. His victory led to the South leaving the Union, fearing that he would abolish slavery. He led the Union in the Civil War, taking decisive action to increase the power of the state to win the war. He abolished slavery in all areas controlled by the Union in 1862 and persuaded Congress to introduce the amendment which ended it everywhere in the USA in 1865. He faced opposition to the war in the North, which he overcame, and won the 1864 election. He was a reluctant abolitionist and wanted a moderate settlement to bring the South back into the Union after the Union's victory. He was assassinated during a visit to the theatre before he could bring about the peace that he had wished for.

KEY TERM

Old South The Southern slave states of the period before the Civil War. It became a term of nostalgia, suggesting that there had been peace and harmony between owners who looked after their slaves and slaves who respected and loved their owners. That was not the reality of a system with considerable brutality and sexual exploitation.

a huge amount of violence in the aftermath of the war for any supposed lack of respect to whites and any attempts to make use of the rights given to them. Also, the amount of segregation increased markedly. The **Old South**, confident of the legal difference between black and white, did not always segregate the races socially. However, as fear of African Americans increased, particularly in some areas where they were more numerous than whites, violence and segregation intensified.

Thus, what characterised the immediate post-war period was uncertainty:

- The US government was uncertain about what to do about the problem of millions of freed slaves and about the Southern 'rebels' whom they had defeated.
- The white population was uncertain about how far to go with measures for greater equality.
- African Americans were uncertain about their role and status in post-war America and how far to press for equality.

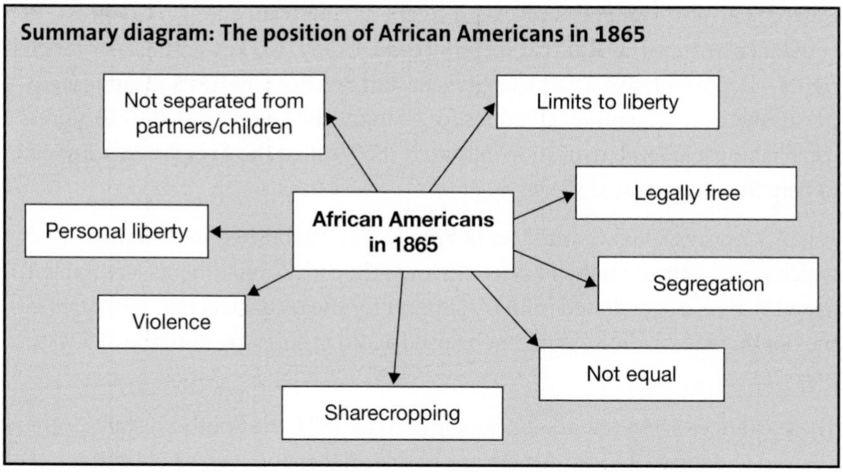

2 The role of the US government in the development of civil rights

▶ *How important was the role of the US government (federal and state) in the development of civil rights?*

In 1865, the defeated Southern states had not yet been readmitted to the Union and were under military rule. This gave Congress an unusual opportunity to take the lead in passing measures to promote civil rights, and the period known as Congressional Reconstruction led to more radical changes than during any other period before the 1960s.

Congressional Reconstruction

Vice President Johnson, who took office in April 1865 after Lincoln's assassination, aimed at a quick return to normality. Once Southerners had sworn an oath of loyalty to the Union they could elect state assemblies which would **ratify** the Thirteenth Amendment. For Johnson, the issue was the Union, not the rights of African Americans. With a sympathetic president, the new state assemblies had the confidence to pass highly discriminatory **Black Codes**, which:

- restricted the right of African Americans to compete for work with white people
- gave states the right to punish vagrants and unemployed former slaves
- gave states the right to return vagrants and unemployed former slaves to forced labour
- allowed those who attacked African Americans to go unpunished, with state officials often participating in attacks.

KEY TERMS

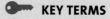

Ratify Officially approve.

Black Codes Southern states' laws to control freed slaves.

KEY TERMS

Radical Republicans
Republicans in Congress who had been active opponents of slavery. They saw the Southern slaveowners as evil exploiters and wanted radical changes to help the freed slaves. They were influential, but had limited support in the North as a whole.

Freedmen's Bureau Set up by Congress in March 1865 to care for former slaves. It provided food, shelter, hospitals and education. It set up two universities, but its 900 agents were subject to intimidation and violence by hostile white Southerners.

Even if state governments and the president did not want change, Congress could take action. The **Radical Republicans**, led by two key enthusiasts for civil rights – Representative Thaddeus Stevens and Senator Charles Sumner – were persuasive and influential advocates for change. They were helped by Congress establishing a federal institution in March 1865, called the **Freedmen's Bureau**, to help the emancipated slaves.

A Joint Congressional Committee of Fifteen was established in December 1865 which pushed through the Fourteenth and Fifteenth Amendments (see Table 1.1, page 19). It also sanctioned military support for the reconstruction measures in the South; federal force would not be used again in this way until the 1950s (see page 26).

These changes seem remarkably modern. After 1877, the Southern states were allowed to deprive African Americans of their rights and it was not until the 1960s that anything as radical was done to help them. The later Civil Rights Act of 1964 forbade racial discrimination in places of public accommodation and the Civil Rights Act of 1965 codified and put into force the Fifteenth Amendment's guarantee that no person should be denied the right to vote on account of race and colour.

A teacher and her pupils in front of a freedmen's school in North Carolina, c.1865–72.

Andrew Johnson

1808	Born in North Carolina
1843–53	Congressman
1853–7	Governor of Tennessee
1857–62	Senator
1864	Lincoln's vice president
1865–9	President
1865	Started Presidential Reconstruction
1866	Clashed with Congress over Reconstruction
1868	Survived impeachment
1875	Died

Andrew Johnson succeeded as president when Lincoln was assassinated in April 1865. A Southerner from a poor background, he was a Democrat representative for Tennessee and governor of the state and later senator in 1856. He was opposed to the abolition of slavery but was passionately for the Union and unsuccessfully opposed Tennessee joining the Confederacy. He was chosen as vice president by Lincoln in 1864. He was quick to issue pardons to Confederates in 1865 and opposed measures to help former slaves. He clashed bitterly with Congress over Reconstruction and was impeached (tried) by the Senate, surviving the trial by only one vote. He remained president with little popularity or credibility until 1869.

Table 1.1 Summary of measures passed during Reconstruction

Date	Measure	Description
9 April 1866	Civil Rights Act	All persons born in the USA were endowed with the rights of citizens: everyone should have full and equal benefit of all laws and equal subjection to penalties for breaking laws
2 March 1867	First Reconstruction Act	The eleven Confederate states were divided into five military districts. There were to be new state constitutions made by elected delegates chosen by all male citizens over the age of 21 of whatever race, colour or previous status
9 July 1868	Fourteenth Amendment	Passed in June 1866 but ratified two years later, this declared that no state could deny any person full rights as an American citizen. All had entitlement to 'due process of law' to ensure 'the equal protection of the laws and to all the rights, privileges and immunities of citizens'
3 February 1870	Fifteenth Amendment	This ensured that 'the rights of citizens … shall not be denied or abridged by any State on account of race'
31 May 1870	First Enforcement Act	This banned discrimination based on 'race, color, or previous condition of servitude'
28 February 1871	Second Enforcement Act	This overturned state laws which prevented African Americans from voting and provided for federal supervision of elections
20 April 1871	Third Enforcement Act	This was also known as the Ku Klux Klan Act (see page 40) and made it a federal offence for two or more persons to conspire to deprive citizens of their right to equal protection of the laws
1 March 1875	Civil Rights Act	All citizens were entitled to 'the full and equal enjoyment of the accommodations, advantages, facilities and privileges of inns, public conveyances, theatres or other places of public amusement'

The Congressional measures of 1866 and 1867 were passed in the teeth of opposition from the president, and a bitter dispute led to Johnson being impeached, or tried, by Congress. His successor, the Union commander Ulysses S. Grant, worked more closely with Congress, and used federal troops to support the legislation. The unity between president and Congress led to the remarkable changes of the period 1868–75.

However, attempts to settle former slaves on confiscated land and to provide some education and awareness of the rights of citizens had been met with brutal opposition since the war ended. In Memphis in May 1866, 46 African Americans were killed in race riots, and in New Orleans 35 also died. State officials and police often participated in attacking African Americans.

The effects of Congressional Reconstruction

From Table 1.2 it is clear that Reconstruction did not achieve equality, but a remarkable number of African Americans (by later standards) sat in assemblies and took part in public life. This level of voter registration and political participation was not seen again after 1877 until the 1970s.

Table 1.2 The political representation in former Confederate states after the Civil War 1867–87

State	Population in 1860	Constitutional Assembly	First Reconstruction legislature	Congressmen 1867–77
South Carolina	412,000 Black 291,000 White	76 Black 48 White	84 Black 73 White	Eight black congressmen
Mississippi	437,000 Black 353,000 White	16 Black 84 White	40 Black 75 White	Four black congressmen (including two Speakers of the House)
Louisiana	350,000 Black 357,000 White	49 Black 49 White	49 Black 88 White	Two elected but neither took seat
Florida	62,000 Black 77,000 White	18 Black 27 White	19 Black 57 White	One black congressman
North Carolina	361,000 Black 629,000 White	15 Black 118 White	19 Black 135 White	Four black congressmen
Alabama	465,000 Black 526,000 White	33 Black 90 White	18 Black 90 White	Three black congressmen
Georgia	465,000 Black 591,000 White	33 Black 137 White	32 Black 214 White	One congressman
Virginia	548,000 Black 1,000,000 White	25 Black 80 White	27 Black 154 White	One congressman

The role of federal institutions in promoting civil rights declined sharply after 1877:

- Congress did not defend the changes it had made.
- Presidents did not generally fully support civil rights.
- The Supreme Court and the state governments worked in opposite directions.

By 1877, Northern voters were tired of the issue of civil rights. The House of Representatives had a Democratic majority. The violence of white opposition to civil rights in the South had produced disorder and was affecting business. In the presidential election of 1876 there were disputed elections in South Carolina, Louisiana and Florida. The fate of the election between the Republican Rutherford Hayes and the Democrat Samuel Tilden depended on the Southern vote. In February 1877, a bargain was struck between Hayes and the representatives of South Carolina and Louisiana. They would cast their votes for Hayes, who would 'give to the people of the States of South Carolina and Louisiana the right to control their own affairs'. This compromise of 1877 ended the period of Congressional Reconstruction. The troops were withdrawn, and Southern states would be able to ignore the Reconstruction legislation.

The rights of states in the South to deal with African Americans as a local issue was restored to the position that it had been in 1865, at the time of the Black Codes. The progress towards civil rights was reversed when Congress and the president accepted the view, expressed in one Northern magazine in 1895, that 'the Negro will withdraw from the field of national politics'.

States' rights

Those who supported states' rights argued that the USA had been founded to protect liberty and if the federal government threatened that liberty, then states had a right to protest and even leave the Union. Thus, the Confederate states asserted their rights in 1861. The government claimed that states' rights did not extend to actually breaking up the USA. The issue was of major importance after the war as the South claimed that the regulation of race relations was a state right.

The role of state legislatures and governments: 'Jim Crow'

The Southern states passed a series of discriminatory measures against African Americans known as the **Jim Crow** laws. Gradually, **segregation** became legalised.

The state of Tennessee segregated rail travel in 1881, and this soon spread through the South. After 1899, there were laws segregating waiting rooms. In the first decade of the twentieth century, there were laws segregating **streetcars**. Segregation affected not only transport, but sports, hospitals, orphanages, prisons, funeral homes, cemeteries and, of course, education.

KEY TERMS

Jim Crow An accepted term for an African American, coined in a music-hall song of the 1830s, used to name discriminatory laws. The laws affected the whole way of life in the South.

Segregation The legal enforcement of division between races by laws passed by state legislatures. Hitherto, segregation had been a fact in some areas (although black and white people had often lived and worked together in the pre-war South), but it was not legalised.

Streetcars Trams.

There were attempts to designate separate residential areas, and while these did not become law because of objections by the Supreme Court, in practice it was possible to achieve areas of predominantly white and predominantly African American residence by intimidation and refusal to rent or sell. This was not confined to the South; the cities of the North also had distinct segregated areas.

Politically, the South was able to remove African American political representatives by intimidation and then by measures against voting.

Measures against voting

In theory, African Americans could vote, as a result of the changes made from 1866. But each state was free to establish its own qualifications. Southern states were able to introduce tests such as literacy tests which were deliberately intended to exclude African Americans. The most outrageous were the so-called 'grandfather' clauses, which said that if a man's family had voted before, say, 1866, then that man could vote. African Americans, of course, were excluded by this clause. Mississippi began the process of setting stringent voter registration tests in 1890 and other states followed. The 13,000 African American voters in Louisiana in 1896 had fallen to 5000 in 1900. If registration did not stop them voting then violence and intimidation could finish the job. A key element in ending the civil rights of African Americans was the lack of action taken over violence and lynching.

Lynching

The illegal killing of suspected persons by vigilante mobs was a feature of US life in the period from 1880 to the 1950s. It was not exclusively used to torture and kill African Americans accused of crimes, but there was a high proportion of black victims. It was particularly prevalent in the years of the Jim Crow laws of the 1890s and 1900s. Lynching became almost institutionalised before its decline from the mid-1930s. There was much popular support for and interest in this illegal form of local 'justice'. Many victims were innocent.

By the 1890s, on average, an African American was brutally killed every two days. Violence was common in the days of slavery; it escalated during the Civil War when African Americans fighting for the Union were often tortured and killed; it grew in the aftermath of the Civil War, and, without federal forces to suppress it, became a regular way of life well into the 1950s.

Congress had played a major role in extending civil rights whereas state governments had played a major role in restricting and weakening those rights. The next sections look at the role of the two other major elements in the constitution – the Supreme Court and the executive – as well as the various presidents and how they dealt with civil rights.

The Supreme Court

The US Supreme Court was a major element in the constitution (see page 11) and could declare legislation agreed by president and Congress to be invalid on constitutional grounds. Its decisions could have major political consequences.

The court as a barrier to civil rights

In 1883, in *United States* v. *Harris*, the Supreme Court ruled the Civil Rights Act of 1875 unconstitutional. It held that private discrimination did not fall under federal jurisdiction. In *Wilkins* v. *Mississippi* in 1898, the court declared that discriminatory voter registration laws were not unconstitutional, as there was no specific mention of race in voting qualifications. This was technically true, although it was obvious that the intention of the court was to disenfranchise African Americans.

The whole development of discrimination was given encouragement by another Supreme Court decision in 1896, *Plessy* v. *Ferguson*. Separation, it was ruled, did not imply any inferior treatment of people of different race or colour. The idea of 'separate but equal' was enshrined in a legal ruling. In practice, facilities, both public and private, were anything but equal – African American schools and homes were always of lower quality.

Plessy v. *Ferguson*

In 1890, Louisiana had passed a Jim Crow law segregating railway transport. In 1892, Homer Plessy, an African American, challenged the law and travelled in a whites-only railway carriage. Plessy was punished in the New Orleans court by Judge Ferguson and appealed to the US Supreme Court, which ruled seven to one that Louisiana was not going against the constitution by segregation. It established the legal basis for segregation laws.

The court as a promoter of civil rights

It was the gradual change in legal rulings from the positions held between 1890 and 1944 that marked a change in attitudes to civil rights. In 1944, *Smith* v. *Allwright* led to a ruling that it was unconstitutional for black voters to be excluded from **party primary voting**. However, a more radical decision in 1954 was the *Brown* v. *Topeka Board of Education* ruling that segregation was illegal.

In 1951, a group of parents, with the help of the National Association for the Advancement of Colored People (NAACP, see pages 45–6), sued the Board of Education in Topeka, Kansas, for not providing appropriate education. The leader, Oliver Brown, said that his daughter Linda had to walk a mile to a segregated school when a white school was much nearer. The District Court ruled against them, quoting *Plessy* v. *Ferguson*. The NAACP lawyer, **Thurgood Marshall**, took the case to the Supreme Court, which ruled in favour of Brown in May 1954, thus ending the legal basis for segregation by a unanimous court decision.

KEY TERM

Party primary voting
Voting for presidential candidates by registered members of the political parties. The 'primaries' precede the actual presidential elections.

KEY FIGURE

Thurgood Marshall (1908–93)
An African American Baltimore lawyer. He studied law at Howard University. From 1934, he worked for the NAACP. He was appointed an appeal judge in 1961 and in 1965 was solicitor general. In 1967, he became a Supreme Court justice, taking a liberal viewpoint on abortion and the death penalty.

This was the most significant federal intervention in civil rights since Congressional Reconstruction. Like Congressional Reconstruction, it led to violence and protests in the South. It required the use of federal armed forces to enforce and it greatly encouraged political participation by African Americans and political organisation:

- *Boynton* v. *Virginia* in 1960 confirmed that segregation on interstate (between different states) bus transportation was unconstitutional, giving rise to the Freedom Rides (see page 46).
- The court maintained the momentum of change in *Alexander* v. *Holmes County* in 1969, insisting on more rapid desegregation of schools.
- *Swann* v. *Charlotte Mecklenberg Board of Education* in 1971 approved plans for enforced desegregation by **busing** children from white suburbs into inner-city areas with more black children.
- In the case of *Griggs* v. *Duke Power Company* in 1971, the court protected African Americans from implicit discrimination by firms who insisted on high-school diploma qualifications for jobs which did not really need them. Many African Americans did not have these qualifications but were capable of doing the work, so were losing higher paid jobs to white workers.
- High points of the court's importance came in 1896, in giving legal backing to segregation, and in 1956, in giving legal backing to integration.

KEY TERM

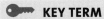

Busing The policy of ensuring that children were in mixed-race schools to help socially disadvantaged African American children, who were thought to do better in mixed-race classrooms, and to promote racial integration. It proved unpopular and controversial among whites and there were disturbances in Kentucky in 1975–6.

The role of the executive: progress 1877–1960

Where the different elements of the federal government acted together, the most progress towards civil rights was made. The most striking progress was made in the years of Reconstruction and in the period after 1963 (see pages 27–8). In the period from 1877 to 1960, however, although individual administrations did advance some elements of civil rights, there was not generally much progress.

In 1960, most of the elements of the situation of the post-1877 period remained:

- African Americans still faced barriers when registering to vote in many areas of the South.
- There was still segregation.
- There was considerable racial prejudice and outbreaks of violence against African Americans.
- Southern congressmen stood against change, as did Southern state governments and legislatures.
- There was a considerable gap between black and white people in terms of income, housing and opportunities.
- Facilities for African Americans were generally inferior to those for white Americans.
- In many areas, in both the North and South, there were distinct districts which were either 'white' or 'black'.

In terms of political participation and hopes for a more equal society, the situation by 1960 was certainly worse than in 1869.

Presidents and civil rights

The record of administrations in the period since Reconstruction had ended was not especially strong. Individual African American leaders were welcomed at the White House. Presidents spoke about the achievements of African Americans, but there was no serious challenge to the segregation of the South. Some presidents, like the otherwise progressive Woodrow Wilson (1913–21), were believers in white supremacy. The most radical of the administrations since Reconstruction was that of Franklin D. Roosevelt (1933–45) and his New Deal of the 1930s (see page 55), which included aid for both black people and white people without official discrimination.

An example of Roosevelt's aid was the creation of the Civilian Conservation Corps (CCC) in 1933 to provide work for unemployed people. The CCC had a statement that 'no discrimination should be made by account of race, color or creed'. This anticipated some of the legislation of the 1960s and 1970s (see pages 28–9). However, this was not on the initiative of the administration, but in response to a demand by a black Republican congressman, Oscar De Priest, who had been elected in 1928 for Chicago. De Priest was the single representative in Congress for 11 million African Americans; he lost his seat in 1935. African Americans benefited from New Deal legislation such as the Fair Labor Standards Act (see page 72), but as it did not cover agriculture or domestic service, many black people were excluded.

The impact of the Second World War 1939–45

The preparations for and onset of war did bring about changes. The long war against Japan and Germany from 1941 to 1945 involved intense mobilisation of US manpower and economic resources. This raised issues of equal treatment for African American workers and soldiers. Additionally, Roosevelt passed Executive Order 8587 in November 1940, which prohibited discrimination on the basis of race, colour or creed. The device of the presidential order was also used in June 1941 to prevent discrimination in the defence industries (Executive Order 8802). However, none of this legislation had as its primary objective any overall plan to increase racial equality or extend civil rights. Roosevelt came under pressure to ensure a supply of labour for defence, and was also influenced by the threat of a 100,000-strong 'March on Washington' organised by the African American labour organiser, Philip Randolph (see page 70).

There were 1,154,720 African Americans in the US armed forces from 1941 to 1945, but they fought in segregated units. In the war for freedom and democracy, racial segregation remained in the armed forces and it was not until after the war, in late 1945, that the armed forces began to be desegregated.

Desegregation

President Truman, after pressure from African American organisations, signed an executive order in 1948 against segregation in the military. Truman had appointed a committee on civil rights in 1946 and he gave a special message to Congress on 2 February 1948 requesting key elements of later civil rights legislation. Truman signed Executive Order 9981 on 26 July 1948, ending segregation in the armed forces.

Truman was praised by African American activists for his open support for civil rights, but there was still no comprehensive civil rights legislation to return the position to where it had been in the early 1870s. The Eisenhower presidency (1952–60) did not see a complete lack of progress. In 1955, yet another executive order stated the principle of equal opportunity in federal employment. Eisenhower was against ending the 'separate but equal' principle but nevertheless gave federal support for the desegregation of schools.

In 1957, a Civil Rights Act became law. African Americans' right to vote was set down in law. The Justice Department now had a Civil Rights Department. The attorney general was given powers to intervene where rights were threatened. However, in the South there were still cases where African American rights were infringed, and local juries did not enforce the law. This Act and a subsequent one in 1960 did not add substantial numbers of African American voters. By 1960, only 28 per cent of Southern African Americans of voting age were registered to vote.

Why was there such limited progress?

- The issue of civil rights was peripheral in comparison with the other issues facing the USA in the period. The prolonged Depression of the 1930s, followed by the Second World War and then the **Cold War**, distracted administrations from difficult and contentious racial issues.
- The influence of the Southern Democratic senators and representatives presented a barrier to passing effective civil rights legislation – bills failed in 1938, 1946, 1948 and 1950.
- There was limited electoral support for civil rights given that so many African Americans could not vote, and the issue was not a popular one in the North until the 1960s.
- Civil rights action would have meant a great deal of intervention in the South, where racism had become firmly established and supported by state and local governments. Presidents faced a revival of civil war hatreds and issues of states rights.
- In the North, the influx of large numbers of African Americans from 1915 had made racial hatred common and made the whole issue of civil rights go beyond dealing with 'backward' Southern attitudes.
- The liberalisation involved in civil rights legislation opened administrations to the charge of being 'Communist' or subverting tradition.
- Even a conservative Southerner such as Truman, who shared many of the prejudices of the South, was bitterly criticised by conservative Democrats for expressing concerns about civil rights and condemning lynching and violence.

KEY TERM

Cold War After 1945, the USA clashed more and more with the Communist USSR and the countries it controlled in eastern Europe and its allies (the so-called 'Communist bloc'). There were two different world views. The USA supported parliamentary democracy and economic freedom, the so-called 'capitalist' free-market system. The Communists had a one-party state, dominated by a dictatorial leader, which controlled economic life through nationalised industry and agriculture. The Cold War lasted until the fall of the USSR after 1989.

What had changed by the 1960s?

- The continuing violence and discrimination of the South had given ammunition to the Communist bloc in the Cold War who saw the USA as merely defending a rotten capitalist system.
- Better communications, especially the spread of television sets, brought racial violence home to Americans nationally.
- The murder of a fourteen-year-old African American, Emmet Till, from Chicago, by two men in Mississippi in August 1955, and the acquittal of his killers by an all-white jury after an hour's deliberation, shocked the USA. Till's crime was that he had talked 'fresh' to a white woman.
- Pictures of Southern mobs abusing a black schoolgirl at Little Rock in 1957 (see the box below) were dangerously bad for the image of the USA.
- Also, by 1960, African Americans were better organised and more skilful in making demands.

The Kennedy administration saw itself as a modernising government, but despite Kennedy's sympathetic speeches and his appointment of more African Americans to positions of authority, he was slow to make civil rights the key element in his administration. His speech to Congress echoed Truman's speech in 1948 as a declaration of support for civil rights. It was all too true to say that 'harmful, wasteful and wrongful results of racial discrimination and segregation still appear in virtually every aspect of national life', but to take decisive action was more difficult given the influence of the Southern white bloc in Congress. Kennedy finally submitted a general civil rights bill to Congress on 19 June 1963.

By 1963, civil rights had been forced to the forefront of national political by two elements. One was ongoing violence, exemplified by the murder of civil rights leader **Medgar Evers** on 12 June 1962. The other was the increasingly effective campaign by various civil rights organisations. The March on Washington on 28 August by 250,000 people demanding civil rights was the largest public demonstration seen in the capital. It also led to one of the most effective speeches by a civil rights leader, when Martin Luther King Jr said 'I have a dream …' (see page 36).

Little Rock 1957

Following the *Brown* v. *Topeka Board of Education* decision (see page 23), the NAACP enrolled nine African American students into Little Rock High School, Arkansas. They were denied entry by angry crowds, supported by the Arkansas **National Guard** ordered in by Governor **Orval Faubus**. The mayor of Little Rock asked for federal help and President Eisenhower sent (white) members of the famous and highly trained 101 Airborne Division and put the Arkansas National Guard under federal control. The students were allowed in, but faced harassment. Faubus shut all public high schools, intending to privatise them and enforce segregation.

KEY TERM

National Guard US states, as well as having police forces, have volunteer part-time military forces which are used in emergencies. They are under the control of the governors of the individual states.

KEY FIGURES

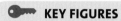

Medgar Evers (1925–63)

A civil rights activist. He had served in the Second World War and afterwards worked in Mississippi with the NAACP. He publicised the case of Emmett Till and helped James Meredith to enrol in the University of Mississippi. He was murdered in June 1963 and his killer acquitted by all-white juries.

Orval Faubus (1910–94)

The son of a socialist, he was elected as governor of Arkansas in 1954. Initially working for desegregation and seen as a liberal reformer, he saw that the Supreme Court ruling against desegregated schools was unpopular and decided to oppose it. He served as governor until 1966.

KEY FIGURE

Lyndon Baines Johnson (1908–73)

Vice president (1961–3) and appointed president after Kennedy's assassination (1963–9). Johnson was a Texan with experience in domestic reform in the New Deal. He passed many reform measures to create a 'Great Society' as president, but his reputation was tarnished by US involvement in the Vietnam War.

However, what made change possible was the assassination of President Kennedy on 22 November 1963. Under the new vigorous leadership of a Southern Democratic president, **Lyndon Baines Johnson**, and with the very emotional rallying cry that Kennedy's vision had to be fulfilled, civil rights legislation became more extensive and effective than at any time since Reconstruction.

Table 1.3 Summary of measures passed after Kennedy's assassination 1964–5

Date	Measure	Explanation
23 January 1964	Twenty-fourth Amendment stated that the right of citizens to vote should not be denied or abridged by failure to pay the poll tax or any other tax	This ended the regulation in Southern states that only those who paid the poll tax could vote, which excluded many African Americans
2 July 1964	Civil Rights Act (Public Accommodations and Employment). Federal courts would hear cases involving discrimination in voting, public facilities and public education	This prevented local juries deciding on cases of discrimination
14 December 1964	The Supreme Court upheld the accommodation aspect of the Civil Rights Act	*Heart of Atlanta Motel* v. *United States* – a Southern motel unsuccessfully challenged the legality of being forced to accept African American guests
8 March 1965	The Supreme Court overturned a Mississippi law discriminating against African American voter registration	*United States* v. *Mississippi*. The decision was backed by Johnson and federal action was taken
6 August 1965	Civil Rights Act (Voting Rights)	This act passed into law the Fifteenth Amendment
24 September 1965	Executive Order 11246 called for affirmative action to end under-representation of racial minorities in the workplace	Discrimination was barred in all federal employment
3 October 1965	Immigration Act	Ended immigration quotas based on national origin, race, religion or colour

The federal government's dismantling of the restrictive laws passed in the period after 1877 was a key feature of the Johnson administration. In 1960, the Supreme Court declared bans on parades, processions and public demonstrations (a Jim Crow law) in Birmingham, Alabama, to be unconstitutional. Restrictions on voting ended and discrimination in public areas and housing was no longer permissible. However, despite changes in the political status of African

Americans, it was more difficult to affect economic equality, which might ensure more stable race relations.

Economic inequality

It was harder for federal authorities to deal with deep-seated economic inequality. President Nixon's Executive Order 11578 required all employers with federal contracts to draft **affirmative action** policies to actively promote African Americans. An Act of 1972 extended equal employment legislation to all federal, state and local governments. The Civil Rights Act of 1991 (Employment) put the burden on businesses to show that any discrimination in employment did not spring from racial discrimination but was based on the genuine requirements of the company.

KEY TERM

Affirmative action
A change in the late 1960s was the policy of not merely trying to give African Americans equality of opportunity but of helping them by a form of positive action and quotas for education and employment. This proved controversial and was reduced under the Republican administration of Ronald Reagan in the 1980s.

The situation by the early 1990s

High unemployment, poverty, poor schools and housing, and unfair treatment by police led to race riots in the summer of 1965. The worst riots were in Watts, Los Angeles, where 34 people died. The failure of federal government to address the underlying causes of racial tension was seen in the re-emergence of serious riots in 1992, again in Los Angeles, triggered by the events surrounding Rodney King (see the box below).

The bulk of the Johnson administration's measures reinforced what had been enacted after the Civil War but had not been implemented after 1877:

- Economic inequality remained. In 1989, 77 per cent of whites graduated from high school as opposed to 63 per cent of African Americans.
- The gap was bigger in college graduation, with 21 per cent of whites graduating as opposed to eleven per cent of African Americans.
- In 1988, unemployment among African Americans was five percentage points higher than for whites – a figure higher than in the 1950s.
- African Americans occupied only half of the managerial and professional occupations of whites.
- Although African American family income doubled from 1950 to 1989 (to $16,800), the gap between African American and white incomes increased far more, from $7000 in 1950 to $12,000 in 1987.
- The average hourly wage for African American men was $6.26 as compared to $7.69 for white men.

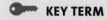

Rodney King

In Los Angeles on 3 March 1991, Rodney King, an African American taxi driver, was speeding to get away from the police who were chasing him. Five white police officers used excessive force while arresting him, badly beating him while he was lying on the ground. The incident was videotaped by a resident who sent the tape to the local news station, which then broadcast it to the world.

The retreat of middle-class blacks into the suburbs left a problematic social gap between suburbs and inner cities. The conclusion of the authors of a major study in the 1990s was that 'Despite the successes of the Civil Rights Acts, harsh economic conditions for America's bottom half have brought disillusion to more and more blacks and disillusion with the political realm with declining turnout in elections and disaffection.'

Summary diagram: The role of the US government in the development of civil rights

Positive			Negative	
Reconstruction		1865		
			Jim Crow laws	
			US v. *Harris*	1883
			Plessy v. *Ferguson*	1896
		1900		
			Wilson's presidency	1913–21
		1930		
Roosevelt and the New Deal	1933–45			
		1940		
Smith v. *Allwright*	1944			
Desegregate military	1948			
		1950		
Brown v. *Topeka*	1954			
Right to vote	1957			
		1960		
Boynton v. *Virginia*	1960			
Civil rights legislation	1964–5			
		1970		
Equal employment	1972			
		1990		
Civil rights employment	1991			

3 The role of African American individuals in the development of civil rights

▶ *How important was the role of individual African Americans in the development of civil rights?*

In the period following Reconstruction, African American leaders faced difficult choices:

- They could organise, resist white violence and intimidation, and hope to regain the political influence of the period after 1865.
- They could withdraw from all attempts at political and social equality, accept segregation and focus on improving their education, and by hard work try to make progress without antagonising the whites, collaborating with them but not challenging their authority.
- They could work within the accepted legal system and use the courts to challenge denial of the constitutional rights established in Reconstruction.
- They could attempt to establish a separate state within a state, withdrawing from the hostile white world.

Aspects of these different choices can be seen throughout the period to 1992. Resistance to violence was seen in the Colored Farmers' Association of the 1880s and by individuals like **Ida B. Wells** of Memphis, who openly carried two guns strapped to her waist. The emergence of later twentieth-century resistance movements and groups, such as **Black Power** and the **Black Panthers** (see pages 50 and 57), had precedents.

The belief in remaining within the law and using it had its origins in the view of **E.J. Waring**, an African American lawyer from Baltimore. He anticipated the leaders of the NAACP by urging lawsuits to test discrimination. The idea was advanced by Thurgood Marshall and other leaders of the NAACP (see page 45) and was a constant thread throughout the period.

The idea of separatism emerged early after the Reconstruction period. A former Kansas state official who had lost his job after 1877, Edwin McCabe, tried to set up a separate African American community in Kansas. Although it failed, the idea remained. Its most prominent advocate was Marcus Garvey (see page 33). The idea of withdrawal from the white man's world underpinned organisations like the **Nation of Islam** (NOI) (see page 48) and the Black Power movement. If African Americans could not be equal, they could be separate, but on their own terms.

Those who had attempted to ensure that African Americans enjoyed equal rights and participated equally in the political process had the Reconstruction

KEY FIGURES

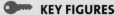

Ida B. Wells (1862–1931)

The daughter of slaves, she went on to be a reforming journalist, leading an anti-lynching campaign in the 1890s. She anticipated the campaigns of the 1950s by protesting against being ordered from a segregated train carriage in 1884. In 1896, she formed the National Association of Colored Women. She campaigned for women's rights as well as being anti-racism.

Everett J. Waring (1859–1914)

Like Martin Luther King Jr, Waring was an active Baptist in Baltimore. He studied law at Howard University. He acted for the Mutual Brotherhood of Liberty, a civil rights organisation, by challenging segregation and campaigning against lynching. He also formed a savings banks for African Americans. He was the first African American to be a judge in Baltimore.

KEY TERMS

Black Power A movement or ideology determined by African Americans to gain power for themselves.

Black Panthers A nationalist and socialist African American organisation formed in 1966 and lasting until 1982.

Nation of Islam A religious organisation founded in 1930.

leaders as models. This thread ran throughout the period with activists such as W.E.B. Du Bois, Philip Randolph and many local leaders and campaigners. It culminated in the leadership of Martin Luther King Jr and his fellow supporters of the 'dream' of equality.

However, the most influential African American leader of the later nineteenth century, Booker T. Washington, did not share these ideas.

Booker T. Washington 1856–1915

Booker Taliaferro Washington was famous as an educator and for both gaining the confidence of white Americans and his moral authority among African Americans. He believed that hard work, education and seriousness of purpose would lead to African Americans showing their true worth, increasing their prosperity and gaining white confidence. The hostility shown by the whites during Reconstruction and their obvious fear of domination by a poorly educated underclass of agricultural workers convinced him that political civil rights should be abandoned in favour of personal improvement. The success of his institute and the hopes brought about for gradual improvement without political or social change won support. The millionaire industrialist Andrew Carnegie gave Washington $600,000 in bonds. His ideas were most clearly stated in Atlanta in 1895 and in his autobiography. He told African Americans to 'dip your bucket' – to take responsibility for their own progress and accept white supremacy. Given the huge problems of resisting the Jim Crow laws and the lack of any developed white support for radical political change, this seemed to many to be quite rational and practical. Washington was invited to the White House by President Theodore Roosevelt in 1901 and he became an informal adviser to both Roosevelt and President Taft.

The following should be factored in when considering the impact of Washington on civil rights:

- One study suggests that 'For some twenty years Washington practically ruled Black America.' Education was the key to the emergence of other leaders, like Martin Luther King Jr.
- Cooperation with white leaders did, in the end, yield progress in civil rights in the 1960s.
- The stress on economic improvement anticipated the post-1964 direction of the civil rights movement, which sought more economic opportunity and saw the key to progress as reducing poverty.
- Washington promoted some opposition to Jim Crow laws behind the scenes and in secret, but was too concerned about antagonising the white South and ending long-term progress in education and economic opportunity.
- Like King, he was criticised by those who sought more radical aims and was hugely respected by the white community – the first African American to achieve this fame and respect.

W.E.B. Du Bois 1868–1963

Later civil rights leaders were hard on Washington, and there is more continuity with his former follower, William Edward Burghardt Du Bois. None of Washington's writings had the impact of Du Bois's *The Souls of Black Folk*, published in 1903. The division between the followers of Washington and those of Du Bois were later mirrored in divisions between King's passive resistance and integrationist ideas and the more radical and separatist views of the Black Power movement. Du Bois's idea was that there should be an elite – the Talented Tenth – who would lead African Americans to equality and social and political equality and integration. He was appalled by the lynchings – 1700 deaths between 1885 and 1894 – and spoke with a passion that anticipated the rhetoric of King much more than the dry rationalism of Washington. 'Why did God make me a stranger and outcast in my own house?' The **Niagara Movement**, founded in 1905, pressed for more radical change and laid the foundation for the NAACP in 1909 (see page 45). Du Bois accepted the alliance with white supporters and as director of research and publicity he was the only African American to hold office in the organisation, publishing the influential journal *The Crisis*. Du Bois recognised that there had been gains: by 1913, African Americans owned 550,000 homes, 937,000 farms and 40,000 businesses; there was a 70 per cent literacy rate, 40,000 churches, 35,000 teachers and 1.7 million pupils in public (state-funded) schools. However, Washington's vision was hardly fulfilled. President Wilson introduced segregation in federal bureaus; lynchings and violence continued unabated and the movement of African Americans northwards had produced race riots in 1917. The worst were in St Louis, and Du Bois organised a protest march in New York, anticipating later civil rights marches. The wave of racial violence which swept the USA in 1919 produced condemnation from *The Crisis* in the so-called Red Summer, but Du Bois's interest shifted to international affairs and **pan-Africanism**.

The following should be factored in when considering the impact of Du Bois on civil rights:

- Du Bois had shifted attention to the need to publicise civil rights through the press and to organise, but his radicalism led him along different paths.
- His interest in pan-Africanism was shared by another radical figure of a much different type, Marcus Garvey, and his belief in organising was shared by Asa Philip Randolph. These men show the wide variation in individual leadership.

KEY TERMS

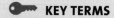

Niagara Movement
A black civil rights organisation formed in 1905. It opposed Booker T. Washington's ideas of working with the white system and wanted an end to desegregation. It was founded by a group of activists but its leading inspiration was W.E.B. Du Bois. Splits and disagreements led to its decline in 1909.

Pan-Africanism A belief in the need for unity and solidarity among Africans all over the world. Its modern origins go back to the late nineteenth century. It recognises the distinct values and the common heritage of all Africans in terms of history, culture, values, achievements and rights. It was given expression by the Organisation of African Unity in 1963 but its supporters think that Africans in all countries should unite.

Marcus Garvey 1887–1940

Marcus Moziah Garvey was born in Jamaica. Politically radicalised by his support for a printers' strike when he was an apprentice, he travelled in central America and studied in London. In 1912, he set up the Universal Negro Improvement Association (UNIA) in Jamaica. He corresponded with Booker T. Washington and wanted to set up an industrial institute in Jamaica.

Marcus Garvey in a plumed hat and uniform in 1922. Compare Garvey's style to that of Martin Luther King Jr in the photograph on page 37.

While in the USA to raise funds in 1916, he established his association there and set up a shipping company called the Black Star Line to trade with Africans worldwide. He was a strong believer in pan-Africanism and a separate African state. Like Washington, he saw the importance of economic development and set up the Negro Factories Corporation to promote manufacture and trade among Africans. His speeches drew large crowds and he stressed the proud African traditions and the inherent strength and worth of Africans. He claimed that the UNIA had 4 million members, making it the largest of the organisations. He was opposed by Du Bois, who thought that the effort should be focused on equal rights within the USA and attempting to integrate African Americans and secure justice and equality for them, not stressing their separate identity. His commercial schemes collapsed when he was accused of and imprisoned for fraud. He returned to Jamaica and later planned a scheme whereby 12 million

African Americans would be taken to Liberia, the state established for former slaves on the west coast of Africa. This came to nothing and he died in London in 1940.

The following should be factored in when considering the impact of Garvey on civil rights:

- Garvey's slogan 'Africa for the Africans at home and abroad' and his glorification of Africanism in some ways prefigured Black Power, but his eccentricity makes him a lone figure.
- He claimed that God and Jesus were black and set himself up as the president of the Republic of Africa with a sort of Napoleonic aristocracy of dukes, ceremonies and parades.
- He collected the considerable sum of $10 million and attracted very large amounts of support.
- Because the economic ventures failed, and because of his imprisonment and later schemes, he has been seen as an isolated and bizarre figure, but this was not the view of many contemporaries.
- His organisation was not matched by anything before 1917 and not again until the mass movements of the 1960s.

Philip Randolph 1890–1979

The more integrationist policies were continued by (Asa) Philip Randolph. He was influenced by Du Bois's writings and moved to New York, where he was active as a union organiser for African American workers (see page 70). Randolph pressured Roosevelt to end discrimination in the war industries in 1941 by threatening a mass march on Washington. This major tactic was new: Du Bois had organised a march in New York in 1917 and it led to the highly effective tactic of the mass march on Washington in 1963, which King dominated but Randolph organised.

The following should be factored in when considering the impact of Randolph on civil rights:

- Understanding of the power of non-violent mass demonstration was Randolph's key contribution to the civil rights movement.
- He used the economic power of organised labour.
- He put considerable pressure on Truman to end segregation in the armed forces in 1948.
- The use of marches, demonstrations and effective organisation, working with white sympathisers and putting pressure on administrations paid off in the long run, and these key tactics (derived in part from resistance to British rule in India under **Mohandas Gandhi**) moved the civil rights movement on more than other leaders had done, and laid the basis of King's success.

Du Bois was the inspiration but did not organise support in comparable numbers. Washington saw the importance of economic development but had

KEY FIGURE

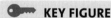

Mohandas Gandhi (1869–1948)

Born in India, he studied law in London and worked in South Africa, where he campaigned against racial segregation. Back in India in 1916, he became a leading figure in the campaign for independence. He used only non-violent means like civil disobedience and peaceful marches and meetings. Despite being imprisoned by the British, he achieved Indian independence in 1947. He worked for peace between Hindus and Muslims but was assassinated by a Hindu fanatic in 1948.

no interest in political aims or mobilisation. Garvey could attract large numbers but his aims were not specific enough to be achievable. Randolph is a key figure in linking the aspirations and ideals of previous leaders with the organisation necessary to put effective pressure on administrations.

Martin Luther King Jr 1929–68

It was King who brought together many of the previous trends. Like Randolph, he was the son of a minister. This religious background showed him the importance of organisation and gave him a moral vocabulary, although this was not new. The leaders of Reconstruction were well versed in biblical rhetoric and Garvey was able to inspire crowds with proud oratory. King was taught about organisation and tactics by Randolph. Local leaders had already laid much of the foundations for change and King was organising in an era when American society was more eager for change than in Du Bois's and Garvey's time. He also faced some of the same criticism that Washington did in seeking to work with white supporters. His leadership produced a similar reaction to that of Washington in the growth of more radical leaders such as Malcolm X (see page 38). Arguably, without the work of all of his predecessors, King could not have made the impact he did, but having said that he brought distinctive leadership qualities and he reflected a lot of previous developments.

KEY TERM

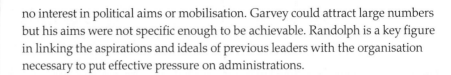

Boycotting Ignoring and isolating a person or an organisation with a view to exerting pressure. Here, African Americans refused to use the buses. As they were the majority of the customers this succeeded in putting pressure on the bus company as revenue fell.

King became the Baptist minister in Dexter Street Baptist Church in Montgomery, Alabama, in 1954. A number of different strands of previous civil rights activity came together in 1955 when King supported other groups in Montgomery in **boycotting** the buses after an NAACP activist, Rosa Parks, was arrested for refusing to vacate a whites-only seat on a bus (see page 46). Local civil rights supporters had been waiting for an opportunity to act. King saw the value of concerted action and organisation – he formed, with others, the Southern Church Leadership Conference (SCLC) in 1957. Like Randolph, he saw the moral power of Gandhi-like non-violence and visited India in 1959. Like Garvey and Randolph, he saw the power of mass demonstrations. What was striking was the religious element. He was inspired by the mass enthusiasm of the preacher Billy Graham and was also conscious of the power of the Southern churches to unite support behind civil rights. Unlike Garvey, he also aimed at links with white supporters. In this respect, he went back to Washington and Du Bois. His aims were not separatism but integration and equality, with white cooperation. He was aware of the importance of the modern media. If marches and sit-ins provoked a violent reaction from the white authorities in the South, then this time they would be shown on television both nationally and internationally and would amount to excellent publicity. Finally, King understood the power of rhetoric and the telling phrase. His speech in Washington in August 1963 contains some of the most powerful words of any US oratory: 'I have a dream that my four little children will one day live in a

Martin Luther King Jr, speaking in Washington in 1963, with the media taking a close interest.

nation where they will not be judged by the color of their skin but by the content of their character.'

Delivered in Washington to the greatest civil rights demonstration to date, King's speech combined oratory of a religious character with a direct emotional appeal to a large crowd, demonstrating a high level of organisation, to a mixed audience showing white support in a non-violent protest. More radical activists like Malcolm X were critical of the fake show of unity, the lack of emphasis on the key issue of economic inequality, its obvious appeal to the white community and its false sense of unity in referring to the 'American dream'.

King, unlike the other leaders, took a major role in the marches and demonstrations. He was arrested 29 times. From the first of the major marches in Atlanta in 1961, he faced hostility from the white authorities. On the whole, they played into his hands. Police chief **Eugene 'Bull' Connor** in Birmingham in 1963 obliged by using water hoses, beatings and arrests. King's 'Letter from Birmingham Jail' thus was given added emotional appeal. The non-violent marches – although not always as controlled as King made out – also allowed white sympathisers to join. King took care that a march in St Augustine, Florida, was joined by Northern white supporters. The march from Selma to Alabama, despite two false starts, achieved legendary status.

KEY FIGURE

Eugene 'Bull' Connor (1897–1973)

A former sports broadcaster elected as commissioner for public safety in 1937 in Birmingham, Alabama. He was a committed segregationalist. His harsh treatment of the civil rights march in Birmingham in 1963 had the opposite effect of its intentions, gaining support for and accelerating civil rights legislation.

The following should be factored in when considering King's impact on civil rights:

- The scale of activity made it possible for civil rights legislation to be passed as a matter of urgency.
- Randolph had succeeded in achieving changes in the law, but not as fundamentally as King.
- Other leaders, like Garvey, may have achieved considerable followings, but no reform emerged.
- Both Garvey and his successor Malcolm X may have achieved a higher level of awareness among African Americans but not the positive outcomes of 1964 and 1965 (see page 28).
- However, King engendered criticism and disapproval in a similar way to Washington for working too closely with white supporters and presidents.
- King was criticised by some of his fellow activists for inconsistent and hesitant leadership.
- He, like the Reconstruction leaders, found that achieving constitutional rights did not solve fundamental economic and social problems.

After 1965, King's campaigns for economic equality and withdrawal from Vietnam met with considerably less success, as the aims were wider and less immediately achievable. He was assassinated in Memphis in April 1968.

King faced a similar dilemma to other African American leaders before him. Achieving political reform was dependent on the support of the US government. The only effective action had taken place with that support, as in the Reconstruction period. However, first, there was no guarantee that political equality would lead to economic equality. Continuing poverty imposed its own segregation. Second, many African Americans did not think that joining the system which had enslaved their forebears and consistently discriminated against them for 90 years was the way forward. King found himself seen as a latter-day Booker T. Washington. Another side of African American activism was represented by Malcolm X.

Malcolm X 1925–65

Malcolm Little was, like King, the son of a civil rights activist and minister, Earl Little. However, Earl had been a follower of Marcus Garvey and a strong believer in African separatism and nationalism. The family, as a result, suffered racist persecution both in their hometown of Omaha and in Michigan, and Earl was found dead in 1931. Malcolm's mother had a mental breakdown in 1937 and Malcolm drifted to Boston, where he became a professional criminal. He was imprisoned from 1947 and 1952 and underwent a conversion to Islam, joining the small radical group the NOI. Like other leaders, his skill was in speaking and writing, and he was responsible for a rapid growth in membership from around 400 in 1952 to possibly 40,000 or more by 1960. Unlike any of the other major leaders, he preached violent revolution, urging African Americans not to reject any means for change. The range of his ideas went beyond that of his predecessors, linking socialism with pan-nationalism, anti-colonialism and radical Islam. This, and concerns about Elijah Muhammad's genuine belief in Islamic moral principles, led to a break with the NOI in 1964. By then, Malcolm X was becoming less committed to violence and more to the force of purely spiritual values. Just as King became more politically radical in later life, so Malcolm X ironically softened his approach, particularly after his trip to Africa and the Middle East and completing the ***hajj***. Like King he was assassinated, at a meeting in Manhattan in 1965.

KEY TERM

Hajj The pilgrimage to the shrine of the Prophet Mohammed at Mecca. It is the duty of Muslims to make the journey at least once in their lifetime.

The following should be factored in when considering Malcolm X's impact on civil rights:

- The influence he had, for instance on the emergence of the Black Power movement, was considerable.
- Given the aims, it was not possible for him to claim the sort of success that King could claim over the civil rights legislation.
- He had less popular support than Garvey at his height and perhaps a less coherent strategy.
- He had considerable influence in promoting a sense of pride and identity among African Americans that did not depend on integration or accepting white values.

Conclusion

By 1992, it was still not clear which of the approaches outlined on page 31 had been or would be the most effective. Washington, Garvey and Malcolm X, in different ways, saw the way forward as separation. African Americans should prove their worth by their own efforts in their own spheres (Washington). They should see their culture and identify as part of a wider African world and develop economically (Garvey). They should see themselves as separate from and superior to the white world and not plead for but demand, if necessary supported by force, their rights and values be respected (Malcolm X). The other path was to enter the system and integrate with its values and ensure that African Americans were represented in order to achieve wider aims. This had been the hope of the Reconstruction leaders, of Du Bois and Randolph and King – to work within the system, to accept the American way. It is still not clear which underlying vision was most realistic and effective.

Summary diagram: The role of African American individuals in the development of civil rights

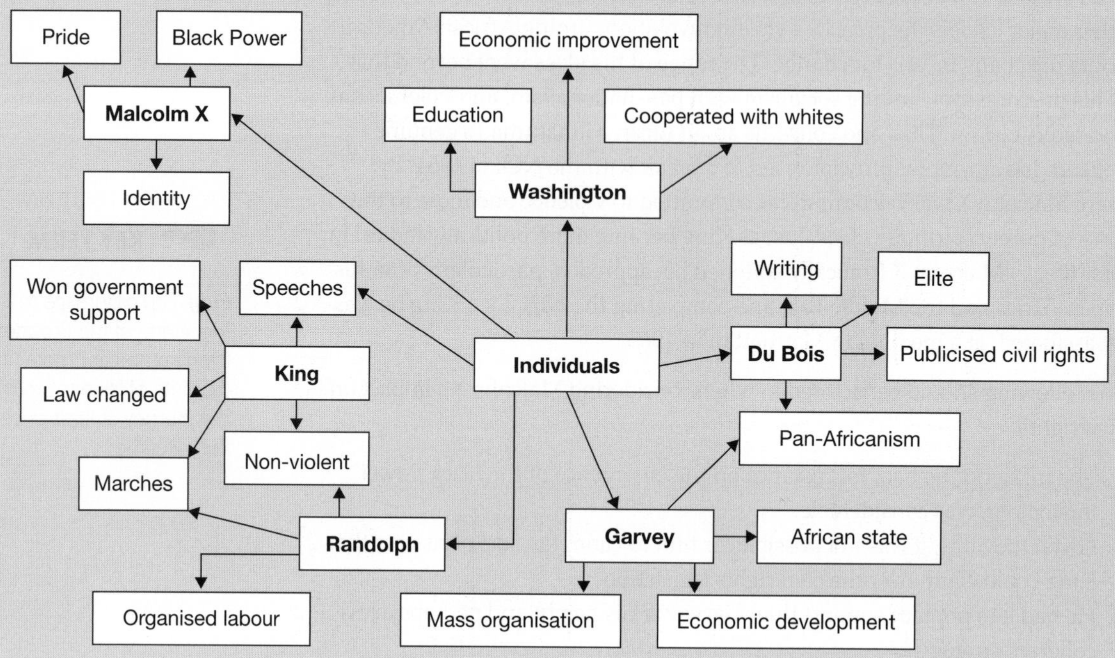

4 The opposition to civil rights

▶ *How strong was the opposition to civil rights?*

The sudden change in the status of African Americans in 1865, together with the bitterness of the Civil War, was bound to bring opposition from the white South. In the face of Congressional Reconstruction and military rule, the Southerners resorted to secret organisations and a resumption of some of the **guerrilla warfare** they had practised in the war itself. The most notorious organisation was the Ku Klux Klan.

KEY TERM

Guerrilla warfare Warfare conducted by irregular forces rather than 'normal' armies, often behind enemy lines. It often involves raids on enemy troops and supply lines and usually little mercy is shown as the usual rules of war are not applied.

The Ku Klux Klan

The origins of the Klan go back to a secret society formed in Tennessee in December 1865. Overall coordination was attempted in 1867 at a meeting in Nashville, and the Confederate General Nathan Bedford Forest was a notional national leader or 'Grand Wizard'. Their ideology was one of white supremacy and their political aim was to undermine Republican domination of the South. Their strongest characteristic was not, however, national organisation but localised groups of people with a variety of grievances, pursuing personal grudges and indulging in racist violence and intimidation.

A group of masked and hooded Ku Klux Klan members acting out the lynching of President Abraham Lincoln, *c.*1867.

Methods of the Ku Klux Klan members

- They used intimidating methods: white hoods, flaming crosses and secret oaths.
- They physically attacked, beat, lynched and murdered African Americans, destroying their property and on occasion setting off bombs.
- Powerful sexual elements, of white women in danger, were employed, that would recur for the next century.
- Freedmen's Bureau members were targeted in the 1860s, and again in the 1950s and 1960s, when civil rights workers were killed.
- Efforts were made to stop African American voters from registering and voting. These were later institutionalised as Jim Crow laws.
- They attacked African Americans to stop them from attending desegregated schools – something that again reappeared in the struggle for desegregation in the 1950s. A formidable precedent was set in this period for white opposition to civil rights.

The scale of violence was quite considerable. There were 2000 deaths and injuries in Louisiana alone in the run-up to the 1868 presidential election. President Grant, elected in 1868, was prepared to suspend ***habeas corpus*** and use federal troops to suppress violence, for example, in South Carolina in 1871. The Klan's methods also led to Republicans and African Americans uniting

KEY TERM

Habeas corpus The right only to be detained by lawful arrest.

against it, having the opposite effect of its supporters. Effective indictments by federal courts began to have their effect by the early 1870s and the national organisation was not strong enough to resist federal powers. State legislatures also turned against it. The Klan itself withered away but individual acts of terrorism continued.

Attitude and actions of state governments

From 1877, the opposition to civil rights did not centre on illegal terrorism but came from the activities of legally constituted state governments, the indifference of Congress and the administrations, and the judgments of the Supreme Court. The new direction of the court was seen in a judgment in 1882, which declared legislation against the Klan unconstitutional (see page 19). The situation in the South descended to official restrictions on African American political rights with the Jim Crow laws and ridiculous voting qualifications (see page 21), while the traditions of the Klan period were maintained in the growth of lynchings (see Figure 1.2), which the local and state authorities did not do much to control. The federal government looked on and did little. The situation reverted to the pre-Civil War period where the South was allowed to regulate its own affairs with regard to race. In place of slavery there was segregation, sharecropping and inequality before the law in social and economic matters, and the application of random and terrifying localised violence. The Ku Klux Klan became inactive because there was no real necessity for it to exist.

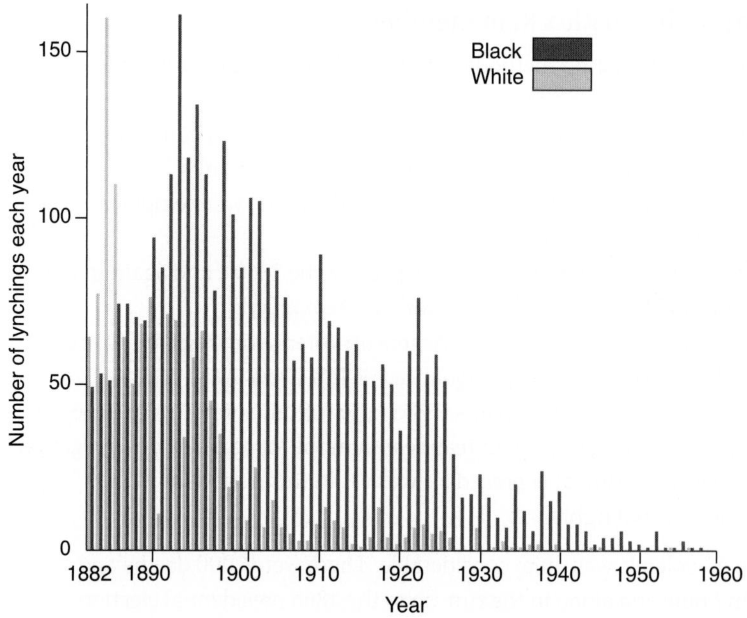

Figure 1.2 Lynchings by year and race 1882–1960 (based on data from the archives at the Tuskegee Institute, February 1979).

The revival of the Ku Klux Klan in the twentieth century

The Klan was reborn in 1915 on the basis of a myth. The film ***The Birth of a Nation*** portrayed the Klan as part of a heroic struggle against Northern domination and black control.

A group led by William Joseph Simmons in Georgia revived the 'historic' costumes but the agenda was considerably wider. It attracted anti-urban, anti-immigrant Protestant racists. Its enemies were not specifically African Americans trying to 'get above themselves' but included Jews, Catholics, foreigners and opponents of the prohibition of alcoholic drink. As its targets were more widespread, the effects on African American civil rights were much less – especially as they had to all intents disappeared in the South. By the mid-1920s, the Klan was in decline. Racial attacks continued, but violence was sporadic – for example there were several attacks on African Americans in 1927. However, Klan membership fell from 4 million in 1920 to 30,000 in 1930. The Klan lingered on in the South throughout the period.

Resistance to civil rights in the 1950s

Civil rights activists faced resistance from a number of sources:

- The state governments, legislatures, senators and representatives. The Republicans did not penetrate the 'solid South'. The Democrats' political dominance was built on their defence of segregation and supremacy and they presented a formidable barrier even to strong presidents like Truman and Kennedy.
- The entrenched opposition of the judicial system in many areas of the South, with police forces, local councillors, courts and juries being determined to hold back change.
- The vestiges of the Klan and similar organisations and the traditions of violence and lynchings among the white population. Access to weapons was easy and white juries were unwilling to convict in the matter of racial crime. Civil rights was often seen as Northern interference, much as abolitionism and '**carpet bagging**' had been seen before and after the Civil War.

With the changes stemming from the Second World War and the greater pressure for change, a revival of political violence in the South was apparent. There was a wave of bombings of homes of African Americans who had become more prosperous in Birmingham, Alabama. The sympathies of police chief 'Bull' Connor allowed attacks to go ahead without investigation. When the Freedom Riders appeared in Birmingham, Connor allowed Klan members to attack them for fifteen minutes without taking action. There were attacks on the homes of members of the NAACP in Florida in 1951. The assassination of the civil rights leader Medgar Evers in 1963 in Mississippi was not an isolated instance of political violence.

KEY TERMS

The Birth of a Nation The Southern film-maker D.W. Griffiths offered a notorious historical drama in 1915 showing a Confederate veteran meeting injustice and corruption when he returns home in 1865 and taking a heroic stand by joining the Ku Klux Klan. It was immensely controversial.

Carpet bagging The South objected violently to Northern officials and businessmen after the Civil War interfering in their affairs and using corruption to gain the votes and support of the former slaves. Such intruders were often portrayed as carrying bags made out of carpet material, hence the name.

KEY TERM

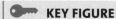

White Citizens' Councils
Formed in the South following the Brown decision of 1954. They had a more middle-class membership than the Klan but their aim was similar. They wanted to intimidate African Americans into not claiming their rights. Their members used not only violence but also their economic power, for example in pressuring insurance companies to cancel policies of African American church members. The councils were active into the 1960s.

KEY FIGURE

George Wallace (1919–98)
A lawyer and Democrat politician. He was initially seen as a moderate but came to support opposition to segregation and voter registration of African Americans. He became governor of Alabama in 1963, advocating hardline conservative policy. He opposed enrolment of black students at the University of Alabama and the desegregation of schools. He ran for president in 1968 for the American Independence Party. He was shot in 1972 while running as a Democratic presidential hopeful. He stood again for president in 1976. In the late 1970s, he had a change of heart and as a born-again Christian rejected his earlier opposition to segregation. He was governor of Alabama for four terms, ending his period of office in 1987.

The 16th Street Baptist Church in Birmingham was bombed in 1963, and the murder of three civil rights workers in Mississippi (the subject of the film *Mississippi Burning*) showed the failure of radical white opposition to appreciate any change in the tide of public opinion. However, continuing violence had produced a similar reaction in the 1870s, with greater energy put into law enforcement and revulsion at the impact on the USA's international reputation.

However, as with the 1870s, it proved impossible to prevent acts of violence, which continued sporadically in the 1970s and 1980s. A turning point was the execution of a Klan member for the lynching of an African American in 1981 in Alabama, although it took sixteen years for punishment to be inflicted. That was the first time in the period that a white man had been convicted and executed for racial murder since the 1870s.

Although disturbing, the opposition to civil rights by Southern authorities and individuals and groups such as the **White Citizens' Councils** was not nearly as effective in the 1950s and 1960s as it had been in the Reconstruction period. Defiantly segregationist white governors, like Orval Faubus, who tried to prevent desegregation of schools in Arkansas, and **George Wallace** in Alabama, only served to push reluctant administrations to use federal authority to enforce Supreme Court decisions because of media attention.

Greater television coverage meant that discrimination, segregation, violence and disregard for the law could not be hidden away as they had been in the period from 1877 to the 1940s. Effective opposition depended on support from Supreme Court rulings and the political indifference of the federal government. Once that had changed, as a result of more effective civil rights organisation and the inspiration of individual leaders, then opposition seemed merely old fashioned, desperate and dangerous to the USA's reputation.

Summary diagram: The opposition to civil rights

KKK	State governments	1950s
• Intimidated • Lynched • Beat • Claimed white women in danger • Stopped African Americans voting/ registering • Prevented attendance at desegregated schools	• Legislated in favour of KKK • Restricted African Americans voting • Did little to stop lynching • Allowed segregation	• State governors and senators • Democrats in the South • Judicial system • Tradition: KKK • Police: 'Bull' Connor • White Citizens' Councils

5 The importance of organisations in the development of civil rights

▶ *How important were organisations in achieving civil rights?*

The experience of the loss of rights after the Reconstruction period showed the dangers of African Americans relying on individual leaders or the protective power of the federal state. There had been instances of African Americans banding together to protect their lives and property, but no overarching organisation had formed to safeguard rights.

The National Association for the Advancement of Colored People (NAACP)

The first major organisation had to wait until the early twentieth century and then was not predominantly led by African Americans. The NAACP proved to be of major importance. Of the 37 major civil rights organisations in the USA today, the NAACP is the only one from the major period of civil rights agitation to remain. The NAACP originated from concerns about race riots and lynchings expressed in the so-called Niagara Movement.

The NAACP included African American campaigners W.E.B. Du Bois and Ida Wells, and liberal white social reformers and campaigners. Its initial founding dates from 1909 and the name was chosen in 1910. Du Bois was its only senior black committee member. Its aims concerned suffrage rights, equal justice, better education, equality before the law and employment opportunities according to ability. This was an organisation more *for* African Americans than *by* them and it was initially dominated by Jewish white liberals.

The main thrust of its campaigns was legal. The target was to challenge the Jim Crow laws of the South, which ran contrary to constitutional amendments. It also campaigned in a relatively restrained way against President Wilson's policy of segregating federal employment and in favour of allowing African Americans to serve as officers in the armed forces. It established 50 local branches and a journal, and set up marches in protest against the film *The Birth of a Nation* and against race riots in St Louis in 1917. However, it did not recruit a mass following: it had only 6000 members by 1915. It used its middle-class membership more for legal challenges against voting restrictions in the South and it effectively blocked moves to make segregation of African Americans into distinct districts illegal in 1917. A more dynamic recruitment policy led to an increase in membership in the 1920s but law remained its main tactic. It defended African Americans sentenced to death in Arkansas after rioting, who claimed they had been tortured. It also publicised the evils of lynching.

The NAACP's achievements were relatively modest:

- The NAACP achieved a Supreme Court ruling in 1944 that it was illegal to deny African Americans the right to vote in primary elections.
- Its long and steady legal campaigns increased the role and reputation of the black lawyer Thurgood Marshall.
- There was a steady attack on segregation, which culminated in the *Brown* v. *Topeka Board of Education* ruling in 1954. However, the actual enforcement of the policy was beyond the resources of the NAACP.
- Local activists spearheaded one of the most significant developments of the post-war period in 1955, when Rosa Parks challenged the segregated bus regulations in Montgomery, Alabama. Her arrest was quickly followed by the issue of 52,000 leaflets calling for a bus boycott. This changed the nature of the NAACP's work and introduced the idea of using organisation and economic pressure and also exploiting the publicity of a celebrated case. However, when the NAACP was barred from Alabama all it could do was to challenge the decision in the courts and leave the state until 1958. This opened the way for more dynamic local organisations using mass campaigning. Thus, the 1955 bus boycott was a high point but also an indication of the limitations of the NAACP.
- It was instrumental in the campaign in 1959 to integrate the schools in Little Rock.

Thus, the most famous incidents of the 1950s were the work of the NAACP, but after its participation in the March on Washington in 1963, which it did much to organise, its days of greatness seemed to be over.

The Congress of Racial Equality (CORE)

Organisations such as the NAACP and the Congress of Racial Equality (CORE) shared strengths and weaknesses. They united white liberal opinion and expertise and they had specific targets which often resulted in tangible progress. The legal challenges mounted by the NAACP led to key Supreme Court decisions. The campaigns of CORE, which was founded in 1942, with two-thirds of its initial membership being white, were focused on key areas.

CORE's impact includes the following:

- It was CORE which began the Freedom Rides in 1947, when eight white activists challenged segregation on buses in the South.
- This was repeated to more effect in 1961. This time, opposition was more pronounced, as was publicity.
- It provoked mob violence in Anniston and Birmingham and savage ill-treatment of the African American Freedom Riders in Jackson, Mississippi.
- As Kennedy was led to authorise the Interstate Commerce Commission to desegregate interstate transport, it had, as with the NAACP's actions, an immediate result.

- A similar example of focused action was the campaign to desegregate schools in Chicago; an indication that action for segregation following NAACP's court victory had been slow.

Later developments

There had been a proliferation of civil rights organisations. The NAACP Youth Council of 1958 had organised sit-ins to challenge desegregated lunch counters, most notably at Greensboro, North Carolina, in 1960. The Montgomery Bus Boycott showed the effectiveness of local organisations, not only the local NAACP but also the Montgomery Women's Political Council. To sustain the boycott, the Montgomery Improvement Association had been formed by Martin Luther King Jr and his allies, and out of this came the influential SCLC with its headquarters in Atlanta, which was backed by highly competent organisers. This organisation was different in that it had a guiding political philosophy and a highly articulate figurehead in King. One of its founders was influential in forming the Student Nonviolent Coordinating Committee (SNCC) in April 1960. The different elements came together in the Council of Federated Organizations in February 1962, with a strategy of increasing voter registration in the Deep South. The Council of Federated Organizations included both the CORE and the NAACP, as well as the SCLC and the SNCC.

Mass demonstrations

The most famous actions derived, however, from King and the SCLC. The emphasis moved away from carefully planned campaigns and legal challenges to more mass demonstrations and a broader appeal for change. Aware that in Kennedy, who had been elected in 1960, there was a mood for change, the SCLC and King's actions were as follows:

- The avowed philosophy was non-violence.
- The campaigns looked for white liberal support.
- They won support from organised religion in the South.
- They wanted to demonstrate mass feeling.
- They looked to invoke the constitutional right of freedom of expression over local state laws which prevented demonstrations.

The first demonstration in Albany, Georgia, in 1961 was thwarted by careful preparation from the local police chief, Laurie Pritchett, who restrained his men and was sure to have King released after his initial arrest. However, in Birmingham, Police Chief Connor (see page 37) obliged by the use of force, all the more shocking since the organisers used children to carry on the protest when the adult marches and sits-in were failing. King gained maximum publicity from his arrest and his time in Birmingham jail.

The greatest expression of non-violent, multiracial protest with the various organisations working together was the March on Washington in August 1963. King's rhetoric, numbers, publicity and the support of the presidency came together to create an event seen as historic and watched throughout the world. The scale was greater than anything attempted since 1865 or after.

A key element was the gathering of white support, which was at its strongest since Reconstruction. In 1964, at a march in St Augustine, the world saw the spectacle of the 72-year-old mother of the governor of Massachusetts being arrested for breaking segregation laws which seemed part of a remote and unsavoury past.

Although earlier organisations had achieved favourable Supreme Court decisions or executive orders, the Civil Rights Acts of 1964 and 1965 seemed triumphs for effective mass organisation.

Separatism

Another tradition of African American organisations had not sought the same aims as King and others. From the isolated attempts after Reconstruction to form distinct African American communities to the widely supported Universal Negro Improvement Association (UNIA), a key strand had been separatism and black nationalism. Garvey's UNIA was short lived but spectacular. His newspaper had a large circulation. The parades in New York in 1920 were among the largest ever seen in the city, and membership may have reached a million. This was a clearly nationalist black-based organisation which stressed the worth of African Americans in a wider context. It did not pursue the aims of white Americans, but rather used the economic power of modern capitalism to generate enterprises and a major shipping line. It inspired activism such as that of Malcolm X's father and was an obvious forerunner to Black Power. In many ways, it was the high point of organisation by and for African Americans:

- It did not focus on highlighting black victims and showing harsh treatment. It celebrated African values and strengths.
- It stressed economic improvement and enterprise from the start.
- It had international support.
- Like King, it used religious-type fervour and had a dynamic and charismatic leader.

There was, however, little chance of an alliance with white liberal America and although Garvey had a private army, it could not save him from arrest and imprisonment. Also, unlike the NAACP and CORE, its goals were difficult to define and achieve in the short term.

Nation of Islam (NOI)

The vein of radicalism and separatism was kept alive by the NOI. Founded in Detroit by **Wallace Fard Muhammad** and dominated until 1975 by

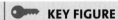

KEY FIGURE

Wallace Fard Muhammad (c.1893–c.1934)

His origins are obscure. He may have been born in New Zealand and may have been a criminal from Oregon. He began a preaching mission in 1930 in Detroit urging African Americans to return to Islam. In a bizarre narrative, he saw black origins as a Shabazz tribe who had created the white race, who had then enslaved them. His NOI temple had 8000 followers by 1934. He was pursued repeatedly by the police and disappeared.

Elijah Muhammad (born Elijah Poole in Georgia), this organisation expanded considerably in the 1950s with the help of convert Malcolm X. Although described as the oldest nationalist and separatist organisation, it came after the UNIA, with which it had common features. Both depended on charismatic leaders, both saw the struggle in the USA of African Americans in a broader context, and both relied on a vibrant newspaper and clear ideas of black superiority.

The impact of the NOI includes the following:

- The links with the Islamic religion increased the emotional appeal of the NOI, and the belief that African Americans were the chosen people of Allah gave the movement a religious strength akin to the power of Southern baptism behind the SCLC and distinct from the more rational and secular NAACP and CORE.
- The ideology was much stronger than other civil rights organisations, as was its separation from support from white America or alignment with its values.
- In the much more spiritually intense atmosphere of both the UNIA and the NOI, matters of voter registration and equal political rights were not priorities.
- For members of the NOI, the efforts of King and the demeaning spectacle of police hoses playing on passive black resisters were objects of hatred. The achievements of the Civil Rights Act seemed irrelevant when the superiority and power of the black race were not accepted.

Changes in the civil rights movement

The more critical outlook of the NOI passed into the Black Power movement, and by 1964 the civil rights movement was losing its unity, as many saw King and his organisation as little more than 'Uncle Toms' excessively dependent on white handouts. The limitations of King's achievements were shown when James Meredith – the first ever African American to enter the University of Mississippi in 1962 – was shot dead on a civil rights march in 1966. The years between the Civil Rights Acts and this murder had seen increasing racial tension and the often slow implementation of reform and change. The previously non-violent SNCC and CORE embarked on a new course. SNCC member **Stokely Carmichael**, in a rally following the murder, said simply 'What we need is black power'.

The mood changed from cooperation with white America to isolation and confrontation. SNCC and CORE groups began to exclude whites and to celebrate African culture, music, food and hair, and to make much more radical political demands.

KEY FIGURES

Elijah Muhammad (Poole) (1897–1995)

The son of a Georgia sharecropper. He moved to work in the car industry in Detroit and met Wallace Fard Muhammad in 1932. As a disciple he established a temple in Chicago, building up the NOI into a large organisation with a 250,000-strong membership. He saw Wallace Fard Muhammad as a living god.

Stokely Carmichael (1941–98)

The son of West Indian immigrants. He studied at Howard University, was involved with the student activism of the SNCC and was a Freedom Rider, suffering imprisonment in the South. He broke with the moderate and non-violent organisation, urging Black Power as an end to dependence on white liberalism: 'we must dismiss the fallacious notion that white people can give anybody their freedom. No man can give anybody his freedom. A man is born free.' He was blamed for the riots in Washington in 1968 following King's murder. He joined the Black Panthers, but broke with them and spent most of his later life in Guinea supporting pan-African nationalism.

The Black Panther movement

Huey Newton and **Bobby Seale** extended previous ideas of armed black groups to found the Black Panther movement in Oakland, California. Weapons were carried openly and defence groups were formed against police brutality. In some areas, fighting broke out in the streets. The distinctive Black Panther salute was made by two African American athletes in the 1968 Olympics, much to the consternation of white America. The 1972 Black Power convention excluded whites.

Political demands had gone considerably beyond those of the mid-1960s' mainstream movement. Black Panther aims included the following:

- economic equality
- an end to capitalist exploitation
- compensation in the form of land and housing
- separate juries for black people and protection from police intimidation.

Essentially, this was a conflict between a white state and a separate black culture. The Black Power movement was going back to Washington's idea of 'dipping your bucket', being self-reliant, but in a very different way. It had more in common with Garvey's organisation but it did not attract the huge membership and was heavily influenced by the Nation of Islam. However, its goals were too diffuse to be easily realised. What the separatist organisations gave rise to was a new confidence and pride in being black and a sense that white values could be challenged rather than accepted. The achievements of the civil rights legislation began to look as limited as the achievements of Reconstruction in promoting a harmonious society.

KEY FIGURES

Huey Newton (1942–89)

Born in Louisiana but brought up in California. He was a cofounder in 1966 of the Black Panther Party for Self-Defense. His ten-point programme called for better jobs and housing for African Americans and he believed in armed self-defence and the threat of force to bring about change. Clashes with police were common and he was accused of killing a policeman but after public protests the case was dropped. He lived in Cuba from 1974 to 1977 to escape arrest. He was shot dead by a drug dealer in 1989.

Bobby Seale (1936–)

Born in Texas but educated in California. After serving in the US Air Force he met Huey Newton at a political protest rally in 1962 and founded the Black Panthers with him in 1966. He was involved in a gun battle with police in 1968. He was imprisoned for four years for contempt of court after being arrested during protests in Chicago. When the Black Panthers declined, he turned to writing and working with younger activists.

The civil rights movement until 1992

The violence in US cities in 1965 and the rise of militant African American groups disappointed moderate supporters of civil rights. The movement split and King's later campaigns against poverty and the Vietnam War were less successful. The problem seemed to be that despite the gains in voter registration and laws against discrimination, the economic inequality of African Americans was a bar to equal opportunity and fuelled more extreme African American opposition. Recognising the need to do more to reduce discontent and unrest, President Nixon took up positive discrimination in his Philadelphia Plan, and Congress and the Supreme Court backed the policy. The Equal Opportunity Employment Act of 1972 helped to increase African American employment. Civil rights had taken on a wider aspect than merely political rights.

Jesse Jackson

1941	Born in South Carolina to an unmarried mother
1959	Graduated from high school
1964	Graduated from North Carolina A&T, a black university
1966	Worked in the civil rights movement
1968	Ordained as a Baptist Church minister
1971	Founded People United to Save Humanity
1984	Stood unsuccessfully for president
1988	Second unsuccessful bid for presidency
1991–7	Senator for Washington DC

Jackson was a college-educated Baptist minister. He took part in SCLC activities and was one of King's inner circle. However, his ambition and assertiveness alienated him from the mainstream SCLC leadership and he resigned in 1971. He formed People United to Save Humanity (PUSH) and the Rainbow Coalition, which aimed to unite all civil rights groups. He was notable for being the first possible African American candidate for the presidency, obtaining 3.5 million votes in the Democratic primary contest in 1984 and 7 million when he stood again in 1984.

An attempt was made by Jesse Jackson to re-create the enthusiasm for change of the King era when he stood for Democratic Party presidential candidate in 1984 and 1988. The idea was ambitious – to unite African Americans who had divided between integrationist and separatist and to re-create the alliance with the white liberals. With more African Americans registered as voters, an African American candidate was a possibility. However, Jackson failed both times to win the nomination.

There were limitations to progress, both political and economic, and the case of the beating of Rodney King in 1991, the acquittal in 1992 of the white policemen who had beaten him and the subsequent race riots showed that the past held the USA in a firm grip.

Another area of improvement was desegregating education: the radical idea of busing children from different areas into desegregated schools did make a difference. However, it was unpopular and declined in the 1970s as middle-class parents found suburban areas where there was no integration policy. Both Nixon and his Republican successor, Ford, supported parental opposition to busing.

By the mid-1970s it was the Democrats who were more likely to do more for the African American cause. However, President Carter (1977–81) was greatly criticised for his limited measures. The problem was that economic problems had come to dominate, with higher oil prices causing inflation and a general slump in the US economy. This disadvantaged African Americans as it had in the 1930s. It made quotas for jobs unpopular and reduced opportunities for many African Americans, a disproportionate number of whom were dependent on state welfare.

Even during the conservative administration of Ronald Reagan, there was some progress towards civil rights. The Voting Rights Act of 1982 strengthened penalties against discrimination and there was a Civil Rights Restoration Act.

There was also a general increase in the number of African Americans holding public office (100 in 1964 and 8000 in 1992). However, Reagan's reductions of welfare benefits fell disproportionately on the African American population. Without a central unifying issue and faced with complex economic and social problems, the activities and membership of the civil rights organisations declined from the high points of the 1960s.

The dynamic leadership of King was an inspiration for one of his followers and it seemed that there might be a chance of an African American president, but Jesse Jackson could not command the support he needed.

Summary diagram: The importance of organisations in the development of civil rights

Organisation	Contribution
NAACP	• Right to vote in primaries • Legal campaigns • Attacked segregation • Bus boycott
CORE	• Freedom Rides • Mob violence and ill-treatment • Desegregation on interstate transport
SCLC and King	• Mass demonstrations • March on Washington • Won white support
UNIA	• Worth of African Americans • International support
NOI	• Links with Islam • Religious strength
Black Panthers	• Armed • Defence groups vs police brutality • Pride

Chapter summary

The main drivers of civil rights in the period were the federal government, key individual African American leaders and a range of organisations. The biggest changes came at the start and towards the end of the period in terms of constitutional change and greater political and social equality. The middle years saw the growth of white supremacy in the South, bolstered by the Democratic Party in Congress, by local white organisations and by sheer violence and intimidation. After uneven progress in the 1950s and as a result of a great deal of pressure from well-organised African American political activity and effective leadership, there was progress in the years 1964–5. However, the problems of African Americans did not disappear when they had more opportunity to vote and participate in the political processes and public offices. The end of the period saw more halting progress against a background of economic depression in the 1970s and conservative reaction in the 1980s.

Refresher questions

Use these questions to remind yourself of the key material covered in this chapter.

1. How much was achieved for African Americans by Congressional Reconstruction after the Civil War?
2. Why, despite the Fourteenth and Fifteenth Amendments, did African Americans not enjoy equal civil rights after the 1870s?
3. Why was it so hard to challenge segregation effectively?
4. What did Booker T. Washington contribute to African American progress?
5. Why was the Supreme Court so important for African American civil rights a) in the 1890s and b) in the 1950s?
6. What was the significance of the two world wars for African American civil rights?
7. Why was there so much more progress in the 1960s than in the 50 years before for African American civil rights?
8. What contribution was made by Martin Luther King Jr to African American civil rights?
9. Why was there so much opposition to African American civil rights in the South?
10. Which of the organisations did most for civil rights from 1909?
11. How important was non-violence in bringing about success for civil rights organisations?
12. What characterised Black Power?
13. What contribution did Malcolm X make to the advancement of civil rights?
14. Assess the importance of affirmative action.
15. What were the main issues concerning African American civil rights that remained by 1992?

In-depth studies and debates

The examination requires you to study three topics in depth and for this unit they are:

- Civil rights in the Gilded Age
- The New Deal and civil rights
- Malcolm X and Black Power.

This section will go into more detail about these periods and introduce you to some of the key debates about civil rights so that you will have enough depth of knowledge to be able to evaluate passages that are set on any of these topics.

? Assess the view that little was achieved by African Americans in the period of the Gilded Age.

Key debate 1: should the Gilded Age simply be seen as a period of reaction and lack of progress in African American civil rights?

The historian Kevern Verney in *Black Civil Rights in America*, published in 2000, gives a bleak picture:

> *There was a popular campaign against tyranny and corruption, the so-called 'redemption period' 1875–7. In these years, white democrats regained political control of the South by the systematic use of electoral fraud, violence and intimidation. Black voters, dependent for their livelihood on whites, were subject to wholesale economic coercion. In the 1880s, the white planter class or 'Bourbon' aristocracy enjoyed political power across the South. In the wake of the Populist movement, state governments in the South sought to exclude blacks from political life altogether. New laws were introduced that required applicants for voter registration to pass literacy tests. The Supreme Court declared these were constitutional. Black disenfranchisement persisted largely unchecked until the 1960s.*

The historians Larry Schweikart and Michael Allen in *A Patriot's History of the United States*, published in 2004, offer a rather different perspective:

> *Outside of the largest cities, blacks found that although the law was infrequently an ineffective weapon for addressing racial injustice, the wallet worked somewhat better. Their buying power gave them important leverage against white businesses. They set up their own insurance and banking companies and formed their own all-black unions. Georgia blacks built 1,544 schools that educated more than 11,000 students. Long segregated from white Protestant churches, blacks had established the African Methodist Episcopal church in 1816 and by the end of the Progressive era, it had grown dramatically. Blacks created all-black universities such as Howard (1867), Spelman (1881), Fisk (1866), Tuskegee (1881), Morehouse (1867), Lincoln (1854), Atlanta (1865), and Hampton (1868) – the so-called black Ivy League or the elite eight. The fact that the 'slave race' had founded its own universities and businesses and had developed a sophisticated debate over the nature of a full and equal place for African Americans in society said just as much about their progress as Jim Crow and Plessy vs. Ferguson.*

The figures for lynchings, the passing of the Jim Crow laws and the Supreme Court decisions do paint a picture of the African Americans being outside the remarkable assimilation of different nationalities and cultures of the Gilded Age. However, African Americans had achieved constitutional guarantees, even if they were not enforced, and in the industrial age it was possible for them to own businesses. It is one of the ironies of history that the infamous 'deal' of 1877 between Hayes and Tilden took place in a hotel owned by a wealthy African American (see page 21). The support given to Booker T. Washington by Alabama for his institute and the success of many educational establishments laid the basis for a great deal of civil rights agitation later on.

Too much emphasis on the discrimination in the South may detract from a degree of economic success in the North and the part played by African Americans in westward expansion. Up to a quarter of 'cowboys' on Western ranches were African Americans. There were African American trappers, farmers, miners and shopkeepers. One African American cowboy, Nat Love (1824–1921), wrote about his Western adventures, which earned him the nickname 'Deadwood Dick' as a formidable shot and cattle roper. There were all-black towns in the West such as Allensworth, California, and Dearfield, Colorado. A former slave, Mary Fields (1832–1914), was a stagecoach driver who earned a formidable reputation. There were also African American lawmen like Bass Reeves (1838–1910). Reeves was a Deputy US Marshal who won a reputation for arresting thousands of criminals and shooting fourteen outlaws. The West was often more indifferent to colour than the South.

Mary Fields with her rifle.

Key debate 2: how much did African Americans benefit from the New Deal?

How significant an impact was made by the New Deal on civil rights for African Americans?

Historian Wallace E. Davies in *New Perspectives in American History*, published in 1964, offered this view:

> *The Negroes particularly benefited from the relief program (of the New Deal), the slum clearance, the public housing projects, and the efforts to alleviate the problems of rural tenancy. The colored people were also impressed when Mrs. Roosevelt resigned her membership of the Daughters of the American Revolution after it had refused to allow Marian Anderson to sing in its hall in Washington because she was a Negro. No first lady had ever shown such concern for them before. And then Secretary of the Interior Ickes invited Miss Anderson to sing instead on the steps of the Lincoln Memorial on Easter Sunday. The result of these actions was that the Negroes turned en masse from being Republican, as they had been since the days of Lincoln, to voting Democrat.*

An alternative vision is described by the historian Jim Powell in *FDR's Folly: How Roosevelt and His New Deal Prolonged the Great Depression*, published in 2003:

> *Roosevelt's New Deal, for instance, has been hailed for its lofty goals of reforming the American economy and helping the underprivileged. Yet mounting evidence,*

> *developed by dozens of economists across the country, shows that the New Deal prolonged joblessness for millions, and black people were especially hard hit.*
>
> *The flagship of the New Deal was the National Industrial Recovery Act, passed in June 1933. It authorized the president to issue executive orders establishing some 700 industrial organizations, which restricted output and forced wages and prices above market levels. The minimum wage regulations made it illegal for employers to hire people who weren't worth the minimum because they lacked skills. As a result, some 500,000 blacks, particularly in the South, were estimated to have lost their jobs.*
>
> *Marginal workers, like unskilled blacks, desperately needed an expanding economy to create more jobs. Yet New Deal policies made it harder for employers to hire people. FDR tripled federal taxes between 1933 and 1940. Social Security excise taxes on payrolls discouraged employers from hiring. New Deal securities laws made it harder for employers to raise capital. New Deal legal actions to prevent the domination by large industrial concerns (Trusts) harassed some 150 employers and whole industries. Whatever the merits of such policies might have been, it was bizarre to disrupt private sector employment when the median unemployment rate was 17 percent.*
>
> *The Agricultural Adjustment Act (1933) aimed to help farmers by cutting farm production and forcing up food prices. Less production meant less work for thousands of poor black sharecroppers. In addition, blacks were among the 100 million consumers forced to pay higher food prices because of the AAA.*
>
> *The Wagner Act (1935) harmed blacks by making labor union monopolies legal. Economists Thomas E. Hall and J. David Ferguson explained: 'By encouraging unionization, the Wagner Act raised the number of insiders (those with jobs) who had the incentive and ability to exclude outsiders (those without jobs). Once high wages have been negotiated, employers are less likely to hire outsiders, and thus the insiders could protect their own interest.'*

Powell argued that Roosevelt adapted his plans to meet the demands of the largest US trade union, the American Federation of Labor (AFL), and dropped a provision in his labour legislation which called for the prohibition of racial discrimination. The unions, he claimed, were allowed to exclude African American workers.

By giving labour unions the monopoly power to exclusively represent employees in a workplace, the Wagner Act had the effect of excluding blacks, since the dominant unions discriminated against blacks. The Wagner Act had originally been drafted with a provision prohibiting racial discrimination. But the AFL successfully lobbied against it, and it was dropped. AFL unions used their new power, granted by the Wagner Act, to exclude blacks on a large scale. It has also been suggested that most of the New Deal's spending programmes went not to the South to help poor black Americans but to the West and East because these were areas where the president needed to gain political support.

- The numbers of African Americans on relief remained high through the 1930s.
- The Social Security Act did not apply to the mass of African sharecroppers in the South.
- The reforms of the New Deal did not include a Civil Rights Act.
- Little was done to increase African American voting or end segregation, which remained the rule in the armed forces throughout America's war for freedom after 1941.
- In the 1930s, the Roosevelt administration was too conscious of the political influence of Southern Democrats to pass direct measures on African American rights.
- The New Deal gave federal support to African American culture, intellectuals, writers and musicians, which helped to boost the status of African Americans and may have paved the way for post-war changes. Lena Horne, Duke Ellington and Richard Wright were all aided by the federal arts projects and cemented the influence of the so-called 'Harlem Renaissance' in the arts in the 1920s.

KEY FIGURE

Ernesto 'Che' Guevara (1928–67)

An inspiration for many radicals in the USA. A middle-class Argentinian, he joined Fidel Castro's Cuban revolutionaries in 1954 and played a leading part in Castro's revolution in 1959. He was killed trying to spread revolution in Bolivia and became an iconic figure.

Key debate 3: how far did Black Power promote the cause of African American civil rights?

Did Black Power have a positive or negative impact on African American civil rights?

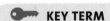

Derrick Murphy, Kathryn Cooper and Mark Waldron are critical of the Black Power movement in their textbook *United States 1776–1992*, published in 2001:

> *The most extreme manifestation of Black Power was the Black Panther Party for Self Defense. This was founded in October 1966. The Black Panthers identified more with Cuban revolutionary* ***Che Guevara*** *than with Martin Luther King. In 1969 27 Black Panthers were shot by the police and 750 were arrested. By 1970 the* ***Federal Bureau of Investigation (FBI)*** *infiltration had broken the back of the Black Panther leadership. Never numbering more than 5000 members, the Black Panthers gained publicity far greater than their real influence deserved. The supporters of Black Power who criticized King's campaign strategy achieved far less for African Americans. It is significant that many historians conclude their studies of the civil rights movement in 1968 with King's death.*

KEY TERM

Federal Bureau of Investigation (FBI)
The US intelligence and security organisation founded in 1908. J. Edgar Hoover, its director from 1935 to 1972, called the Black Panthers 'the greatest threat to the internal security of the country'.

Jeffrey O.G. Ogbar is a historian who takes another view of the importance of African American radicalism (*Black Power: Radical Politics and African American Identity*, published in 2005):

> *By 1960 the Nation of Islam had become a national organization with name recognition in every major black community. It … provided a visible contrast to civil rights organizations. The vilification of whites and endorsement of self defense was anathema to the humanistic language of the SCLC, SNCC and CORE. … NOI brought attention to the ubiquity of white supremacy and its effects on black people, such as unemployment, police brutality, and housing and job discrimination. It also made organizations like the NAACP and SCLC seem attractive alternatives to*

white America … By 1963, concessions from the white power structure were more common, partly … because of the fear of the Muslims.

Thus, on one hand there was a dead-end of violence, with radicals unable to resist the power of the state and not achieving the sort of change that King's peaceful campaigns had led to. The clashes with the police led nowhere and merely strengthened the hand of opponents of civil rights. Black Power also could not achieve the mass support that King had done.

On the other hand, the traditional civil rights organisations were not addressing the problems of white supremacy and were even perpetuating them. King's appeal was much less in the North, as opposed to the Black Power movement, and his attempts to apply the tactics of the peaceful marches in support of opposition to poverty and the Vietnam War had not met with success. The radical African Americans, however, not only encouraged a great consciousness of black identity and awareness of grievances but their real threat acted as a prod to the white establishment to make concessions that a more peaceful and less confrontational movement would not have done. In this view, the radicalisation was vital not only for energising African Americans, but actually for achieving aims.

Study skills: thematic essay question

How to plan the essay

The title of the unit, 'Thematic study', makes it clear that the essay section should be approached thematically rather than chronologically, particularly if you want to reach the higher mark range. In answering essay questions, you are required to make connections, comparisons and links between different elements of the period and aspects of the topic. In the opening paragraph you should try to establish a hypothesis based on the question; this should be tested in the main body of the essay before reaching an overall judgement. This is much easier to do if you approach the essay through a thematic structure. In your answer you will need to cover the whole period, and answers should look to establish patterns of change and continuity and similarity and difference.

Given the large amount of material that you will have to handle, it is very important that you spend time planning your answer. As the essay should adopt a thematic structure, it makes sense if the plan follows the same format and is therefore not chronological or just a list of dates.

In developing your skills to answer essay questions for units 1 and 2, you will have considered the wording of a question. Although you will also have looked at planning an answer, the requirements for these types of question are, as was suggested above, somewhat different, as you will need to establish the themes you will consider.

Consider the question below:

Was Martin Luther King Jr the most successful African American individual leader in this period?

In this essay you need to consider how you would deal with 'success'. This is better than trying to make a list of other leaders and dealing with them in turn. What could 'success' entail?

Consider the example essay plan below:

Getting mass support for the cause of civil rights

King did get encouragement for his campaigns from local support at Montgomery to the March on Washington 1963 – although others organised. He was more successful than the Black Power groups and the NOI in this respect, although Garvey also had a very large following.

Inspiring followers

The high point was 'I have a dream'. However, Washington was a charismatic figure as was Du Bois in his own way. Garvey won intense devotion from his followers and Malcolm X was highly inspiring. Also King was criticised for indecision and too many links with the authorities.

Gaining allies from white America

This was a vital element in success, especially with King and Washington. Du Bois worked with white liberals but the NAACP was too dominated by them in 1909. Randolph saw the importance of influencing Roosevelt but Garvey, the NOI and the Black Power movement eschewed white cooperation as a sign of weakness and misguided aims.

Having effective tactics in campaigns

King's orchestrated campaigns were not always successful, for example, the first march in Georgia and the later marches, but at their height they were highly effective in revealing the strength of purpose of the African Americans taking part; the moral superiority of non-violence and the way that publicity was obtained. Compare with less effective campaigns involving violence.

Achieving his aims

King's success in seeing civil rights legislation being passed might be seen as evidence of aims being achieved more than other leaders. However, his campaigns against poverty and for an end to the war were less successful. As Washington's aims were more narrow, perhaps he achieved them more; those whose aims were too broad were less successful.

Conclusion

In terms of increasing awareness of African American culture and values it may not be King so much as Garvey or Malcolm X. In terms of setting down economic *and educational goals for future growth and development then it may be Washington. However, overall in terms of inspiration, using organised pressure, outlining goals and also having a focused approach to specific goals, King is probably the most successful.*

The plan does not simply list the individuals, but offers a comment about their importance in different aspects of leadership, and the conclusion offers a clear line of argument, which has been supported in the previous paragraphs. Planning an answer will help you to focus on the actual question and marshal the large amount of knowledge you have, in this case about King and the other leaders. It should prevent you from writing all you know about the different leaders in turn so that no judgement is made.

How to write the opening paragraph

Having planned your answer, you are in a position to write the crucial opening paragraph, in which you should set out your line of argument – establish your thesis – and briefly refer to the issues you are going to cover in the main body of the essay. This will help you to remain focused on the actual question. In establishing your thesis, it might be helpful to consider the following questions:

- What was the situation at the start of the period?
- What was the situation at the end of the period?
- Were there any parts of the period where there was considerable change or does the pattern remain the same throughout the period?

These questions will help you to remain focused on the key elements being tested in this unit: continuity and change.

The following is an example of a good opening paragraph in answer to the question:

> The federal government was the most important element in achieving civil rights during this period. How far do you agree?

Response

The federal government was highly significant in civil rights at key points in the period, notably in the Reconstruction years after 1867 and in the 1960s. Where president, Congress and the Supreme Court agreed then reforms were made quickly and decisively and enforced effectively. However, this was not true throughout the period. The Supreme Court had a long period in which it prevented desegregation. After 1877, presidents and administrations were unwilling to tackle the block of 'Old South' senators and representatives. For long periods, impetus for change came either from individuals or from organisations, with very little hope that the federal government would put its weight behind their cause.

Analysis of response

- The opening offers a clear view about the importance of the federal government as a cause and the period during which it was relatively important.
- It outlines some of the other factors that will be considered and offers a view as to their relative importance.
- It reaches a judgement as to the most important cause – it is this line of argument that should be carried through the rest of the essay.

The focus of this section has been on planning and writing a good opening paragraph. Use the information in this chapter to plan answers and write the opening paragraph to the questions below.

Essay questions

1 How far did obstacles to greater civil rights for African Americans remain the same in the period 1865–1992?
2 Did organisations or individuals play the greater role in advancing the course of African American civil rights in the period 1865–1992?
3 Was the Second World War the greatest turning point for the progress of African American civil rights in the period 1865–1992?
4 Was the period of Congressional Reconstruction the most significant period for the development of African American civil rights in the period 1865–1992?

Study skills: depth study interpretations question

How to plan the essay

The specification identifies the three topics from which the interpretations question will be drawn. In answering this question, you have to assess and evaluate the arguments in the passages by applying your own knowledge of the events to reach a supported judgement as to which is the stronger interpretation.

The question will require you to assess the strengths and limitations of the two interpretations of an issue related to one of the specified depth studies. You should be able to place the interpretation within the context of the wider historical debate on the key topic. However, you will not be required to know the names of individual historians associated with the debate or to have studied the specific books of any historians, and it may even be counterproductive to be aware of particular historians' views, as this may lead to your simply describing their view, rather than analysing the given interpretation.

How should the question be approached?

Using the question and the two passages below on the problems faced by African Americans in the Gilded Age, it might be helpful for you to think of a four-paragraph structure to your answer:

- In the first paragraph, explain the interpretations in the two passages and place them in the wider debate about the advances and problems of African Americans.
- In the second paragraph, apply your own knowledge of the situation after Reconstruction to Interpretation A to evaluate the validity of its view about the problems. What knowledge do you have of the problems that either supports or challenges the view of Passage A?
- Repeat the second point, but for Interpretation B: what knowledge do you have of the situation after Reconstruction that either supports or challenges the view of Passage B?
- In the final paragraph, reach a supported and balanced judgement as to which passage you think is more convincing as evidence for the problems.

Evaluate the interpretations in both of the passages and explain which you think is more convincing as an explanation of the problems facing African Americans in the Gilded Age.

PASSAGE A

The white supremacists after 1877 tolerated a lingering black voice in politics and showed no haste in raising the barriers of racial separation. A number of them harbored at least some element of benevolence towards blacks. A former slave-owner, said an editor from South Carolina, 'had no wish to browbeat, maltreat and spit up on the colored man' because he saw no threat to his status. Blacks sat in the state legislatures of South Carolina until 1900 and Georgia until 1908. The South sent black congressmen to Washington in every election until 1900. The disenfranchisement of black voters remained inconsistent but it was enough to ensure white control of the Southern states. In segregation, the color line was drawn less strictly than it would be in the twentieth century. In 1885 a black journalist reported from South Carolina that he rode first class cars on the railways and saw blacks dining with whites at train stations. Very soon, though, after Plessy v Ferguson the principle of social segregation extended into every area of southern life, including street railways, hotels, restaurants, hospitals, recreations, sports and employment.

(From G.B. Tindall and David Shi, America: A Narrative History, *W.W. Norton, 1996.)*

PASSAGE B

In the '80s the long subdued poor whites of the South exploded in an orgy of agrarian agitation. Talented and unscrupulous political leaders came forth to do battle for them and discovered that Negro baiting was highly popular with those whose only distinction was a white skin. Southerners of all classes made solidarity an article of faith. Crossroads rang with declarations that White Womanhood was threatened. Negro baiting became more violent. Victims were roasted over slow fires and their bodies were mutilated. Men and women were charged not only with rape but testifying against whites in court, seeking another job, using offensive language, failing to say 'mister' to the white man. To escape in the Exodus of 1879 some 40,000 African Americans left for the Midwest. Random movements continued through the period. Some went to Canada. Some to Africa.

(From Lerone Bennett, Before the Mayflower: A History of Black America, *Penguin Books, 1969, p. 236.)*

Using this model, a developed plan to the same question might look something like this:

1 The two passages agree that there was discrimination. Passage A offers a more balanced view, but does not ignore injustice, whereas Passage B places more emphasis on social violence and poor white participation.

2 Passage A deals with some areas of continuity with the more relaxed relations between the races before the war and also sees some continuity with the Reconstruction period, although it notes an increase in severity of discrimination.

3 Passage B focuses less on any balance and not on the ruling class but the incitement of racial hatred among the poorer whites and the sheer violence of the lynchings, which is not a feature of Passage A.

4 Both passages acknowledge that the problems were considerable but Passage B offers more on day-to-day violence, while Passage A talks more about the development of segregation.

How to write the opening paragraph

Now look at this possible opening paragraph in answer to the question above (on page 62).

Response

These two passages both suggest considerable problems for African Americans in the Gilded Age. Both deal with discrimination. In Passage A it is segregation of a considerable range of social activities and amenities. In Passage B it is more direct action against breaking social norms, for example in simply addressing white people and being falsely punished for trivial offences.

Passage A suggests a gradual change, perhaps making it all the more difficult for African Americans as they would have been used to some measure of respect which was gradually denied them. Passage B shows some horrifying violence not seen in Passage A and also the desperation that caused some African Americans to migrate in quite large numbers, such as the 40,000 who left for the Midwest in 1879. Both passages show tactics employed by white supremacists but Passage A shows more of the impact of the external judgement of Plessy v. Ferguson while Passage B shows the cynical exploitation from within the white community. One shows gradual and inconsistent discrimination; the other more complete ruthless and determined oppression.

Analysis of response

- The student is aware that both interpretations acknowledge that the problems were multicausal.
- The student is aware that the two interpretations put forward different views of the nature, methods and extremity of the racial problems generated for African Americans.
- The student is able to identify the key differences.

CHAPTER 2

Trade union and labour rights

The struggle for union and labour rights across the period was focused on a number of issues, from the right for unions to even exist to the right of workers to strike. This chapter will consider how, why and the extent to which unions were able to improve the position of their members. It will also assess the reasons for improvements in the position of organised labour and the problems faced in achieving its goals, and consider how far the gains made were maintained. The chapter will analyse the developments under the following headings:

★ The position of unions and organised labour
★ Industrial growth and economic change
★ Federal government attitudes and actions
★ The First and Second World Wars
★ Union unity
★ Union action and membership

It also considers the debates surrounding the three in-depth topics:

★ To what extent did improvements in the economy during the Gilded Age benefit workers and unions?
★ Did the New Deal bring about an improvement in the position of workers?
★ Did the Black Power movement help to improve the position of workers?

Key dates

1869	Knights of Labor founded
1873	Molly Maguires
1886	Haymarket Affair
	American Federation of Labor founded
1890	Sherman Anti-Trust Act
1892	Homestead strike
1894	Pullman strike
1905	*Lochner* v. *New York*
1914	Clayton Anti-Trust Act
1925	Brotherhood of Sleeping Car Porters and Maids established
1933	NIRA and NRA
1935	Wagner Act
1937	Congress of Industrial Organizations
1947	Taft–Hartley Act
1955	Merger of AFL and CIO
1970	Occupational Safety and Health Act
1981	PATCO strike

1 The position of unions and organised labour

► *How far did the position of unions and organised labour improve in the period from 1865 to 1992?*

KEY TERMS

Labour The workforce or workers as opposed to the employers or owners of the factories and other industrial enterprises. (Spelled as *labor* in the USA.)

Mediation Negotiations between employers and employees to resolve disputes and reach a settlement.

Capitalism An economic system based on private enterprise, rather than state control, of the economy. Companies are privately owned and consumers therefore have a choice of which goods to buy.

Collective bargaining Workers' representatives join together and negotiate over issues such as pay and conditions.

No-strike clauses Provisions in workers' contracts to forbid striking.

This period of history gave rise to many issues around the position of union and **labour** rights in the USA, such as:

- the right for unions to exist
- recognition of unions
- the involvement of unions in negotiations over pay and working conditions
- the establishment of systems for **mediation**
- the freedom of workers to withdraw their labour without fear of punishment.

Progress in these areas was not continuous. There were periods either when improvements did not occur, or were very limited, as employers and, very often, the government, were reluctant to support unionisation. Economic change, the growth of **capitalism**, the amount of immigration and other factors all influenced the progress of union and labour rights during this period.

At the start of the period, the rights of workers and unions were completely dependent on what workers could negotiate with their employers. However, there was no requirement for employers to even recognise unions, let alone negotiate with them. This meant that workers had no representation or protection from their employers and could therefore be exploited.

By the end of the period, workers had won the right to join a union, although some employers had also been able to create workplaces where unions were forbidden (workers had been forced to accept this because of the actual fall in wages and fears they would lose their jobs because of the decline in the economy). Unions had also secured the right to **collective bargaining**, but, as with the right to join a union, this was limited in practice. Without union representation, the workers were in a weak position to improve their rights, yet they did not want to risk confrontation with their employers for fear of losing their jobs. Unions had also secured the right for workers to withdraw their labour and go on strike, but once again this was limited in practice as some employers had brought in **no-strike clauses**, which prevented workers from taking industrial action. Therefore, although the position of workers had certainly improved since the start of the period, the gains that they had made in earlier parts of the period were not always maintained.

The extent of labour and union rights by the First World War

The position of unions improved in the period leading to the outbreak of the First World War in 1914. This was reflected in the growth of union membership, but, initially, many of the gains were limited to white, male workers. And even by 1914, there was no guarantee that these gains were permanent.

The unions that did exist in 1865 represented only skilled workers in craft industries such as shoemakers, yet the USA was undergoing a period of rapid **industrialisation** (see Table 2.1), which meant that many of the new, unskilled workers were excluded from unions and therefore had no representation or protection. Employers also hired unskilled workers under contracts, rather than permanent employment, and this meant that workers could be laid off (be put out of work) when there was less need for their work. Workers were working long hours in factories where safety precautions were limited, which resulted in a large number of accidents. Despite this, employers would often not introduce health and safety standards as it would reduce their profits through greater supervision. Workers who suffered industrial injuries received little or no support from their employers and even the courts considered that industrial injury was a risk that the employee had to take.

Unions in the late nineteenth century

However, the increasing industrialisation did result in the development and growth of a number of unions. The most notable of these were **the Knights of Labor (KOL)** and the **American Federation of Labor (AFL)**. The KOL reached a membership of 700,000 by 1886, having had only 20,000 members in 1881, suggesting that its successful strike action was crucial in its growth. However, after the violence of the Haymarket Affair (see page 94) its reputation collapsed and its membership fell to just 100,000 by 1890. Additionally, in 1905, the **Industrial Workers of the World** or 'Wobblies' was established, but this union was less effective. Its militancy and violence meant that it was disliked by employers. It did attract some 100,000 members by 1923 but went into decline thereafter.

It was not just the violence of the Haymarket Affair that affected membership of unions (and hence their influence), but also the obvious divisions within the workforce. In this period, the arrival of African American workers in the labour market after the abolition of slavery and the end of the Civil War (see the box on page 68) meant that white workers no longer enjoyed a monopoly of the labour market. Former slaves were now available for employment in the growing industries and most accepted lower rates of pay. Employers exploited this by laying off (firing) white workers and replacing them with African Americans. Their position was made more difficult by the arrival of new immigrants from Europe, as well as Asia, which only added to the available pool of workers.

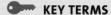

KEY TERMS

Industrialisation
The development of large-scale industries, such as steel and textiles, across much of the country.

Knights of Labor (KOL)
Founded in 1869 and developed in the period after 1879 under the leadership of Terence Powderly. It conducted a successful strike against the Wabash Railroad in 1885, which further encouraged workers to join. However, it lost influence following the Haymarket Affair of 1886.

American Federation of Labor (AFL) This replaced the KOL and attempted to unite all unions, so that by 1914 it had some 2 million members.

Industrial Workers of the World This union was set up in 1905 and had a reputation for violence and militancy, but did attempt to fight for the rights of poorer workers and immigrants. However, their violence meant that they were constantly under pressure from the authorities.

Table 2.1 Steel production in the USA 1860–1910

Year	Production (tons)
1860	920,000
1870	1,000,000
1880	1,200,000
1890	5,000,000
1900	10,300,000
1910	28,200,000

Existing unions saw these arrivals as a significant challenge and therefore refused to allow them to join the unions, which further limited the size of the unions and therefore their ability to exert pressure on employers. A divided, rather than a united, workforce made it easier for employers to exploit them.

The American Civil War

The Civil War between the Northern and Southern US states had lasted from 1861 to 1865. One of the main causes of the conflict was the issue of slavery, which was used in the Southern or Confederate states on cotton and other plantations. President Abraham Lincoln had promised an end to slavery with his Emancipation Proclamation issued in 1863. This was put into practice with the Thirteenth Amendment to the constitution in 1865, which abolished slavery everywhere following the defeat of the Southern states (see page 14).

The progress in obtaining rights for workers was further weakened by two other strikes: the Homestead strike of 1892 (see pages 94–5) and the Pullman strike of 1894 (see page 82). The Homestead strike virtually bankrupted the Amalgamated Association of Iron and Steel Workers, and resulted in a decline in union membership from a high of 24,000 in 1891 to just 6300 by 1909. Similarly, the Pullman strike, which developed from the employer's refusal to recognise the right of workers to use collective bargaining to protect their living and working conditions, also showed the difficulties unions faced in trying to gain recognition.

It would therefore appear that, by the outbreak of the First World War, little had been achieved in advancing union and workers' rights. However, the apparent lack of progress should be balanced against how:

- Union membership across the USA had grown to over 2 million members.
- Unions had begun to put pressure on candidates in elections to support workers' rights.

Yet, there were more factors that suggest the position of organised labour was no stronger than it had been in 1865:

- Unions represented only twenty per cent of the non-agricultural workforce.
- Many industries, such as steel or car manufacturing, did not have unions.
- Although there were often negotiations between employers and unions, many of the unions were not legally recognised and therefore lacked real power over decisions.
- Workers were divided by ethnicity, gender and level of skill. These divisions were exploited by employers (see page 89).
- The gains that had been made were often limited to white, male, skilled workers.

The First World War and interwar years

The period of the First World War, the **New Deal** and the Second World War witnessed some progress, more due to necessity than willingness on the part of employers.

The First World War 1914–18

During the First World War, the position of workers and unions improved. As factory owners saw an increased demand for their products, such as textiles for uniforms or steel for weapons, and there was therefore more opportunity to increase profits, they were more willing to be conciliatory towards their workers. To ensure that production was maintained, the government recognised and negotiated with unions through the **National War Labor Board (NWLB)**. As a result, the length of working hours was limited to eight, but in return workers agreed to a no-strike policy.

The boom of the 1920s

The economic boom that followed the war resulted in a rise in **real wages** and a decline in unemployment. It also appeared as if workers had made further gains compared with the period before the war. Employees were often offered benefits such as a reduction in working hours, pensions, insurance and other services. However, the development of **welfare capitalism** was usually in return for no-strike agreements and abandoning the right to negotiate wages, as employers feared that workers would take advantage of the low rates of unemployment to demand more money. Additionally, in some industries, company unions were set up, which meant that in practice workers lost their independence and were sometimes forced to sign a '**yellow-dog contract**'.

Many employers still refused to recognise unions, as had been the situation before the First World War. The most notable of these was Henry Ford. He exerted a tight control over his workforce and it would take until 1941 before he would recognise any union for collective bargaining. The struggle for recognition was also evident at the Pullman Company, which manufactured railway carriages. The company employed a significant number of African Americans as **porters**, who had few rights:

- Their working conditions were poor.
- They relied on tips for much of their income.
- Promotion was denied as the job of conductor was limited to whites.
- The company also prevented any effort to organise a union, sacking leaders and sometimes assaulting them.

KEY TERMS

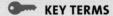

New Deal The early period of F.D. Roosevelt's presidency from 1933 to 1939, during which time a large number of reforms were passed to tackle the economic and social problems caused by a stock market crash and the resulting Great Depression.

National War Labor Board (NWLB) First created by President Wilson in 1918 to settle disputes between workers and employers. This ensured that production would not be interrupted by strikes.

Real wages Used to describe what wages can actually buy. Wages might rise, but if prices rise faster then real wages are falling, and if wages rise faster than prices then real wages rise.

Welfare capitalism A policy followed by employers during the boom of the 1920s to reduce industrial unrest. It entailed offering workers improved working conditions and other benefits such as pensions, in return for the establishment of unions under the control or direction of the employers.

Yellow-dog contracts Contracts that workers signed whereby they agreed not to join a union.

Porter Someone who looked after train passengers, particularly in sleeping cars, preparing the coaches and cleaning them after use.

(Asa) Philip Randolph

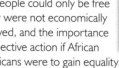

1889	Born in Crescent City, Florida
1911	Moved to New York
1913	Married a widow, Lucille Green
1917	Founded the *Messenger* magazine
1920	Stood for election as Comptroller of New York State
1922	Stood for election as Secretary of State for New York
1925	President of the BSCP
1950	Co-founder of the Leadership Conference on Civil Rights
1963	Led the March on Washington
1979	Died in New York

Early life

A. Philip Randolph's father was a minister and his mother a seamstress. He attended the only academic high school in Florida for African Americans, excelling in many areas. At first he worked odd jobs, but moved to New York in 1911 and took social science classes at college. In 1913, he married Lucille Green, a Harvard graduate.

Early career

Randolph began his career as an academic and member of the Socialist Party, familiar with the concepts of the Industrial Workers of the World (see page 67). During this period, he developed two notions that would influence his beliefs: the idea that people could only be free if they were not economically deprived, and the importance of collective action if African Americans were to gain equality.

Union activity

This began in 1917 when he organised his first union, and in 1919 he became president of the National Brotherhood of Workers of America. However, his greatest triumph was in 1925 when he became president of the BSCP. In 1955, he became vice president of the merged American Federation of Labor and the Congress of Industrial Organizations or AFL-CIO (see pages 74 and 89).

Civil rights leader

Randolph's union success allowed him to emerge as a major figure in the civil rights movement. He persuaded President Roosevelt to end racial discrimination in federal government and President Truman to end segregation in the armed forces. In 1950, he co-founded the Leadership Conference on Civil Rights, which coordinated campaigns on all civil rights laws. He joined Martin Luther King Jr in the campaign to end segregation in schools and helped to teach King how to organise peaceful protests. In 1963, he was the head of the March on Washington at which King delivered his famous speech.

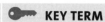

KEY TERM

National Mediation Board The US government established the agency to regulate labour relations in the railway industry. Its aim was to resolve disputes and prevent strikes through arbitration.

The porters appointed Philip Randolph to lead their counter-campaign, and set up the Brotherhood of Sleeping Car Porters (BSCP) union. The Pullman Company countered, established its own union and banned meetings of the BSCP. Although nearly half the porters joined the BSCP, they had not gained recognition by 1928. Some union leaders then wanted to strike to force the company to negotiate, an issue which divided the union. However, by 1934, under President Roosevelt, a change in the law, with the passing of the Railway Labor Act, meant that the BSCP could claim the right to represent the porters. Randolph was able to demand that the **National Mediation Board** officially declare the BSCP as the porters' representative. The union defeated the company union in elections to decide who should represent the workers, and in 1935 finally gained recognition and Pullman began to negotiate with them. Within a year the union had enrolled 51 per cent of all porters.

Pullman strike of 1894. Examining the wreckage of burned freight cars at a Chicago, Illinois, railway yard. Photograph from a contemporary American newspaper.

The Great Depression 1929

The improvements in living standards that some workers had made during the boom years were brought to an end by the Great Depression, which began with the **Wall Street Crash**. It might be expected that, in a period of high unemployment, labour and union rights would suffer as employers could exploit the weak position of workers who feared for their jobs. Employers took tough action against strikers during this period, often calling in the police or their own **strike breakers**. As a result, union membership fell, as being unable to strike severely undermined the workers' position and union strength.

President Roosevelt's New Deal

However, the introduction of President Roosevelt's New Deal shortly after the Wall Street Crash, in 1933, has led some historians to argue that this was a high point in labour rights. Roosevelt introduced a wide range of legislation, some of which was beneficial to the labour movement, to tackle the economic problems the USA faced and get people back to work. The first Act passed was the National Industry Recovery Act (NIRA) of 1933, which encouraged firms to agree to codes of practice which dealt with improving hours, wage rates and union rights. Perhaps one of the biggest changes was that it enshrined in law the right of workers to organise unions and take part in collective bargaining. Although this was a major step forward in union rights, the effects were limited as not all employers signed the code (for example, Henry Ford). Additionally, the Supreme Court declared the Act unconstitutional and therefore many of the gains for workers were reversed.

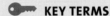

KEY TERMS

Wall Street Crash
In October 1929, the prices of shares fell dramatically on Wall Street in New York, the USA's financial centre. This led to a loss of confidence and the prices of shares continued to fall, which sent the economy into recession. Workers were laid off and unemployment soared, not just in the USA; much of the world also went into recession.

Strike breakers Workers who are willing to work while others are on strike, thus making the strike ineffectual.

Although the NIRA did not necessarily improve the position of workers, there is little doubt that the National Labor Relations Act, or Wagner Act, of 1935 did benefit them. It represented a great step forward from the pre-war period:

- It established the National Labor Relations Board (NLRB), which could negotiate on behalf of workers and prevent companies from using their own unions. It also looked into accusations of unfair labour practices and reached a judgement on issues brought before it.
- Workers were given the right to elect their own representatives to undertake collective bargaining.
- Just as importantly, this Act was declared constitutional.
- Workers were also given the right to join unions, while using spies against unions was banned.
- The Act recognised the role of unions, unlike any other legislation, and this resulted in the rapid expansion of union membership, rising from 3.7 million in 1933 to 9 million by 1938.

The increasing number of unionised workers also increased their power. Although some firms initially resisted, most, including General Motors, one of the three big car manufacturers and employing over 80,000, were forced to accept the change in circumstances. A sit-in strike in 1936 resulted in the recognition of the United Automobile Workers' Union and then the Steel Workers Organizing Committee was recognised by US Steel in 1937.

Table 2.2 Union membership in the interwar years

Year	Membership
1930	3,401,000
1935	3,584,000
1940	8,717,000

The passing of the Fair Labor Standards Act of 1939 also gave workers a minimum wage. It therefore appeared as if the position of workers by the time of the outbreak of the Second World War in 1939 was far stronger than it had been at the end of the First World War in 1918. The benefits of New Deal legislation were reflected in the growth of union membership during this period (see Table 2.2).

Unfortunately, these improvements benefited only some workers. Many unskilled workers did not have rights and therefore many in mass-production industries, such as car manufacturing, still lacked the gains that had been made. It was those, particularly at the lower end of the pay scales and probably most in need of protection, who did not benefit. In practice, this meant that many from ethnic minorities, particularly African Americans and Mexican immigrants, were still in a very vulnerable position – as were women, who were almost always paid less than men. Moreover, the National Labor Relations Act did not give agricultural workers the right to join unions. Attempts to improve their position would have to wait until the 1960s when the United Farm Workers union, under Cesar Chavez and Dolores Huerta, was founded (see pages 74–5).

The Second World War

The improvement in the position of labour continued during the Second World War as, once again, workers proved essential to war production. The strong position of workers was reflected in wage increases, which went up by some 70 per cent during this period. Unemployment fell to such an extent that there was a virtual labour shortage. The improved position was also reflected in the continued growth in union membership, boosted from 9 million in 1938 to nearly 15 million by the end of the war. In such a situation the power and position of unions had increased considerably, particularly in comparison with the situation in 1918. Some historians see this as the high point or turning point of the union movement.

It is hard to disagree with this view. Not only had unions gained recognition, but laws were also in place to ensure that labour rights were recognised. Union membership had soared, which gave workers a more influential voice in politics. The balance of power between workers and employers had moved in favour of workers, although many employers were still unwilling to fully accept this shift or see it as permanent.

The post-Second World War period

The period immediately after the war witnessed a large number of strikes and, it was probably this that resulted in a decline in the position of the unions. Additionally:

- Many people in politics believed that the unions had become too powerful under Roosevelt.
- The **Taft–Hartley Act of 1947** limited the power of unions. Although this development appeared to represent a backwards move, there were some individual victories. In 1948, workers at General Motors negotiated a pay agreement linked to the cost of living, and a pension package.

The economic changes that followed the Second World War also threatened to undermine the position of workers. The growth in the number of **white-collar workers** and subsequent decline in the number of **blue-collar workers** meant that fewer workers were joining unions. Overall membership fell between 1945 and 1950 because many of the new jobs were in government posts and these workers signed no-strike agreements. The position and influence of unions were also hit because many workers were now so much better off than they had been, having gained paid holidays, healthcare, pensions and pay rises linked to the cost of living, and so they were less interested in union activity.

KEY TERMS

Taft–Hartley Act of 1947 Prevented unions from running a closed shop, where one union dominated and all workers had to belong to it, and regulated the relationship between unions and employers.

White-collar workers Those who work in professional, technical or clerical work.

Blue-collar workers Those who carry out manual work.

The 1960s

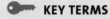

Workers did make some gains in the 1960s. President Kennedy's administration passed the Equal Pay Act in 1963, which gave men and women 'equal pay for equal work'. Those workers who lived in poverty or close to the poverty line benefited from Johnson's 'Great Society' policy. Although primarily the Great

Society was an attack on poverty, laws passed under it helped workers in other ways. The Civil Rights Act of 1964 outlawed discrimination based on race, colour, religion, sex or national origin, while the Economic Opportunity Act of 1964 increased training opportunities and the Age Discrimination Act of 1968 protected those aged over 40 years. Workers also gained from the merger of the American Federation of Labor and the **Congress of Industrial Organizations** (AFL-CIO), which had taken place in 1955. This merger brought together some 85 per cent of union members and gave the movement more influence and power with its 16 million members. More unions could now:

- bargain over conditions
- bargain over wages
- negotiate over contract conditions
- gain medical and dental insurance
- negotiate paid holidays
- gain pensions
- negotiate unemployment insurance.

These gains gave membership of unions an increased attraction, particularly as union workers' pay was often twenty per cent higher than that for non-union members. Despite this, the position for many African American workers had seen little improvement, and their position worsened even more because of the changes in industry. The demand for more skilled and technically advanced workers disadvantaged many African Americans. They simply lacked the necessary education, as a result of the majority of them living in poverty and being ill-educated from the poor-quality schools provided for many African Americans (in stark contrast to the education most white Americans received).

Although economic changes in the period from the 1950s to the end of the 1960s threatened the position of unions, this period had seen unions consolidate their position. There was little doubt that the right to join a union, which had not been possible a century earlier, was now firmly established. Unions were now collaborating with employers and the confrontations that had characterised the earlier period, in the nineteenth century, appeared to be in decline. Workers had certainly gained many benefits, but some of these were given as part of a policy to reduce the likelihood of workers going on strike. This appears to have been a success, according to Table 2.3.

KEY TERMS

Congress of Industrial Organizations (CIO) Originally the Committee for Industrial Organizations, it was established in 1935 and made up of eight unions from the American Federation of Labor (AFL). These unions remained within the AFL, but were expelled in 1936 because of suspected links with communism. The CIO broke away, but rejoined the AFL in 1955.

United Farm Workers (UFW) A major union for farm labourers that resulted from the merger of two workers' rights organisations, the AWOC and the NFWA. The alliance between the two groups resulted in a series of strikes in 1965 in the grape farming community and led to the creation of the UFW.

Table 2.3 Strikes in the period 1950–65

Year	Number of workers striking
1950	3,030,000
1955	2,650,000
1960	1,320,000
1965	1,545,200

Cesar Chavez

Farmworkers had been one group of workers who had not gained from the benefits that organised labour in industry had gained. However, from the 1960s there were attempts to improve the position of farmworkers. Initially, they gained from the merger of two workers' rights organisations: the Agricultural Workers Organizing Committee (AWOC) and the National Farm Workers Association (NFWA), founded by Cesar Chavez, joined to become the United Farmworkers Organizing Committee in 1966, which then became the **United Farm Workers (UFW)** Union in 1972.

Cesar Chavez

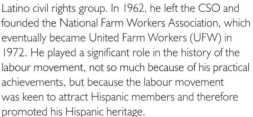

1927	Born in Yuma, Arizona
1942	Left school
1944	Joined the navy
1952	Organiser for the Community Service Organization
1962	Founded the National Farm Workers Association
1968	Fasted for 25 days
1972	Fasted in protest at an Arizona law that prohibited boycotts and strikes during harvest season
1993	Died

Early life

Chavez was born Césario Estrada Chávez. His family owned a small grocery store and ranch, but lost land during the Great Depression. Ultimately, the family lost their home and moved to California to become migrant farmworkers. Chavez left school in 1942 so that his mother did not have to work in the fields. In 1944, he joined the navy, but did not enjoy it. On returning after two years, he married and moved to San Jose, California.

Labour leader

Chavez worked in the fields until 1952. During the 1950s, Chavez worked for the Community Service Organization (CSO), a Latino civil rights group. In 1962, he left the CSO and founded the National Farm Workers Association, which eventually became United Farm Workers (UFW) in 1972. He played a significant role in the history of the labour movement, not so much because of his practical achievements, but because the labour movement was keen to attract Hispanic members and therefore promoted his Hispanic heritage.

Decline

Chavez was involved in clashes with other union members in the 1970s. It appeared as if he had abandoned his union activity as he became involved in real estate development, which caused an embarrassment as non-union workers were used. However, he returned to agricultural issues and in 1988 organised another, final, grape boycott over the exposure of workers to pesticides. This ended in failure and he therefore undertook another fast, which damaged his health and was abandoned after 35 days.

Chavez adopted a policy of non-violence and turned the struggle of farmworkers into a moral cause, which won national sympathy. His tactics forced growers to recognise the UFW as the bargaining organisation for field workers in California and Florida. In the early 1970s, the UFW organised strikes and boycotts, including the Salad Bowl strike, the largest farmworker strike in US history, which won higher wages for those working for lettuce and grape growers. He was also involved in the struggle to limit immigration, as he believed that it undermined the position of workers born in the USA while it also exploited immigrants.

As part of his protests, Chavez went on a series of fasts to promote non-violence and in response to legislation passed in Arizona that prohibited boycotts and strikes by farmworkers during harvest time. The UFW eventually declined in the 1970s, but, in 1975, he secured victory in California when the California Agricultural Labor Relations Act established the California Agricultural Relations Board to oversee collective bargaining for farm labourers.

The late 1960s saw a decline in union membership, not because of the failure of unions to protect workers, but because of the technological changes that resulted in a more skilled workforce that did not look to unions to protect their position.

Towards the end of the period

The falling union membership (see Table 2.4) continued until 1992. The power and importance of unions were reduced compared with both the 1960s and the period of the New Deal, but the rights that had been won largely remained. Organised labour was certainly in a stronger position than at the start of 1865.

The decline in union membership was a reflection of the continuing change in the structure of the American workforce and economy, but also due to events such as the Professional Air Traffic Controllers Organization (PATCO) strike in 1981 (see pages 85–6) and the change in attitudes among both the government and public towards unions. The number of strikes and the number of workers taking part in those strikes also decreased (see Table 2.4). The lack of public sympathy for the air traffic controllers' actions discouraged other strikes and was a further indication of a decline in union power and influence.

Table 2.4 Strikes in the USA 1970–90

Year	Number of strikes	Workers involved
1970	381	2,468,000
1980	187	795,000
1985	54	324,000
1990	44	185,000

In the 1980s and early 1990s, unions were under attack from all sides:

- Both the government and employers had their issues with unions (see pages 95–6).
- Divisions within the union movement, with others unwilling to support the PATCO air traffic controllers, whom they perceived as well paid, further weakened the position of workers.
- The decline in the size of factories and businesses meant that it was more difficult to organise workers and this also impacted on union recruitment, as reflected in Table 2.5.
- This decline in membership was further encouraged by the continued provision by employers of generous welfare packages. As a result of these gains, many workers were no worse off than in earlier periods, but saw little to be gained from union membership.
- There were also an increasing number of female and white-collar workers who were less interested in joining unions.

Table 2.5 Trade union membership 1970–90

Year	Membership
1970	19,381,000
1975	19,611,000
1980	19,843,000
1985	16,996,000
1990	16,740,000

The period also witnessed the growth of non-unionised firms. This meant that employers were able to ignore the law and deny workers their rights. This became an increasing trend when employers discovered that they were able to effectively get away with it. The NLRB (see page 72) was less willing to defend union rights and this resulted in employer interests taking precedence over those of the workers. The employer was now in a stronger position than during the period of the New Deal and Second World War.

While union power and influence had been reduced, it would be wrong to see workers in the same position as they were in 1865. By 1992, workers had the right to:

- join a union, although there were non-union firms
- collective bargaining, but the threat of unemployment weakened their position
- strike (although some government workers were forbidden, and there were some firms where employees had signed no-strike clauses).

The position of female workers had also improved with advances towards equal pay and opportunity. However, the changes had not brought the same benefits to all groups of workers; many African Americans and Hispanic workers were still in vulnerable positions and were often low paid. The following sections will consider the factors that both encouraged and hindered the development of union and labour rights.

Summary diagram: The position of unions and organised labour

How did it improve?	Why did it change?
Right to exist	Economic changes
Recognition	Growth of capitalism
Negotiate pay and conditions	Immigration
Mediate	Impact of war
Strike	Role of government

2 Industrial growth and economic change

▶ *Did industrial growth and economic change help or hinder union and labour rights from 1865 to 1992?*

The American economy fluctuated wildly over the period from 1865 to 1992. Economic downturns such as the Great Depression as well as the periods of growth such as the Gilded Age had a great impact on the position of unions and labour rights for workers.

The Gilded Age

A term used to describe the period in US history from *c*.1870 to 1890. It was a period of rapid economic growth, particularly booming in the Northern and Western states. In particular, industries such as railways, mining, iron and steel and the financial sector grew. Workers gained from high wages, which attracted large numbers of immigrants from Europe. However, many of the immigrants lived in poverty and did not benefit from these gains.

Labour rights during periods of industrial growth and economic change

Growth in the American economy usually resulted in an increased demand for workers but this did not always result in the actual development of union rights. Employees were often in a stronger position than in times of economic downturn, such as the Great Depression and the 1930s, where the fear of being made unemployed did not always result in the gaining of labour rights. A growing economy may have allowed labour organisations to increase pressure on employers, at first for union recognition and then better pay and conditions. However, this was not always the case as in the latter part of the period the improvements in workers' living conditions meant that many were less interested in union activity. Therefore, while industrial growth improved workers' conditions, it may not have helped in the struggle for union rights.

Skilled and unskilled workers in the nineteenth century

Workers' organisations were able to use the growth in the number of industrial workers from 885,000 to 3.2 million in the period from 1860 to 1900 to win some concessions from employers. This economic growth increased the demand for unions, resulting in the formation of the KOL in 1869, the AFL in 1886 and the Industrial Workers of the World in 1905 (see page 67). The creation of a large number of unskilled workers, due to the development of mass production and growth in **heavy industry**, resulted in a new wave of workers who wanted

KEY TERM

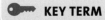

Heavy industry Industries such as coal, iron and steel, and textiles.

representation and protection. Although progress in obtaining rights was slow, union membership grew from 500,000 at the end of the nineteenth century to 2.5 million in 1915 and 5 million by 1920. The sheer number of workers increased pressure on employers to recognise unions. Although much still depended on fluctuations in the economy, the changes had resulted in some progress.

The 1920s

The boom in the economy in the 1920s allowed some of this process to continue. In order to meet a growing consumer demand for new goods, such as washing machines, refrigerators and cars, not only were more workers taken on but real wages rose. The increased demand for workers and the low level of unemployment forced some employers to take conciliatory action, either in the form of union recognition or through 'welfare capitalism'. Although it can be argued that welfare capitalism limited the rights of workers, there were some gains with employers such as Henry Ford, who cut the working day to eight hours, doubled the daily wage to $5 and introduced profit-sharing.

The 1950s

The developments of the 1920s were very similar to those in the 1950s. Once again, a period of prosperity resulted in the rapid improvement in the economic position of workers, with average income by the end of the 1950s some 35 per cent higher than it had been at the end of the Second World War. Workers were therefore able to take advantage of the availability of consumer goods, with 75 per cent owning cars and 87 per cent owning at least one television. However, as with the 1920s, although the standard of living for workers had risen it was not always reflected in an improvement in their rights. Moreover, increasing prosperity made many workers less likely to support unions and risk their gains through industrial action. This trend continued into the 1970s, with those involved in **high-tech industries** and skill-based industries witnessing significant rises in their wages, but therefore having less concern for workers' organisations.

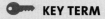

> **KEY TERM**
>
> **High-tech industries** Industries such as computer-based enterprises that require a highly skilled and trained labour force.

Growth or depression?

It is possible to argue that it was not just periods of boom that saw an increase in the position of unions, but also periods of depression. This is particularly true of the Great Depression and the 1930s. Although the high levels of unemployment (rising from 3 per cent in 1929 to 25 per cent by 1933) made workers vulnerable and often just grateful that they had a job, the legislation that was introduced as part of the New Deal to get people back to work had a profound impact on union rights. However, this development was more the result of government action (see page 84) as it attempted to deal with high levels of unemployment and increased conflict between employers and employees.

Did industrial growth and economic change hinder labour and union rights?

At the start of the period, the increase in mass production was the main factor limiting union rights, whereas in the period after the Second World War it was the growth in white-collar employment, with the development of high-tech and service industries, that had the largest impact. Additionally, economic change, and the resulting change in the composition and nature of the workforce, had a particularly limiting impact at the start and end of the period.

The nineteenth century

The exceptional growth in the American economy, particularly during the Gilded Age, created an unprecedented demand for unskilled labour in industries such as construction, machine tools and clothing. The craft unions that existed saw the addition of these workers to the job market as a threat to their position and therefore were unwilling to allow them to join their unions. This division (see page 89) served only to weaken the union movement, as even when unskilled workers attempted to establish their own unions, employers could often resist because of the lack of unity among workers. The change in industrial structure and the frequent failure to gain union recognition for the unskilled workers resulted in large numbers of workers being exposed to dangerous conditions and long hours with no organisation to protect them.

The booms of the 1880s and 1920s

The end of the Gilded Age negatively impacted on the position of workers. The fall in demand meant that fewer workers were needed and therefore employers were able to lower wages, as there was a readily available workforce. Workers were unable to combat this as the unions lacked the power to take on employers and, when they did, the violence that often ensued further weakened the union movement (see pages 94–5). However, as the previous section has shown, a decline in the economy did not always result in a worsening of the position of workers (see page 79).

In some ways, the Gilded Age was similar to the period after the First World War, when the ensuing boom of the 1920s did little to advance labour rights. Although workers did gain from a rise in real wages and 'welfare capitalism' (see page 69), in practice welfare capitalism limited their independence.

Economic change post-Second World War

Both the boom and the changing nature of the American economy after the Second World War had a negative impact on the position of unions:

- New technology and increased automation in many industries during the 1950s saw the number of blue-collar workers decline. Union membership in these industries fell by some 50 per cent, weakening the bargaining power of the unions.

- As well as this, the changes in the economy saw a growth in the number of white-collar workers, particularly in the service industries and in the government sector. Some workers were forced to sign non-union agreements. Both developments limited the influence of the unions.
- This was further reinforced by the growing number of women in employment, as often they did not join the male-dominated unions.

The result was a decline in the percentage of the workforce who were members of unions during the 1950s and 1960s because of the technological changes and the changing nature of the workforce.

Economic change in the USA from the 1970s only added to the difficulties for organised labour. Not only did economic growth slow, often as a result of foreign competition, but there was also a decline in productivity. This caused:

- A rise in unemployment and a fall in real wages, particularly among the unskilled.
- An increased reliance on high-tech industries, which required more skilled and white-collar labour workers who were more reluctant to join unions.
- Relocation: high-tech industries also often relocated to areas outside major cities and were usually much smaller enterprises than the large factories of earlier periods. This meant that the workforce was more dispersed and therefore harder to unionise.
- A general reluctance of highly paid skilled workers, who were often given incentive packages, to support unions.
- An increase in new industries employing a large number of women, who, as in the 1950s and 1960s, were less interested in joining unions.

For these varying reasons, many workers were less willing to either join unions or take part in union action, which weakened the position of organised labour at the end of the period.

Summary diagram: Industrial growth and economic change

Period	Economic change	Union rights
1860–1900	Growth	• Some concessions
1920s	Growth	• Welfare capitalism • Unions gained little
1950s	Growth	• Real wages rose • Less interest in unions • Decline in unions

3 Federal government attitudes and actions

► *How far did government action and the attitudes of the federal government help or hinder the development of labour rights?*

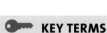

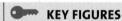

American governments intervened in the economy only at times of emergency. This meant that, for most of 1865–1992, they adopted a ***laissez-faire*** policy. In practice, this favoured the employers as it allowed them to form large business corporations and, for some individuals in the late nineteenth and early twentieth centuries, such as **John Rockefeller** and **Andrew Carnegie**, to build up large industrial enterprises. By doing this, manufacturers were able to exploit their employees and deny them a voice to complain. This was probably the most consistent way government action and attitudes hindered the development of union rights. Throughout much of the period, the government therefore allowed capitalism to thrive and businesses to work together to make large profits.

The Pullman strike 1894

Government action in support of workers was therefore unusual in the early years of this period, with the passing of the **Sherman Anti-Trust Act** of 1890 being an exception to the pattern. The government's *laissez-faire* attitude usually ensured that any intervention would be on the side of the employers. This was certainly the case during the Pullman strike of 1894. Initially, the attorney general had issued an **injunction** which stopped anyone from interfering with the movement of mail. President Cleveland then sent in some 2000 federal troops to break the strike despite claiming it was only to ensure the movement of mail. Troops fired at the protesters and killed four people, showing that the government was willing to kill its own people. A clear indication that federal authorities were willing to act to prevent unions from exerting their rights was shown by the Supreme Court legalising the use of injunctions, and issuing the Omnibus Indictment Act which prohibited strikers and workers' representatives from trying to persuade others to strike. This Act remained in force until the passing of the Wagner Act in 1935 (see page 72). In this instance, it meant that when the indictment was read and the workers did not disperse they were declared in contempt and the strike illegal. Therefore, the nineteenth century was certainly characterised by the government upholding the position of employers against unions.

The two world wars

The government also intervened in 1914 with the passing of the Clayton Anti-Trust Act, which limited the use of injunctions against striking workers and allowed peaceful **picketing**, provided protesters did not damage property. A general lack of legislation meant that owners could reduce wages and lay

KEY TERMS

Laissez-faire A belief that the government should not interfere in the economy and that businesses and owners should be allowed to manage their affairs free from regulation.

Sherman Anti-Trust Act An attempt to restrict monopolies by which large companies were able to control a trade.

Injunction A legal order preventing an action from being carried out or, in some instances, forcing an action to be carried out.

Picketing During a strike, workers may stand outside a place of work to discourage other workers from entering the business.

KEY FIGURES

John Rockefeller (1839–1937)
A US businessman who controlled 90 per cent of US oil refineries. He built up a personal fortune of over $1 billion.

Andrew Carnegie (1835–1919)
He controlled 25 per cent of US iron and steel production. He sold the company in 1901 for $250 million.

workers off at times of depression. The unwillingness of the government to intervene ensured that workers had no means of seeking redress of grievances.

It was the need for the production of war goods during the First World War that saw the government's first move towards supporting organised labour. It recognised unions and established the NWLB to negotiate with unions (see page 88). However, it must be remembered that this was done not out of sympathy for unions but because of the need to sustain production and prevent strikes. As such, it was successful as **Samuel Gompers**, leader of the AFL, ordered his large number of workers not to strike. The improvement in the position of unions as a result of government action helped to increase union membership during the war years.

A similar process was repeated during the Second World War when the government re-established the NWLB. Once again, the improved position of unions encouraged workers to join and membership rose considerably. Government action had improved the position of workers, but as with the First World War, this was because their efforts were essential to the war effort rather than because of any sympathy with the workers.

In contrast, support for employers was seen after the Second World War. Many in government, particularly **Republicans**, who had won the 1946 election, believed that the power of unions had grown too strong. As a result, they passed the Taft–Hartley Act in 1947 to restrain union power. They also sought to reduce the influence of **Communists**, whom they believed dominated much of the labour movement. This policy served to weaken the CIO as they expelled Communist-led groups from the organisation, thus reducing its membership.

The role of the Supreme Court

The Supreme Court had played a crucial role in limiting the rights of workers through its use of injunctions to break the Pullman strike (see page 82). This policy of supporting employers and hindering the progress of workers' rights continued into the twentieth century with the *Lochner* v. *New York* case of 1905.

In *Lochner* v. *New York*, the Supreme Court rejected the law that limited the number of hours a baker could work each day and week. The court did not accept the argument that the law was needed to protect the health of bakers and decided that the law was an attempt to regulate the terms of employment, which it described as 'unreasonable, unnecessary and arbitrary interference with the right and liberty of the individual to contract'. This judgment began a series which invalidated laws to regulate working conditions during the period up to the Second World War. In this period it:

- allowed yellow-dog contracts in the *Coppage* v. *Kansas* case of 1915
- stated that minimum wage laws violated the due process clause in the *Adkins* v. *Children's Hospital* case of 1923.

KEY FIGURE

Samuel Gompers (1850–1924)

Leader of the AFL, he ensured the acceptance of the AFL by employers.

KEY TERMS

Republicans One of the two main political parties in the USA. The Republican Party is usually seen as being on the right of the political spectrum, believing in low taxes and little government intervention in the economy.

Communists People who believe that the economy should be state controlled and planned.

The intervention of the Supreme Court reached its climax in 1935 when it found the NIRA to be unconstitutional. The case involved the Schechter Brothers, a firm selling chickens that were not fit for human consumption. They were prosecuted by the NIRA for breaking its codes, but the court ruled that it was not a matter for the federal government. This meant that not only could the federal government not intervene in internal state issues, but if they could not prosecute firms for breaking NIRA codes then the NIRA codes were unconstitutional. This was because the federal government had developed the codes, but they were imposed on individual firms in different states. The court declared that the federal government had no right to intervene in matters that were the concern of individual states and that the federal government had acted unconstitutionally by taking the power to implement the codes. Ultimately, NIRA, which had brought in measures to regulate relations between employers and employees and had done much to improve the position of workers, was destroyed.

How important were presidents in the development of labour rights?

The impact of President Roosevelt

Perhaps the most significant government intervention that helped workers was during Roosevelt's presidency. The collapse in world trade that followed the Great Depression necessitated the introduction of a programme to get the large numbers of unemployed back to work, and to stop the industrial unrest that the collapse had triggered. New Deal legislation transformed the position of workers and organised labour. More government legislation not only helped to reduce clashes between employers and employees and thus maintained production, but also gave the right to workers to organise unions and take part in collective bargaining, allowed **closed shops**, prevented companies from using **blacklists** or company unions, and established a minimum wage. This was done through:

- the National Industry Recovery Act (NIRA) of 1933 (see page 71)
- the National Labor Relations, or Wagner Act, of 1935 (see page 72)
- the creation of the National Labor Relations Board
- the Fair Labor Standards Act of 1938 (see page 72).

As a consequence, this legislation reduced the power of employers and prevented them from limiting the rights of their workers. Roosevelt had been reluctant to increase the power of workers. He may have seen the potential advantage for the Democrats in winning their support, but it is more likely that his main concern was to bring stability to industry by ending conflict between employer and employees. The growth in union membership that followed these reforms certainly suggests that government action played a crucial role in the growth of unionism during his presidency.

KEY TERMS

Closed shop A workplace where one union dominates and workers have to belong to that union.

Blacklist A list of workers who are regarded as unacceptable.

The impact of the presidents of the 1960s and 1970s

Perhaps the only time that government advanced the cause of workers, outside war and national emergencies, was in the 1960s and 1970s. During the 1960s, legislation was introduced as part of the wider civil rights movement and the desire to reduce the number of people living below the poverty line. Therefore, as part of President John Kennedy's '**New Frontier**' and President Lyndon Johnson's '**Great Society**', a number of reforms that improved the position of workers were introduced:

- the Equal Pay Act (1963), which made wage discrimination on the basis of gender illegal
- the Civil Rights Act (1964), which helped African Americans and Hispanics who had been discriminated against at work
- the Economic Opportunity Act (1964), which provided funds to train people and increase their employment opportunities
- the Age Discrimination in Employment Act (1968), which prevented discrimination against people aged between 40 and 65.

This legislation did much to help those who had suffered discrimination through gender, ethnic origin and age.

Similar policies that helped workers were also seen under the presidencies of Richard Nixon and Jimmy Carter. Nixon brought in the 1970 Occupational Safety and Health Act, which aimed to provide a working environment which was free from hazards and insanitary conditions and reversed the position whereby the health and safety of workers had been largely ignored. Moreover, the Department of Labor set the standards, which meant that employers had little influence. Carter's presidency saw the establishment of a minimum wage, but attempts by the unions to persuade him to reform the National Labor Relations Act failed, showing that there were still limits to the government's willingness to support workers. This would become even more evident under Reagan.

The impact of President Reagan

It was towards the end of the period that presidential action played its most significant role in reducing the influence of the labour movement. On becoming president in 1981, Ronald Reagan was determined to reduce the powers of unions. His aim was to remove restrictive regulations that admittedly hindered US industry, but often protected workers. He also wanted to privatise publicly owned businesses, which again was not in the best interest of workers. It is clear that he believed that the pendulum had swung too far in favour of employees. This is most evident in the government's response to the PATCO strike of 1981. The strike occurred because the government was unwilling to allow air traffic controllers to be paid more for working fewer hours.

KEY TERMS

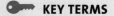

New Frontier Kennedy promised that the pioneering tradition would be maintained in a new way, by space exploration, by changes in US society and by new attitudes of commitment to the American way of life.

Great Society More changes were actually made during the presidency of Kennedy's successor, Lyndon Johnson, and the responsibilities of federal government in social reforms and civil rights expanded considerably to create a 'Great Society'. The feminist movement grew in the context of greater expectations in the Democrat era after 1960, of a fairer and more progressive society.

Members of the Professional Air Traffic Controllers Organization striking in Detroit in 1981.

The government was also concerned that such a strike would have a serious impact on the economy, let alone disrupt holidays. The strike was also in contravention of a 1955 Act which prevented government workers from striking. Reagan announced that if the workers did not return within 48 hours, their contracts would be ended. Those who did not strike were augmented by supervisors and military air-traffic controllers to keep air traffic moving and a training programme for new controllers was speeded up. Some have seen this as a turning point as it redefined industrial relations, and this was reflected in the decline in strikes and union membership that followed (see page 76). The government had given a clear message as to how they thought relations with unions should proceed and this was continued with the membership of the Labor Relations Board. Appointments to this board were made by the president and he ensured that those appointed supported his views and thus ensured that any disputes that went before it were likely to favour the employer.

Summary diagram: Federal government attitudes and actions

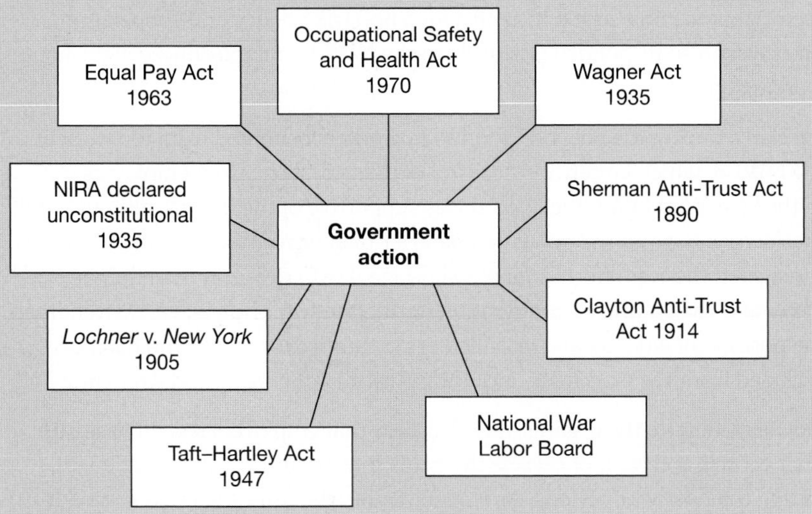

4 The First and Second World Wars

▶ *What was the impact of the First and Second World Wars on labour rights?*

The increased demand in production created by the two world wars offered employers the opportunity to increase their profits, but also meant that they had to adopt a more conciliatory attitude towards unions and their members (see pages 69 and 72–3). At the same time, the wars encouraged government intervention in the economy, which also benefited the workers. This is reflected in the increased union membership that occurred during the periods 1914–18 and again between 1939 and 1945. During the First World War, union membership rose from 2.7 million in 1916 to some 5 million by 1920, and during the Second World War from 8.9 million in 1940 to 14.8 million by 1945.

Not only did workers gain from the more conciliatory approach because of the demands for their labour, but they also gained from a rise in real wages. During the First World War, real wages rose by twenty per cent, whereas during the Second World War wages rose by a staggering 70 per cent owing to increases in overtime pay. These rises obviously raised the standard of living for industrial workers.

During the First World War, these benefits were further aided by the NWLB (see page 69). It recognised the unions as representing workers and guaranteed their rights to join a union in return for a no-strike policy and cooperation. Employers also responded positively to the NWLB and introduced eight-hour working days.

Similarly, during the Second World War, workers benefited from the work of the NWLB, which largely took control of industry away from employers. As in the First World War, the NWLB was supportive of the unions, although the president was given the power to take control of factories where strike action threatened the war effort. A labour shortage due to the growth in the armed forces and the ending of immigration during the war also helped to strengthen the position of workers and provided opportunities for many who had been excluded from the workforce, including African Americans and women.

However, despite these gains, it is also clear that employers sought to regain their control and limit or reverse the gains that organised labour had made during the post-war periods. As a result, industrial unrest was a common feature of both 1919–20 and 1946–7, with 1919 seeing some 4 million workers involved in industrial action and 1946 witnessing over 4.5 million. Therefore, although workers did make gains during the war years, these were often temporary.

Summary diagram: The First and Second World Wars

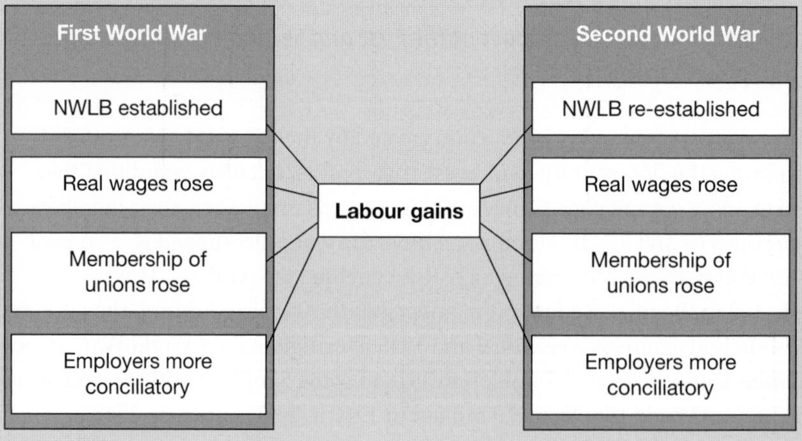

5 Union unity

► *How important was union unity in the development of labour rights?*

It was much easier for either the government or employers to restrict the position of unions if workers were divided. There is little doubt that throughout the period this was a constant problem, although it can be analysed under three main areas:

- skilled and unskilled workers
- ethnic divisions
- gender divisions.

Skilled and unskilled workers

At the start of the period, in the 1860s, the unions that existed were to protect those in skilled or craft industries (see page 78). They admitted only craftsmen and this meant that the idea of strength through numbers was ignored. Unions did not allow unskilled workers, women or African Americans to join. Despite attempts to develop unions for unskilled workers, this was still a problem on the outbreak of the First World War. Although skilled workers were trying to protect their positions, their opposition to unskilled workers limited the size of union membership and therefore the pressure that the workers could exert on both employers and government in this period. This division was also evident during the years of the New Deal, when large numbers of unskilled workers, particularly in the mass-production industries, were still denied their rights, with organisations such as the AFL being more concerned with protecting and unifying craft unions.

However, the situation began to change in the 1930s, and worker solidarity became more evident. The decision in 1935 by some unions to break away from the AFL, which was more interested in amalgamating craft unions than helping unskilled workers, began the process of union solidarity. This breakaway group set up the Committee on Industrial Organization, which by 1937 had become the Congress of Industrial Organizations (CIO). Initially, this split weakened the labour movement, but did establish unions in many of the new mass-production industries and therefore gave many unskilled workers representation. In 1955, the CIO merged with the AFL to become AFL-CIO, bringing 85 per cent of union members into one unit. This gave the organisation a membership of some 16 million workers and allowed it to exert pressure over wages and conditions. Unions had recognised that the changes in the American economy meant that workers were under increasing pressure and that the best way to protect their interest was through greater solidarity.

Post-Second World War

In the period after the Second World War, divisions continued to limit the influence of unions. However, this time the situation was reversed. The change in the American economy had resulted in an increase in jobs in the white-collar and service industries. These workers were less likely to join a union and were also more willing to sign no-strike agreements. As a result, the proportion of workers in unions dropped to 31 per cent of the workforce by 1960 and, as with the start of the period, limited union membership and the power that it could exert. This division between more highly skilled workers and others was also evident in the PATCO strike (see pages 85–6). The lack of worker solidarity was further reinforced by the continued decline in the 1970s and 1980s of the number of blue-collar workers, who were more supportive of unions, and the continued increase in white-collar workers, who were less interested in joining unions, as they were already well paid and enjoyed benefits such as pensions and healthcare schemes.

The success of the merger between the CIO and the AFL is also clearly seen in the 1960s, when, despite changes in the nature and structure of the economy, the AFL-CIO secured benefits for its members such as contract negotiations, regulations for promotions and opportunities for workers to voice grievances. Perhaps the most evident example of its success was that wages of union workers were some twenty per cent higher than non-union workers during this decade. The organisation was also important in the 1970s and 1980s. With unions under increasing pressure and membership in decline, AFL-CIO had seen its influence reduced. However, this development ignored the growing number of union members in the **public sector** and the AFL-CIO established a department to look after their interests.

KEY TERM

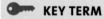

Public sector Industries or businesses which are owned and managed by the state as opposed to being privately owned and managed.

Ethnic divisions

The division between white workers and other ethnic groups remained throughout much of the period. White workers were particularly concerned about African Americans, and immigrants from southern and central Europe and Asia, taking their jobs or working for lower rates of pay. As a result, many unions did not allow these ethnic groups to join, especially in the early period, or, when they did, offered little support to them. Although some African Americans established their own unions, many remained non-unionised and this allowed employers to exploit the divisions and employ them for low wages and in poor conditions.

Abolition and immigration

At the start of the period it was not only the division between white native-born Americans and African Americans that weakened the union movement, and prevented the development of unity needed to win workers' rights, but also the arrival of immigrants from Europe. The abolition of slavery meant that many African Americans joined the industrial workforce, but many whites were unwilling to work with them, as were many of the European immigrants. However, this meant that at times of industrial unrest the employers were able to lay off the white workers and replace them with African Americans, which limited the ability of workers to strike as they feared that they would be replaced. It also meant that employers were able to sack any workers who attempted to organise action, which resulted in the removal of the very men who might have been able to effectively lead unions. Therefore, at the very time workers' organisations needed to be united in order to gain rights and be recognised, the employers were able to ignore their demands and exploit the divisions within the workforce.

This had been further exacerbated by the arrival of large numbers of immigrants who were willing to work for low pay, and this was a particular problem in some cities where they accounted for over half the population. They made up much of the semi-skilled and unskilled workforce and therefore the refusal of white, native-born Americans to allow them to join unions further weakened organised labour.

Continuing division in the twentieth century

This weakness continued in the twentieth century, and can be seen in the Pullman strike, when the company attempted to prevent the organisation of unions by sacking its leaders. Additionally, while the AFL did not exclude African Americans, many of its affiliates did, making it harder for the porters to organise effective action. It was therefore hardly surprising that the struggle for recognition for the porters lasted until 1937, when the union finally reached a collective bargaining agreement with the Pullman Company. This type of struggle was only reinforced by racial divisions and the policy of economic separation, outlined by Booker T. Washington (see page 32), as many African Americans would not join unions led by white people. Furthermore, some African Americans created their own unions, and although this played a role in helping in the wider struggle for African American civil rights, it weakened the unity of the workforce further in the late nineteenth and early twentieth centuries. These divisions continued to be a barrier to unity within the labour movement until after the Second World War.

Even during the period of the civil rights movement divisions still remained. Unions did not help promote equal opportunities for African American workers. Some smaller unions did not welcome members of different races and ethnic groups continued to struggle to gain support for their rights from unions. In the later stages of the period it was immigration – with some 2.5 million people arriving from Asia, particularly after the Vietnam War (see the box on page 92), in the period from 1971 to 1990 – that weakened the union movement. Many of the immigrants were not only willing to work for lower wages, but also less interested in joining unions or willing to work for firms that ran non-union enterprises, which further weakened the position of the unions.

Vietnam War

Following the withdrawal of US forces from Vietnam, the Communist forces of the north overran the whole of Vietnam. This encouraged many to flee the Communist regime, as had also happened following Communist successes in China, Korea and Cambodia. These immigrants were often joined at a later date by other members of their families.

Gender divisions

The number of women entering the workforce increased during the period, but for much of it they faced discrimination. This was even worse for African American and Native American women. Although women were concerned with improving their position in the workplace, this was initially bound up with their campaign for the vote (see Chapter 4) and they were less interested in union activity.

Women and trade unions in the period to 1945

Women were usually paid lower wages than men even when they were doing the same job, and for much of the period their main concern was to limit their exploitation. Unions were dominated by men and therefore the Women's Trade Union League (WTUL) was established in 1903. Its aim was to encourage women to organise themselves into unions, encouraged by a fire at the Triangle Shirtwaist Factory in 1911 which killed 145 workers. However, the organisation was also involved in the franchise campaign as it saw the gaining of the vote as the best way to ensure that conditions at work were improved. The WTUL also

Women carrying the banner of the Women's Trade Union League of New York in a parade through the city, 1913.

wanted an eight-hour day and a minimum wage, which brought it into conflict with male unions, which believed that it was their role to negotiate over such issues.

The New Deal legislation did not bring equal pay and therefore women continued to campaign for it, but not all male unions supported this, and those that did often did so simply to stop firms employing women because they were cheaper. The Second World War, as with the First, saw a dramatic increase in the number of women in the workforce, some of whom did join existing male unions.

The post-war period

In the period after the Second World War, more and more women entered the workforce and some joined unions and became directly involved in union activity and action. However, many of the jobs that were undertaken by women were in the service industries, where their work was often part-time and they were not interested in joining unions, thus weakening the numerical power of unions. However, this was not always the case, particularly for those who were working full time and were concerned about childcare and paid maternity leave. They saw unions as offering a means to achieve this and were more attracted to unions than the feminist movement (see Chapter 4), with the result that the number of women in unions increased in the 1970s. However, the changing economic situation and decline in union membership from the later 1970s was reflected in the attitude of many women towards unions. Moreover, those women who entered high-tech industries already had the benefits of welfare schemes and were therefore less interested in joining unions or partaking in union activity, further weakening the position of unions.

Summary diagram: Union unity

Division	When?
Skilled/unskilled workers	1865–1930
Blue collar/white collar	Post-1945
White American/African American	*c*.1865–1960
White American/European immigrants	*c*.1900
White American/Asian immigrants	Post-Vietnam
Male/female	Post-Second World War

6 Union action and membership

▶ *What role did union action and membership play in the gaining of labour rights?*

The period from 1865 to 1992 saw much unrest in the struggle for unions to get companies to legally recognise their existence. However, even when this right was gained, many unions were still weakened by divisions within their own organisations, as defined above, along skill, class, ethnic and gender lines.

Union violence

Union violence was a particular issue in the first half of the period. It discouraged some workers from joining unions as they did not want to be associated with such acts. There is certainly evidence of union membership declining following periods of unrest. Union violence also encouraged and presented a reason for both the government and employers to resist union demands.

The first clear indication of the impact of violence was seen with the Molly Maguires in 1873. This group of Irish immigrant miners wanted better working conditions. Their derailing of railway carriages, setting fire to coal tips and even the murder of a superintendent resulted in many workers being reluctant to join unions, either because they disapproved of the violent tactics or because they were fearful of the intimidation of the employers which often followed.

The Haymarket Affair 1886

This violence continued with the Haymarket Affair of May 1886. A strike at the McCormick Harvester Plant in Chicago resulted in violence between police and strikers, in which four strikers were killed. This was followed by a protest march during which a bomb was thrown. Seven policemen were killed, which resulted in the police returning fire and killing four more workers. The trouble was blamed on immigrants from Germany and, although no evidence was found, eight were arrested and five were executed. The strikers' actions simply encouraged the dislike of unions, who were blamed for the events. The Haymarket Affair violence also further weakened and divided the labour movement. White, native-born Americans were even more suspicious of immigrants. It also destroyed the reputation of the KOL and led some unions to break away from it and join the AFL or the Industrial Workers of the World.

The Homestead strike 1892

Probably the most famous violent strike was the Homestead strike of 1892 between the Amalgamated Association of Iron and Steel Workers and the Carnegie Steel Company. The dispute at the Homestead Steelworks, near Pittsburgh, Pennsylvania, lasted 143 days and finished with a battle between the strikers and the Pinkerton National Detective Agency, a private security firm. This was not the first occasion of trouble at the works. There had been violence in 1882 and unrest in 1889, but on those occasions the unrest resulted in a growth in union membership. In 1892, it was the company's decision to lock the union out of the plant, following the failure to reach a collective bargaining agreement, which precipitated the trouble. Violence followed the company's decision to advertise for replacement workers, and this culminated with the shooting and then stabbing of **Henry Frick**, who had been brought in to break the union. This led to the collapse of the strike, with a virtual unconditional surrender by the workers. The violence broke the union and resulted in a dramatic decline in membership from 24,000 in 1891 to 10,000 in 1894, and by 1909 it was down to just 6300. Carnegie Steel remained non-unionised for another 40 years. There was not a single steel plant in Pennsylvania that was unionised in 1900. The strike had seriously harmed the progress of workers gaining rights, while employers in other industries became even more suspicious of granting recognition to unions.

KEY FIGURE

Henry Frick (1849–1919)

A self-made millionaire who dominated the US coal industry. He entered into partnership with Carnegie and took over from him when Carnegie retired. He had the reputation of being ruthless, as his handling of the strike showed.

Violence continued into the twentieth century, culminating in outbreaks of unrest in the period just after the First World War. As with the earlier periods, it provided employers with the justification they needed to resist calls for recognition from labour organisations. However, perhaps realising that violence achieved little, union unrest and strikes became more peaceful during the remainder of the period.

The attitude of management to organised labour and strikes

The earlier sections have often made reference to the response of employers to strikes, but this section shows that throughout the period employers often took a hard line against workers, using their powers or appealing to the federal government for support:

- At the start of the period they had resisted the introduction of health and safety measures because it would impact on profits.
- During the Homestead strike of 1892 they locked out the workers, called in the state militia, brought in agents.
- In the Pullman strike of 1894 they appealed to the federal government for help and troops were sent.
- Henry Ford closely controlled his new factory, which opened in 1927. He used security men who attacked and intimidated potential union organisers.

- During the Pullman dispute of the 1920s and 1930s, the company sacked union leaders, used spies and even assaulted union organisers.
- Many companies, particularly in the 1920s and 1930s, set up their own unions. They also offered benefits which attempted to negate the need for unions and discouraged workers from joining them.
- Employers, particularly in the period after the Second World War, made employees sign no-strike and non-union agreements.
- Employers brought in **'scab' labour** to break strikes.
- In order to gain an economic advantage over competitors, some employers ignored the law over wage agreements, hours and conditions, particularly once they were aware that the NLRB was on their side.

KEY TERM

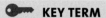

'Scab' labour Similar to 'blackleg'; workers who are willing to work during strikes, often crossing picket lines.

Throughout the period, employers had generally resisted the claims of workers' organisations. In the first half of the period much of their concern had been to break strikes and intimidate workers, which discouraged others from joining. However, towards the end of the period they were able to erode some of the legislative gains that employees had made.

Union membership

Although trade union membership continued to grow until the 1980s, it was not able to attract all workers to its cause. At the start of the period, this was a deliberate policy on the part of the unions, such as its refusal to allow African Americans to join or to take up the cause of unskilled workers. This was often exacerbated by the violence of industrial action, which dissuaded many workers. In the period after the Second World War, the failure to attract all workers was due to changes in the industrial structure and nature of the resultant workforce.

As a result, employers did not have to deal with the large numbers of trade unionists which would have given the movement added strength and increased pressure on the employers to make concessions. Employers were therefore often able to bring in other, non-unionised workers and resist the union demands. By the end of the period, union membership had declined from nearly 20 million members in 1980 to 16.5 million by 1995 and the number of days lost to strikes had been more than halved since 1980. Unionisation was also affected by the decision of some companies to establish factories in developing countries, rather than in the USA, further decreasing the number of union recruits. This was reinforced by the growth in the service sector which, by tradition, attracted fewer union members.

Summary diagram: Union action and membership

Date	Action	Result
1873	Molly Maguires	Disapproval of violence
1886	Haymarket affair	Destroyed reputation of unions
1892	Homestead strike	Union broken and employers reluctant to grant rights
1894	Pullman strike	Troops sent in
1920s–1930s	Pullman strike	Union leaders sacked
1981	PATCO	Workers sacked

Chapter summary

The struggle for labour rights started with the focus on the right for unions to exist and represent their members. As the period progressed, workers took up other issues, such as the right to strike without the fear of losing their jobs and an improvement in working conditions. The struggle to achieve these rights was dependent on a number of factors that at various times either helped or hindered success. Employers were reluctant to grant rights and this view was often supported by the federal government. However, changes in the economy and the structure and unity of the workforce were also important. Despite difficulties, labour, by 1992, had retained most of the rights it had fought hard to achieve and workers were in a stronger position than they had been in 1865.

Refresher questions

Use these questions to remind yourself of the key material covered in this chapter.

1. To what extent did the position of workers improve in the period from 1865 to 1914?
2. In what ways did the years between the wars witness an improvement in the position of workers?
3. Why was it difficult for workers to maintain their gains in the period after the Second World War?
4. In what ways did the 1960s see an improvement in the position of workers?
5. How far did workers lose the gains they had made during Reagan's presidency?
6. Why did economic changes affect the position of workers?
7. Why did the industrial changes of the period from 1950 hinder the development of union rights?
8. How important were the actions of the federal government in promoting labour rights?
9. Did the Supreme Court help or hinder the development of union rights?
10. In what ways did the PATCO strike hinder the labour rights movement?
11. Why did divisions within the labour movement limit the progress of union rights?
12. What was the impact of union militancy on the development of union rights?
13. How important were unions in gaining labour rights?
14. How far had unions declined from 1945 by the end of the period?

In-depth studies and debates

The examination requires you to study three in-depth studies. For this unit they are:

- Civil rights in the Gilded Age
- The New Deal and civil rights
- Malcolm X and Black Power.

This section will introduce you to some of the key debates about these depth studies, so that you will have enough depth of knowledge to be able to evaluate passages that are set on any of the three studies.

Key debate 1: to what extent did improvements in the economy during the Gilded Age benefit workers and unions?

Most accounts of the Gilded Age would agree that the period from around 1875 to the end of the century witnessed a significant growth in the American economy. It has been argued that it was the fastest growing period in the American economy, with a growth rate of some seven per cent per year. However, there is more disagreement about the beneficiaries of that growth.

It can be argued that the Gilded Age was a period of improvement for workers:

- Wages (particularly for skilled workers) rose dramatically, with an increase of some 60 per cent, despite a rapid rise in the available workforce caused by immigration.
- The increase in transport and heavy industry created an increased demand for labour. American heavy industry overtook that of Britain, which had been the world's leading producer of industrial goods.
- The number of craft-orientated labour unions grew.
- Unions such as the Knights of Labor (KOL) saw a rapid growth in membership which went from 20,000 in 1881 to 700,000 by 1886 and included both women and African Americans.
- The American Federation of Labor was established in 1886 and was the first successful national labour federation. It sought to link all unions. Some businesses were willing to work with it and establish mechanisms by which business and workers could negotiate.
- Unions were able to extend their influence into politics at both a national and local level.
- Some sickness clubs, to which workers contributed so that they had some income if they were ill, were established but compensation was limited.

It could also be argued that the period did not witness an improvement for workers:

- It was a period of increasing inequality and poverty for many in the workforce, with two per cent of the population owning 30 per cent of the wealth.
- The wages of unskilled workers were around just 30 per cent of those of skilled workers.
- The demand for skilled workers declined because of the increase in mechanisation.
- The use of the 'contract system' meant that workers could be laid off during quiet periods.
- Workers had few rights, and worked long hours and in dangerous conditions. In 1889 there were 2000 rail workers killed in accidents.
- The violence of strikes, which began with the Haymarket Affair in 1886, did much to damage the reputation of the KOL and its membership collapsed.
- The slump in the economy at the end of the 1880s weakened the position of workers as there was unemployment, job insecurity and a reduction in wages.
- The workforce was divided between white, skilled workers, who made up most of the unions, and African Americans, but this division was exacerbated by the arrival of new immigrants from Europe and Asia. There were fears that these new arrivals would increase the available workforce and result in a reduction in wages. Unions would not allow either the African Americans or new immigrants to join.
- The government's *laissez-faire* policy encouraged large corporations and meant that there was no protective legislation for the workforce.
- The courts also supported the employers and issued injunctions to end strikes.

It would therefore appear as if organised labour, having seen some gains when the economy grew in the period from 1860 to 1880, lost the gains made when economic slumps set in. The position of the workers was not helped by the divisions among the workforce or by the violence and number of strikes, which often led to their suppression by force.

Key debate 2: did the New Deal bring about an improvement in the position of workers?

It is probably to be expected that an economic slump on the scale of the Great Depression and the resulting high levels of unemployment would weaken the position of organised labour. Those who were in work were probably just pleased to have a job. However, despite this, conflict between employers and workers increased, and legislation was passed that improved the position of organised labour.

In arguing that the period brought about an improvement in the position of workers, both government legislation and the growth in union membership could be considered:

- The government passed the National Industry Recovery Act (NIRA) in 1933, which set up the National Recovery Administration (NRA) to improve relations between employers and employees. It aimed to bring about cooperation on matters such as production, wage rates and hours.
- The National Labor Relations, or Wagner Act, was passed in 1935. This gave workers the right to elect their own representatives to take part in collective bargaining, and gave workers the right to join unions. A National Labor Relations Board was established, which had the power to bargain on behalf of workers.
- Union membership grew during this period from 3.7 million in 1933 to 9 million in 1938, which suggests that it was a period of success.
- Some major industries, which had resisted recognition, now recognised unions. A sit-in strike at General Motors in 1936 resulted in the recognition of the United Automobile Workers' Union. The Steel Workers Organizing Committee was recognised by US Steel in 1937.
- A minimum weekly wage was created by the Fair Labor Standards Act of 1938.
- The Committee of Industrial Organizations was established in 1935, becoming the Congress of Industrial Organizations (CIO) in 1937. This not only encouraged whole-industry based unions, but also encouraged African Americans and other ethnic groups to join, thus bringing some unity to the labour movement.

It could be equally argued that the period did not bring about an improvement in the position of workers and organised labour:

- Many employers, including Henry Ford, did not recognise the NIRA or the Wagner Act.
- The Supreme Court declared NIRA unconstitutional in 1935.
- Employers used those willing to break strikes or strong-arm tactics to intimidate workers. There was also continued violence used against workers.
- Unskilled workers, particularly agricultural domestic workers and those at the lower end of the pay range, did not benefit from the improvements, nor did women, as pay differentials were upheld by the NIRA and the Fair Labor Standards Act of 1938.
- Although welfare reforms helped some of the poorer paid, there were limits to this because of conflicts between state and federal rights.

The changes meant that although there was some improvement in the position of workers during the New Deal, the extension of rights to all workers had not been achieved by the outbreak of the Second World War.

Key debate 3: did the Black Power movement help to improve the position of workers?

Despite some improvement in the position of African American workers, trade unions had not been particularly helpful in promoting equal opportunities for black, unskilled workers. African Americans were not well represented on the AFL-CIO leadership body (formed in 1955) even though the organisation followed a non-racial policy, while racism was still evident in some firms. This meant that unions still had a role to play in improving the position of African American workers.

It could be considered that the aims and policies of Malcolm X and the Black Power movement were not influential in improving the position of African American workers:

- Their militancy and violence lost support not just among whites but also among some African Americans.
- Although there was some emphasis on the economic position of African Americans, much of the campaign was about black culture and emphasising the differences from whites, rather than arguing for integration.
- Concern about the economic position of African Americans was just one issue among many in the ten-point programme.
- It further divided both the civil rights movement and the union movement with Black Power's emphasis on African American worker solidarity, rather than worker solidarity.
- In economic terms, the main concern was the poverty in which a large number of African Americans lived and this may have resulted in less support for advancing labour rights.

However, it can also be argued that Malcolm X and the Black Power movement played a role in winning increased civil rights and that this did help the African American workers and improve the position of unions:

- The movement further encouraged the abandonment of any practices within unions that were racist.
- It helped to focus concerns on the question of poverty, which was a greater issue among African American workers. This could be linked to Johnson's 'Great Society', which aimed to reduce the numbers living below the poverty line.
- Some of the civil rights legislation may have been influenced by the movement and this legislation did have a positive impact on the workforce, particularly the Economic Opportunity Act of 1964.
- In the longer term, it may have encouraged Nixon's policy of affirmative action.
- It provided practical help for African Americans who lived in ghettos and kept the issue of ghettos on the political agenda.

The civil rights struggle also encouraged other minorities, such as women, to continue their fight for fair treatment. African American workers did make some gains in this period, but it is difficult to argue that these gains were the result of the Black Power movement, rather than the wider civil rights struggle.

Study skills: thematic essay question

How to develop analysis and write a paragraph that shows synthesis

If you have already studied units 1 and 2 of the OCR course, the essay-writing skills that you have developed are similar to those needed for unit 3. However, there are two key differences:

- On page 2, the title of the unit, 'thematic study', makes it clear that the essay section should be approached *thematically* rather than chronologically, particularly if you want to reach the higher mark range.
- In addition, there is a significant emphasis on *synthesis*. In answering essay questions you are required to make connections, comparisons and links between different elements of the period and aspects of the topic; this is that crucial element of synthesis – the comparison between different parts of the period to show similarities and differences between events or people.

Remember: it is not simply enough to list examples from across the period in each paragraph; you must make direct comparisons between them. You do not need to make comparisons across the whole period in every paragraph, but the whole period needs to be covered in the essay.

Developing analysis

As with the essays for units 1 and 2, you should aim to write analytically. This is perhaps the most difficult but most important skill you need to develop. An analytical approach can be helped by ensuring that the opening sentence of each paragraph introduces an idea, which directly answers the question and is not just a piece of factual information. In a very strong answer it should be possible to simply read the opening sentences of all the paragraphs and know what argument is being put forward.

Consider the following question:

Assess the view that trade union and labour rights in the USA changed more significantly in the 1980s than at any other time in the period from 1865 to 1992.

Possible opening sentences for an answer in response to this question could be as follows:

- Relations with the federal government changed significantly during the 1980s as they became hostile to unions once again, although this was very similar to both the 1890s and 1920s.

- It was the period of the New Deal that saw the greatest change in union rights because of the growth in membership, which greatly increased their power, unlike the 1980s, which saw a fall and thus a loss of power. …
- Although the 1980s saw a loss of union power as a result of government intervention, which undermined the ability of government workers to strike, this had less impact on the position of workers than the 'welfare capitalism' of the 1920s. …
- The 1930s were more significant for labour rights as Roosevelt's government was more supportive of workers than Reagan in the 1980s. …
- The changing demands and expansion of a wartime economy meant that the period of the Second World War was more significant than the 1980s as it gave the unions greater bargaining powers. …
- In terms of improved welfare conditions, it was not the 1980s but the impact of the New Frontier and Great Society programme that had the greatest impact. …

You would then go on to discuss both sides of the argument raised by the opening sentence, using relevant knowledge about the issue to support each side of the argument. The final sentence of the paragraph would reach a judgement on the role played by the factor you are discussing in the development of labour rights. This approach would ensure that the final sentence of each paragraph links back to the actual question you are answering. If you can do this for each paragraph you will have a series of mini-essays, each of which discusses a factor and reaches a conclusion or judgement about the importance of that factor or issue.

Developing synthesis

Some of the opening sentences have already hinted at comparisons between different periods, but this comparison would need to be developed and more of the period covered for answer to reach the highest level. Response A illustrates a weak approach that does not really illustrate synthesis, and Response B shows a strong approach which shows a high level of synthesis, highlighted by the bold points.

Response A

Labour rights changed significantly as a result of the PATCO strike. Not only did the striking workers have their employment terminated, but they also received a lifelong employment ban. PATCO leaders were sent to prison and large fines were levied against the union, which destroyed it. These actions weakened union activity and were significant as they resulted in a decline in strikes. The 1920s were also significant in restricting unions' rights to strike with the establishment of 'welfare capitalism' and 'company unions'. These developments prevented strikes and meant unions did not have the power to negotiate wages. Workers also had to sign 'yellow-dog contracts' which prevented them from joining a union. In some industries, such as Ford, security men were employed to watch over and intimidate potential union organisers and prevent any potential union activity. Labour rights also changed significantly at the end of the nineteenth century as the federal government intervened to suppress the rights of labour. Federal troops were sent in to end the Pullman strike of 1894, which forced the American Railway Union to end the strike. The Supreme Court also legalised the use of injunctions, and employer associations adopted aggressive tactics against workers, a clear indication that workers' rights were severely limited.

Response B

Although the 1980s saw a loss of union power as a result of government intervention, which undermined the ability of government workers to strike, **this had less impact** on the position of workers than the 'welfare capitalism' of the 1920s which allowed only company unions and forced workers to sign 'yellow-dog contracts' which prevented them from joining a union if they wanted to work in big business enterprises. Moreover, **in both the 1920s and 1890s, as well as the 1930s, violence was used against workers, which did not happen** in the 1980s. In the 1980s, the government used supervisors and military air traffic controllers to minimise disruption, **but in the 1890s** the government actually sent in federal troops to end the Pullman strike and the Supreme Court legalised the use of injunctions to prevent strikes. Similarly, **in the 1920s, and even during the New Deal,** violence against workers from the employers, for example at Ford where there was a protection department, was not unusual in order to control workers and prevent them from unionising. Although the PATCO strike did limit the rights of government employees to strike, **the 1890s and 1920s were more significant** because the limits applied to all workers; in the 1920s employers prevented the formation of non-company unions, and employer powers were often imposed in a violent manner, all of **which did not happen** during the 1980s.

Analysis of the responses

Response B is the stronger answer and displays high-level synthesis:

- Response A simply lists and explains three periods of time when union power was limited – 1890s, 1920s and 1980s – but there is no link or comparison between those periods in terms of the significance of the events.
- There is sound detail in Response A, and there is some argument and analysis about the importance of each period, but there is no judgement as to which period was the most significant.
- Response B compares the government response to the PATCO strike with the 1890s and 1920s – as illustrated in bold type – and shows synthesis across most of the period, with examples from the 1890s to the 1980s.
- There is less factual detail in Response B, but there is sufficient to support the argument and own knowledge is being 'used' and not simply imparted.

Activities

1 Write paragraphs similar to Response B for the other themes that were considered in the opening sentences above.
2 Try writing paragraphs for essays from the essay questions below.
3 In order to ensure that you have demonstrated synthesis across the period, highlight the examples of synthesis in your paragraphs and make a checklist to ensure that, over the course of the essay, your paragraphs cover all of the period from 1865 to 1992.

Essay questions

1 The federal government hindered rather than helped the development of trade union and labour rights. How far do you agree with this view?
2 Assess the extent to which internal divisions within the trade union and labour movement limited the development of their civil rights in the period from 1865 to 1992.
3 To what extent was new immigration the most important obstacle to the progress of labour rights in the period from 1865 to 1992?

Study skills: depth study interpretations question

How to evaluate the interpretations

On page 61 of Chapter 1 we considered how to structure and plan an answer to the depth study interpretations question. This section looks at how to evaluate, or apply own knowledge to one of the interpretations to judge its strengths and weaknesses. After you have started your essay explaining the two interpretations and placing them in the context of the wider historical debate about the issue, you need to go on to looking at each interpretation in turn to judge their strengths and weaknesses.

A good paragraph will:

- remain focused on the question
- directly link own knowledge to the view offered in the passage about the issue in the question in order to explain whether the view in the passage is valid or not
- use relevant and accurate knowledge to evaluate the view
- evaluate a range of issues mentioned in the passage.

Read the question and the two interpretations below about trade union and labour rights during the period of the New Deal. Then look at the response, which gives a strong evaluation of the strengths and weaknesses of Interpretation A.

Evaluate the interpretations in both of the two passages and explain which you think is more convincing as an explanation of trade union and labour rights during the 1930s.

PASSAGE A

The mid-1930s was a time of difficult labour relations. Labour unions wanted to exercise the rights afforded them by the NIRA and the Wagner Act. However, many employers did not recognise these. At a time when many large-scale employers such as Henry Ford employed strong-arm men, strikes could often result in violence. There was also considerable anger at the use of 'blackleg' labour during disputes, particularly if the 'blacklegs' were of a different ethnic group to the strikers. The Unions were concerned about the level of violence used against them, which was often condoned and even perpetrated by the authorities. Both sides looked to Roosevelt for help, but he upset both by doing nothing. He had never been especially sympathetic to labour unions: hardly any of the New Deal legislation supporting them had been initiated by him.

There was also an important new development in American labour unionism. The American Federation of Labour traditionally favoured craft unions and did not encourage the semi-skilled and unskilled to unionise. The President of the United Mine Workers wanted to see large industry-wide unions set up rather than small individual craft-based ones. If this happened it would be possible for any dispute to paralyse an entire industry. When the AFL continued to show little interest in this idea at its 1935 conference, the miners and others who thought similarly broke away to form the Congress of Industrial Organisations, which was later renamed the Committee of Industrial Organisations (CIO). It did encourage whole industry-based unions. At General Motors, there were 'sit-in' strikes to gain employer recognition of the United Automobile Workers' Union and on 11 February 1936 the company recognised the UAW. Chrysler followed suit but Ford held out against UAW until 1941.

(Adapted from Peter Clements, Prosperity, Depression and the New Deal: The USA 1890–1954, *Hodder Education, 2008, pp. 175–6.)*

PASSAGE B

The period between the two world wars was one of economic extremes that inevitably impacted on workers. It is clear that significant progress was made in recognising the rights of labour, establishing this in law and putting in place systems and mechanisms to ensure that these laws could operate effectively. Much of this was the result of the New Deal legislation, particularly the National Labor Relations Act (1935) which represented a turning point in the establishment in law of workers' rights.

Measured in terms of union membership, the 1930s must be seen as a high point. Union membership grew. Previously semi-skilled and unskilled workers unionised themselves. However, the divisions between skilled and unskilled workers as well as the inequality determined by racial and ethnic differences remained a barrier to effective solidarity. The increasing membership meant that the unions became a political force, the Democrats being particularly keen to attract the vote of organised labour.

It could also be argued that, to some extent, the uneasy balance between workers and employers had swung in favour of the workers and their unions. To some degree this was a combination of post-Depression imperative to reduce unemployment and to stimulate the economy. This was, however, an uneasy balance that was not readily accepted by employers.

(Adapted from David Paterson, Doug Willoughby and Susan Willoughby, Civil Rights in the USA 1865–1992, *Heinemann, 2009, pp. 133–4.)*

Response

There is certainly some credibility in Interpretation A's view that the 1930s was a time of difficult labour relations**[1]**. The passage makes reference to the struggle between workers and employers that followed the introduction of the NIRA and the Wagner Act and also comments on the violence that occurred at sites such as Ford's**[2]**. There had been struggles at Ford throughout the 1920s, with the company having a protection department to watch over potential union organisers. The view that it was a period of difficult relations is further reinforced by not only an increase in the number of strikes during the 1930s, which rose from 637 in 1930 to 4740 by 1937, but also the growth in union membership, which rose from 3.4 million in 1930 to 4.7 million in 1937, which led to sit-in strikes at firms such as General Motors**[3]**. Moreover, employers called in the police or employed their own strike breakers, as was the case with Ford**[4]**. The passage is also correct to stress the conflict created by the introduction of the NIRA, as firms such as Ford refused to sign it, and even where codes were agreed they usually favoured the employer**[5]**. Moreover, although not mentioned in the interpretation, the period was difficult for the unions because of the divisions within the union movement itself; this is hinted at in the second paragraph and the consequence was that many unskilled workers were still deprived of their rights despite the legislation**[6]**.

Analysis of the response

1. Starts to evaluate the view of the Interpretation about union and labour rights.
2. Evidence from the interpretation is used to support the claim that it is a valid view.
3. Detailed own knowledge is then applied to reinforce and support the evidence in the interpretation.
4. A precise example of strike breaking is supplied to support the claim.
5. There is further evaluation using the example of Ford.
6. The evaluation continues with a comment about division.

The paragraph should continue by evaluating the issues raised in the second paragraph of Interpretation A before a judgement is reached about the overall validity of the view of Passage A. Advice about reaching a judgement is given on page 199.

Activities

- Use information from this chapter to evaluate the second paragraph of Interpretation A.
- Use information from this chapter to evaluate Interpretation B.

It might be helpful to consider the following questions to help you structure your answer:

- What is the view of Interpretation B about trade union and labour rights during the New Deal?
- What evidence is there in the interpretation to support this view?
- What knowledge do you have that supports this view?
- What knowledge do you have that challenges this view?
- Check your work and highlight the evaluative words that you have used.

CHAPTER 3

Native Americans

The period from 1865 to 1992 saw a significant change in the position of Native American Indians, or Native Americans. For much of the period they made little progress in improving their position or quality of life and it was only in the latter decades that they achieved some progress towards self-determination, which had always been their aim. This chapter identifies the losses and gains made, and analyses the factors that both helped and hindered the development of their rights. The chapter analyses the developments under the following headings:

★ The progress and development of Native American rights
★ Federal government attitudes and actions
★ Native American responsibility
★ Conclusion: the improvement of Native American rights

It also considers the debates surrounding three in-depth topics:

★ To what extent did the Native Americans benefit from the Gilded Age?
★ Did the New Deal improve the position of Native Americans?
★ To what extent did the Black Power movement influence Native American protest?

Key dates

1862–7	Plains Wars
1876	Battle of Little Bighorn
1887	Dawes Severalty Act
1890	Massacre at Wounded Knee
1898	Curtis Act
1905	Muskogee Convention
1911	Society of American Indians established
1924	Indian Citizenship Act
1934	Indian Reorganization (Wheeler–Howard) Act
1944	National Congress of American Indians
1953	Policy of termination introduced
1968	American Indian Movement (AIM) established
1969	Siege of Alcatraz
1974	*Oneida* v. *Oneida and Madison Counties, New York*
1975	Indian Self-Determination and Education Assistance Act

1 The progress and development of Native American rights

▶ *How far did the position of the Native Americans improve in the period from 1865 to 1992?*

Native Americans had inhabited America for thousands of years before the arrival of Europeans. Although this chapter largely treats them as a homogeneous group, this was far from the case. At the start of the nineteenth century, some 86 independent tribes had been identified across the USA, which makes generalising about them both difficult and dangerous. There were periods when some tribes cooperated with the American government, while others maintained a consistent hostility. Not only did some fight against the government and each other, but there were occasions when some tribes aided the government against other tribes, thus making the picture incredibly complex. It was only towards the end of the period that there was any evidence of real unity between tribes, and even then some opposed the actions and methods of those leading the campaign for Native American rights.

It is also important to consider the aims of the Native Americans and the aims of the US government. For the majority of the period their aims differed considerably. A large majority of Native Americans wanted to continue to live according to their tribal customs and laws, under their tribal leaders; they wanted the right of self-determination or independence and their own lands. However, the US government wanted to assimilate the Native Americans into American society and this meant destroying tribal customs and culture. The government was unwilling for much of the period to accept the idea of 'nations within' and wanted the Native Americans to become self-supporting. Therefore, there was an almost inevitable clash between the two. The Native Americans resisted the government's policy of assimilation in its various forms as the government failed to understand the strength of the spiritual and cultural legacy of the Native Americans, which could not easily be destroyed.

The largest concentration of Native Americans was in the area known as the Great Plains and they were called the Plains Indians. Most of the tribes who lived there were nomadic, following the buffalo herds on which they depended for everything. White explorers had first come into contact with the Native Americans in this area in the early nineteenth century, but had noted that the region was not capable of sustaining civilised life. So, initially, the Native Americans had been left alone. This meant that they were free to continue their lifestyle, which was in complete contrast to that of the white settlers. They:

- worshipped nature
- were **nomadic**
- had their own tribal laws and governments
- had their own languages
- had their own culture and ceremonies.

However, by 1865, much of this was under threat.

KEY TERM

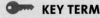

Nomadic The Plains Indians did not have permanent settlements as they followed the buffalo herds. They lived in tepees that could be taken down quickly in order to follow the buffalo, on which they depended for their existence.

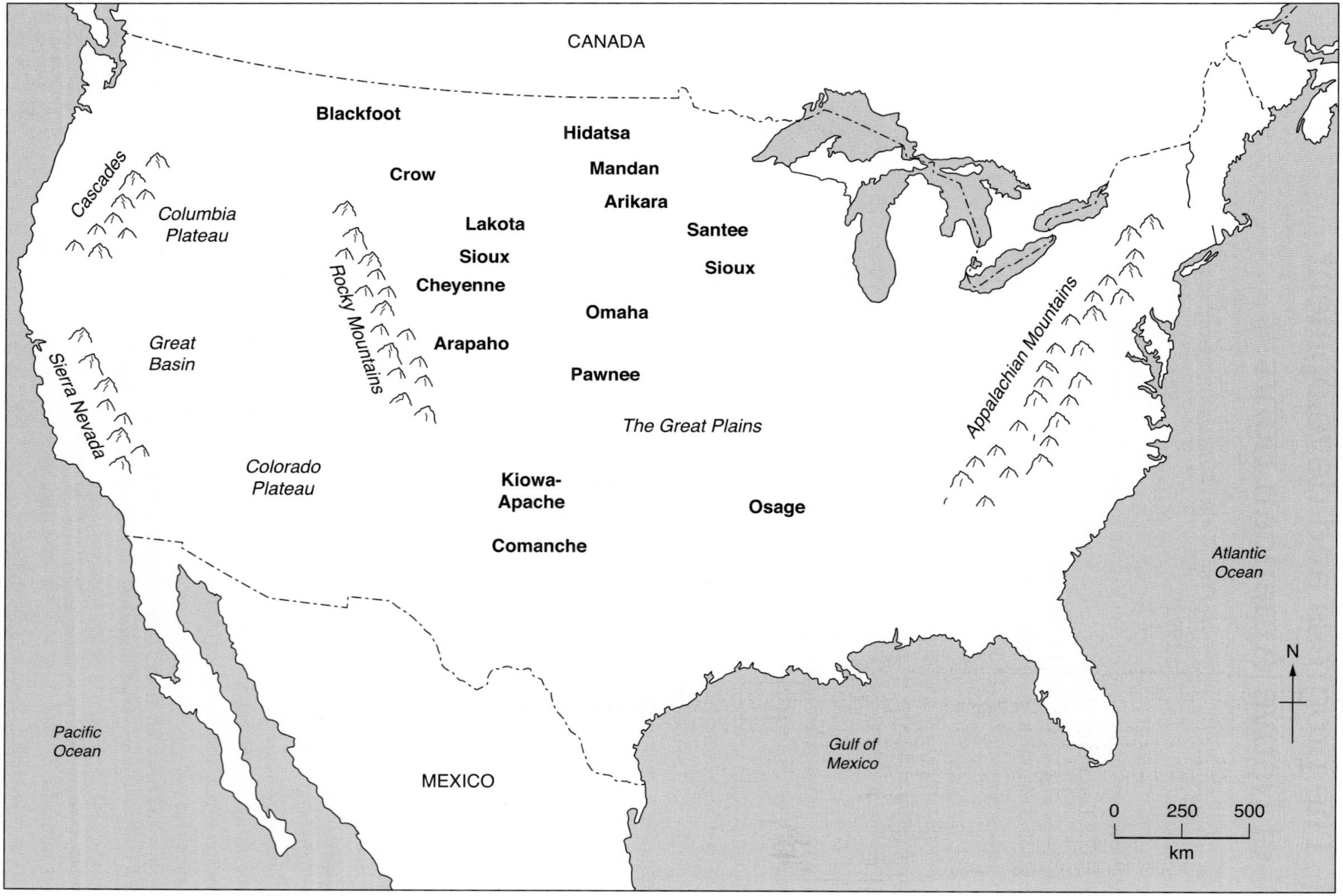

Figure 3.1 A map of the Great Plains showing the main Native American nations by 1840.

Buffalo

The buffalo was a key part of the existence of the Native Americans of the Great Plains, so much so that it was sacred to them. They used every part of it (including the bones, skin, fat and dung). The number of buffalo was greatly reduced as the white settlers and railway companies advanced across the Great Plains. The new settlements also restricted the ability of the Native Americans to follow what remained of the herds and, combined with the decline in numbers, the settlement destroyed the Plains Indians' way of life.

Westward expansion

The main reason why the position of Native Americans was already under threat by 1865 was the impact of westward expansion. American governments had encouraged settlers to move west to open up the rest of the continent for the growing population and because of a belief in **Manifest Destiny**. As a result, the Native Americans were gradually driven out of their traditional lands. The 1830 Removal Act had seen tribes moved from Alabama, Florida, Georgia, Mississippi, Tennessee and Virginia on to the Great Plains in Oklahoma, which was designated as Indian Territory.

This process continued in the 1840s as trails or tracks originally used by fur trappers or mineral prospectors earlier in the century provided routes to the West and encouraged settlers to move to the fertile lands of Oregon and California. This westward movement was given further encouragement by the discovery of gold and other minerals in the region. The new settlers displaced tribes already in those areas. Many of these Native Americans were fishers and if they stayed they were deprived of their fishing rights, but if they moved inland to the Plains, they could no longer continue their traditional practice and so died out.

This westward expansion took settlers beyond the Appalachian Mountains, which had acted as a natural frontier or barrier between settlers and Native Americans, and on to the Great Plains, where many of the Native Americans lived. Chief Washakie of the Shoshone Indian tribe explained the damage that this caused to the Native American way of life:

> *The white man kills our game [buffalo], captures our furs and sometimes feeds his herds upon our meadows. Every foot of what you proudly call America, not very long ago belonged to the red man [Native American]. The* ***Great Spirit*** *gave it to us. But the white man had, in ways we know not of, learned some things we had not learned; among them how to make superior tools and terrible weapons [guns] and there seemed no end to the hordes of men that followed from other lands across the sea.*

KEY TERMS

Manifest Destiny A belief that it was Americans' God-given right to settle the rest of the continent. The term was first used in 1845 in the magazine *Democratic Review*: 'the fulfillment of our manifest destiny is to overspread the continent allocated by Providence for the free development of our yearly multiplying millions'.

Great Spirit The Native Americans believed that there was a supreme being who had made them the guardians of the land, to look after it and pass it on to the next generation. As a result, they argued that the land could not be owned, but was to be shared, hence their tribal way of life.

Unable to resist these advances, a number of tribes had already begun to hand over land to the US government, and this continued after the Civil War, as Table 3.1 shows.

Not only were the Native Americans losing land, but it was having a massive impact on their lifestyle as it affected their ability to follow the buffalo herds. Although the government made promises to ensure that the Native Americans were fed, these assurances were often not kept. This became an even greater problem during the Civil War when the government had more pressing concerns. As a result, many Native Americans, driven by hunger, rose up against the government and this resulted in a series of wars, known as the **Plains Wars**, which lasted on and off from 1862 to 1868.

The American Civil War only added to these problems for the Native Americans. The government withdrew the troops that had been stationed on the Plains. In many instances, the Native Americans had traded with the forts where these soldiers were stationed, but the troops who replaced them were volunteers and often poorly disciplined, with little interest in the Native Americans. This resulted in violence between the two groups, with the most serious incident being the **Sand Creek Massacre** in 1864. Another major incident was the massacre at Wounded Knee, in 1890, when the cavalry killed over 100 Native American men, women and children, including babies and the elderly. Black Elk, a survivor, said:

> *When I look back now from this high hill of my old age, I can still see the butchered women and children lying heaped and scattered all along the crooked ditch as plain as I saw them with eyes still young. And I can see something else died there in that bloody mud, and was buried in the blizzard. A people's dream died there. It was a beautiful dream. The Nation's hoop is broken and scattered. There is no centre any longer and the sacred tree is dead.*

The government was determined to control the land in the West and created federal territories, which were governed by officials. The government's aim was to populate the region with small-scale farmers. To do this, it passed the **Homesteads Act** in 1862. This encouraged even more movement to the West. It is estimated there were some 20,000 people settled on the Plains by 1865. This obviously had serious consequences for the Native Americans.

KEY TERMS

Plains Wars These consisted of a number of clashes, most notable of which were: 1862 Little Crow's War against the Sioux, 1863 Cheyenne uprising, 1867 Red Cloud's War against the Sioux and 1868 Winter Campaign against the Cheyenne.

Sand Creek Massacre An attack by US cavalry on an undefended Cheyenne camp. It resulted in the deaths of many elderly men, women and children.

Homesteads Act This gave farmers a 160-acre plot free on the condition that they farmed it for five years.

Table 3.1 Government treaties with Native American tribes

Year	Treaty	Tribes
1851	Fort Laramie Treaty	Arapaho, Cheyenne, Sioux
1861	Fort Wise Treaty	Arapaho, Cheyenne
1867	Medicine Lodge Treaty	Comanche, Kiowa, Plains Apache
1868	Fort Laramie Treaty	Arapaho, Lakota, Sioux

The burial of dead Native Americans after the 1891 massacre of Wounded Knee. US troops placed the bodies in a common grave.

The railways

The final impact of westward expansion, and an additional threat to the Native Americans, was the development of railways. The desire to develop the US railway network so that it ran from coast to coast had a significant impact on the Native Americans. Not only did some of the lines cross the Plains, but the rail companies encouraged settlers to come and live on the land they had been given by the government. However, it was not just these developments that hit the Native Americans. The rail lines disrupted the buffalo herds and also brought numerous white people to the region to hunt them. This only added to the dramatic fall in buffalo numbers and therefore had a further impact on the life of Native Americans.

As a result of these developments, the position of the Native Americans was already in decline at the start of the period. They had signed a number of treaties with the government and handed over much of their land to be settled by white farmers. This and the development of the railways made it much harder for them to follow and hunt the buffalo herds on which they depended for their food and way of life. Promises of support and aid from the federal government did not always materialise, particularly during the Civil War when the government had other priorities. As a result, much of the population of Native Americans declined through starvation, while those who did survive often suffered poverty. Therefore, even before 1865, the culture and way of life of the Native Americans were under threat and, in many ways, as a result of government policy, this continued for much of the period.

The position of the Native Americans before the First World War

Throughout this period and for the first half of the twentieth century, the federal government's aim was to assimilate the Native Americans, as was made clear in a report of 1877 by an agent of the Yankton Sioux in Dakota:

> *As long as Indians live in villages they will retain many of their old and injurious habits. Frequent feasts, heathen ceremonies and dances, constant visiting – these will continue. I trust that before another year is ended they will generally be located upon individual land or farms. From that date will begin their real and permanent progress.*

The policies to achieve this aim may have changed over the period, but the aim of assimilation remained constant. This aim meant that the government would have to destroy the tribal lifestyle and bonds of the Native peoples. This was to be achieved in a number of ways:

- education
- conversion to Christianity
- turning the Native Americans into farmers
- the establishment of government reservations (see the box below).

The reservation policy prevented the Native Americans from moving freely and pursuing what was left of the buffalo herds. It allowed the government to destroy their way of life as:

- **polygamy** had to be abandoned
- **braves** could no longer demonstrate their skills
- herbal remedies were forbidden
- tribal laws were abolished
- communal living was ended
- the power of the **tribal chief** was ended.

Native Americans were thus forced to become farmers who inhabited a specified area of land.

Additionally, parents were forced to send their children to school, where the children were forbidden from speaking their own language and were made to completely renounce their traditional tribal beliefs (see the photos on page 117).

KEY TERMS

Polygamy The taking of more than one wife. It was the custom so that all women were cared for by a male, which helped to ensure the survival of the tribe. This went against Christian beliefs and was used as further evidence of the need to 'Americanise' Native Americans.

Braves Native American warriors.

Tribal chief The head or leader of the tribe. They presided over the tribal courts and were therefore important in the running of the tribe, or 'nation' as the large tribes were called.

Reservations

Reservations were lands designated by the US government for the Native Americans to occupy as part of the treaties signed with the Native Americans. This process began in the 1850s, but was speeded up in the 1860s as the main way of bringing about assimilation. At first, the boundaries of the reservations were agreed by treaties between the government and the Native Americans, but later the boundaries were imposed by Congress.

Above: a group of Chiracahua Apaches on their first day at the Carlisle Indian School in 1886. Below: the same group after attending school for four months.

Two off-reservation boarding schools were set up because the quality of education provided on the reservations was poor. These schools were in Virginia and Pennsylvania. They provided boys with vocational training and girls with the skills for domestic service. The education provided gave some Native Americans the opportunity to find better jobs, with some working in the Indian agency offices and others working as interpreters, or scouts to army units.

KEY FIGURE

General Custer (1839–76)

A US army officer and cavalry commander in the Civil War and in the Plains Wars against the Native Americans. He is most famous for his defeat at the Battle of Little Bighorn, where he and all his battalion were killed. The battle has gone down in US history as 'Custer's Last Stand'.

KEY TERM

Battle of Little Bighorn
Probably the most famous battle in the history of the Native American struggles. It was the result of General Custer being sent to return a number of Sioux and Cheyenne who had left their reservation and refused to return. Custer attacked them without waiting for his full force to arrive, but his force of some 200 men were defeated and all were killed.

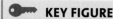

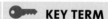

At first, the rights of the Native Americans to determine what happened to their land was agreed. However, after 1871 they lost this right and Congress was given the power to decide on setting up reservations, relocating tribes and redrawing any reservation boundaries. This approach continued and the size of the reservations was further reduced after the defeat of **General Custer** at the **Battle of Little Bighorn** in 1876.

The way of life on reservations

Life on the reservations was far from easy. Native Americans were unable to cultivate much of the land because it was often unsuitable for farming. This meant that they depended on food supplies from the government, which often failed to appear, with the result that many starved. It was also humiliating for them to be dependent on government aid, but the position became much worse in the 1880s when drought hit their crops and disease killed many of the cattle they now kept. This view is made clear by a comment from General George Crook, who had led the Little Bighorn campaign:

> *In regard to the Bannocks, I was up there last spring and found them in a desperate condition. I telegraphed and the agent telegraphed for supplies, but word came that no appropriation had been made. They have never been half supplied. The buffalo is all gone, and an Indian can't catch enough jack rabbits to subsist himself and his family, and then, there aren't enough jack rabbits to catch. What are they to do? Starvation is staring them in the face, and if they wait much longer, they will not be able to fight. All the tribes tell the same story. They are surrounded on all sides, the game is destroyed or driven away; they are left to starve, and there remains but one thing for them to do – fight while they can.*

Moreover, many died from highly infectious diseases such as measles, while others appear to have simply died because they had been moved from their native lands or could not adjust to the new way of life. Their decline was further fuelled by the availability of whiskey, which many Native Americans were not accustomed to. Alcohol addiction may also have become widespread owing to the psychological impact of having had their families broken apart. As a consequence, it is estimated that by 1900 only 100,000 of the original 240,000 Native Americans inhabiting the Plains in 1860 remained. The Native Americans had lost their freedom and were also denied civil rights as they were treated as 'wards of the state' and were not taxpayers. There were exceptions to this trend, best illustrated by the fortunes of the Navajo tribe. They adapted to the new farming practices and built up large flocks of sheep and goats, increased the size of their reservation and witnessed a considerable growth in their own numbers, rising from 8000 in 1868 to some 22,000 by the turn of the century.

The Dawes Act 1887

By placing the Native Americans on reservations, the government had inadvertently ensured that tribal life would continue. It allowed them to retain some of their culture and customs. This outcome had not been the intention of the government and therefore in 1887 it introduced the **Dawes Severalty Act**. Although the Act turned the Native Americans into landowners and gave them full rights of citizenship, because they now paid tax, it further undermined their position as it ignored their belief that land belonged to all creatures and could not be owned by individuals. It also resulted in a decline in land held by Native Americans as much of it was bought by white settlers when the Native Americans were unable to farm it. Although they received money from the sale, they were often unable to manage such sums and therefore slipped further into poverty and debt. The Act also worsened the position and status of many Native American women. This was particularly true of tribes that were matriarchal, such as the Iroquois and Cherokee, where property belonged to the women, but under the Dawes Act the land was given to the men.

The **Five Civilised Tribes** had initially been exempt from the Dawes Act, but in 1898 the Curtis Act ended the exemption. The tribes attempted unsuccessfully to prevent this by proposing that their lands became the state of Sequoyah. As a result of their failure, the Native Americans lost a further 2 million acres of land. The Cherokees challenged Congress's right to deny them their rights to live according to their laws in the *Cherokee Nation* v. *Hitchcock* case of 1902. In 1903, the *Lone Wolf* v. *Hitchcock* case gave the government the right to revoke all treaties made with the Native Americans and stated that they were 'an ignorant and dependent race', who were not citizens of the USA and therefore had no rights.

By the outbreak of war in 1914 the position of the Native Americans had changed, but from their perspective for the worse. Lands that had been given to them by treaty (see page 114) in the 1860s had often been taken away and they were now denied the right to negotiate. Although they had been given civil rights through the Dawes Act, this meant little in practice as they were often discriminated against regardless. The development of the **allotment process** meant that they lost their identity, which had at least been preserved to some extent, albeit unintentionally, through the reservation system. They had also lost their pride and self-respect as they were often dependent on the government for food. Therefore, by 1914, many Native Americans had seen their already miserable lives deteriorate even further.

KEY TERMS

Dawes Severalty Act
Divided the reservations up into plots or allotments which were given to the Native Americans. As a result, they now owned the land.

Five Civilised Tribes
The Cherokee, Chickasaw, Choctaw, Creek and Seminole tribes that were forced to leave their lands and were settled on the Great Plains in 1838. Their journey from their traditional lands to the Plains has been called the 'Trail of Tears' as so many died on it.

Allotment process
The reservation lands were divided into homesteads or allotted, hence the term, by the Dawes Act. This process attempted to turn the Native Americans into landholders, further destroying their tribal culture.

The First World War to the end of the Second World War

The period from 1914 to 1945 witnessed a number of changes in the position of Native Americans. Perhaps the most notable developments were the granting of citizenship and the improvements in the quality of their lives brought about during the period of Roosevelt's New Deal in the 1930s. However, it must always be remembered that many of the improvements were improvements only in the eyes of the federal government and not from the viewpont of the Native Americans.

This was particularly true when considering the granting of citizenship. Native Americans were not particularly interested in gaining citizenship and the right to vote. Many already had the right through the Dawes Act, and the extension of the right to those living on reservations was not intended to increase their political involvement but to increase the speed of their assimilation. The government was simply continuing the process it had started in the nineteenth century and, therefore, for the Native American it appeared as if nothing had changed. The Native Americans had not regained either their sovereignty or nationhood and the devastating impact of the reservation policy had become clearly evident, as their lands had been further reduced. Attacks on their culture continued with the Dance Order, which banned them from practising some of their traditional dances. Additionally, the first part of the period, with the continuation of the allotment policy, saw the continued reduction in the amount of land available to the Native Americans and this only added to their poverty.

These events can be contrasted with the developments of the New Deal period, which saw some improvement in the Native Americans' position, although many of the benefits were abandoned in the period immediately after the Second World War. Central to the improvement in their position was the passing of the Indian Reorganization (Wheeler–Howard) Act of 1934. This was the first move to preserve the Native Americans' culture and involve them in the administration of the reservations. The terms of the Act gave the Native Americans:

- the right to practise their religion
- the right to undertake ceremonial dances and celebrations, thus reversing a law of 1883
- the ability to prevent the sale of Native American lands to individual buyers
- the extension of political rights to women.

The Act also improved conditions on the reservations as agencies of the New Deal built schools and hospitals. It also encouraged women to take on a greater economic role and take up higher education. Most importantly, it brought to an end the allotment policy, although it did not end the policy of assimilation – that was to be achieved through these reforms and the belief that Native Americans would recognise the benefits of the American way of life. Therefore, although there was some improvement, it did not lead to the tribes becoming independent or self-sufficient. Lands that should have been returned under the Act were not given back and much of the funding that was supposed to improve the conditions on the reservations was transferred to the war effort once the USA became involved in the Second World War in 1941. As a result, this period up to 1945 saw, at best, a limited improvement in the condition of Native Americans.

The post-Second World War period

The period from the end of the Second World War to 1992 can conveniently be divided into two parts when considering the position of the Native Americans:

- 1945–69: when a government policy of **termination**, begun in 1953, worsened conditions for Native Americans
- 1969–92: during this time the Native Americans regained many of their rights.

1945–69

The position of the Native Americans deteriorated in the period after the Second World War. There were two major elements to this decline:

- The policy of termination, which ended the recognition of Native American tribes and any remaining treaty rights, and instead treated them as independent and self-supporting.
- The movement of many Native Americans to urban areas.

It might be expected that a move to urban areas would bring the Native Americans all the benefits of American life, but this was not the case. For some the experience was traumatic as they were forced to leave the reservations and relocate, but even for those who went voluntarily the experience was usually far from positive. Most finished up in the worst accommodation and, if they were lucky enough to find jobs, they were poorly paid. Literacy rates remained low and disease high. It is estimated that in 1960 some 25 per cent were 'poor' and the accommodation they lived in was unable to support any extended family. Therefore, many elderly people were forced to return to their former reservations, where they found that conditions had declined even further. The difficulty in finding jobs was reflected in an unemployment rate of up to eighteen per cent. Life expectancy, at 44 years, was some twenty years below the national average. At the same time, the loss of their land continued.

Many who moved to urban areas did not settle as the lifestyle was alien to their culture, and it is estimated that over 50 per cent returned to their reservations. However, when they returned they discovered that the funding of projects, begun under the New Deal, had ended and therefore conditions were worse for them there than in the cities. Those who did stay in the cities often grouped together in ghettos and, unintentionally, this had an impact on helping to preserve their culture as they fought to preserve their heritage. This development would have a considerable impact on the progress made in gaining their rights in the last part of the period, as they witnessed the impact of the civil rights movement and began to develop their own groups to advance their cause. Therefore, it could be argued that although the period witnessed a decline in the position of the Native Americans, with nothing achieved in advancing their rights, it did create the conditions from which they were able to move forward and bring an end to the policy of assimilation.

KEY TERM

Termination In order to speed up the policy of assimilation, which had always been the aim of the federal government, a more aggressive approach was adopted. Native Americans would now be treated as self-supporting Americans and lose any special protection they had been given as 'wards' of the government. It was planned to end the reservation system and encourage them to move to cities, where there was employment, in what can be described as a policy of 'urbanisation' of the Native Americans.

1969–92

The determination to preserve their culture and way of life finally triumphed in this final period. Native American lands were gradually returned to them, some nations that had lost their status regained recognition and rights, while educational opportunities were also improved.

The process of restoring lands was slow, but some tribes did regain some land. Not all aims were achieved. For example, in some cases compensation was awarded rather than the return of land. In a number of instances the compensation offered was considerable, but some tribes, such as the Sioux, wanted the return of their lands instead. They were also able to gain respect for their religious traditions and their right to worship freely, and some 30 states passed laws which protected their burial grounds and remains.

Native Americans also moved nearer to self-sufficiency as tribes were able to negotiate responsibility for health, education and other social services. This process of self-determination was further encouraged by the recognition that Native Americans could live according to their tribal culture. Just as importantly, this restored the self-confidence of many Native Americans, reflected in the census data which saw a rise in their numbers from 800,000 in 1970 to 1.7 million in 1990.

However, the process of regaining land had only just started and today much is still disputed. Education and employment levels were still low and well below the national average in 1992, with the result they are the poorest element in the nation. Their position was also hit by cuts in funding due to the economic decline and this hit areas such as healthcare. Yet, despite these issues, the last part of the period had seen the ending of the policy of assimilation and a significant movement towards achieving self-determination.

Summary diagram: The progress and development of Native American rights

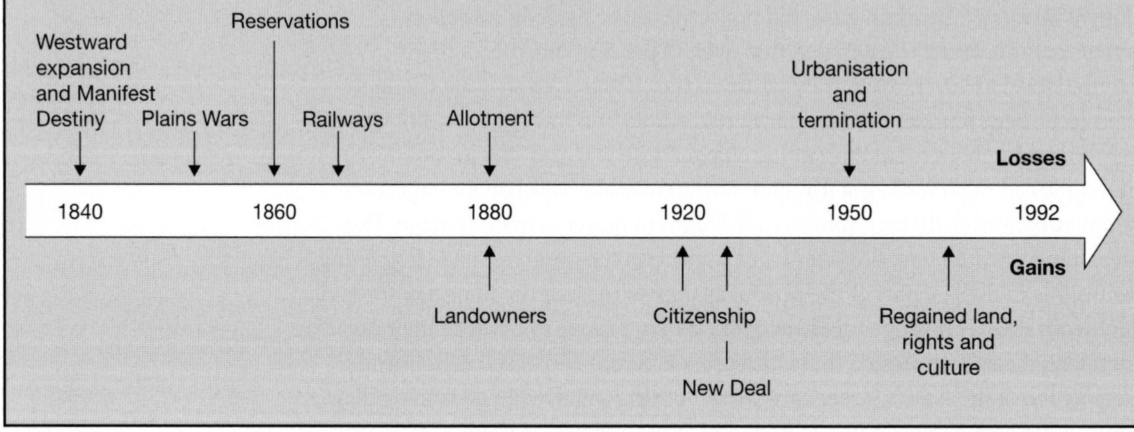

2 Federal government attitudes and actions

► *To what extent did the federal government improve the rights of Native Americans?*

For most of the period, and certainly until the 1930s and Roosevelt's New Deal, the federal government did not support the rights of the Native American peoples. Some would go even further and argue that it was only from 1969 and the presidency of Richard Nixon that US governments did anything to support the desire of Native Americans for self-determination. Instead, federal government was driven by a concern to assimilate Native Americans through a variety of policies ranging from reservations and allotments to termination.

The attitude of presidents and Congress

There were a number of reasons why presidents and Congress not only did little to improve the rights of Native Americans, but pursued a policy that actually aimed to take away their rights.

Manifest Destiny

At the start of the period and into the twentieth century, many Americans, including presidents and members of Congress, believed in the concept of Manifest Destiny (see page 113). The land in the West was seen as representing America's freedom. The government, through its legislation (such as the Homesteads Act), encouraged its settlement and therefore brought the white settlers into contact and conflict with the Native Americans. It was also the government's belief in Manifest Destiny that encouraged it to make grants of land that cut across the Great Plains, where the majority of Native Americans lived, to rail companies. In 1862, the government had passed the Pacific Railway Act, which allowed the companies to take sufficient materials for the building of the line from the land alongside the tracks. It said that 'The US shall extinguish as rapidly as may be the Indian titles to all lands falling under the operation of the Act.' As a result, the government granted some 155 million acres between 1850 and 1871, thus depriving the Native Americans of large tracts of land. The government took the view that the Native Americans must simply accept this and adapt.

The outlook of the presidents and Congress

The period from 1865 to 1930, and immediately after the Second World War, saw much continuity in attitudes towards the Native Americans. Initially, the government had at least allowed the Native Americans the right to determine what happened to their lands, but even this was ended in 1871. From then until the 1930s the government destroyed their rights.

The US government followed a consistent policy of attempting to assimilate Native Americans into the US nation. The government saw them as a problem. The previous section showed that their possession of land was an obstacle to the concept of Manifest Destiny, but just as importantly their tribal way of life was at odds with the American way of life. The tribal structure meant that they had some self-determination and their tribal laws meant that they were not subject to the full law of the country. The nomadic, tribal and communal lifestyle of the Native Americans was alien to the settlers. The nomadic lifestyle of following the buffalo herds contrasted with the permanent settlements that the new settlers established. There were also stark differences in their religious practices and use of hallucinatory drugs during tribal ceremonies. As a result, many saw Native Americans as savages who needed to be brought under control and 'Americanised'. In practice, this meant converting them to Christianity, educating them and providing them with permanent land which they could farm.

In order to destroy this tribal way of life the government implemented a series of policies, which in practice all had the same aim of assimilation:

- reservation policy 1871–87
- allotment policy 1887–1934
- termination 1953–69.

The reservation policy

The government believed that putting the Native Americans on reservations would end their nomadic life and separate them from the buffalo, on which such a lifestyle depended. It would allow the government to control them and prevent them from leaving the reservations. Moreover, while they were on the reservations it would be much easier for the government to educate them and remove all elements of tribal customs. The government defined those living on the reservations as wards or dependants of the state, and so did not allow Native Americans civil rights.

At first, the government had established the reservations as part of the treaties with the Native Americans, but after 1871 the Native Americans lost that right as the government pursued a more aggressive policy of assimilation, encouraged by the idea of Manifest Destiny. This meant that if the government required the land they were unwilling to negotiate with Native American chiefs in order to obtain it. The governor of Colorado outlined the reasons why Congress believed they should be able to take the land without consultation:

> *God gave us the earth and the fullness thereof. I do not believe in donating to these indolent savages the best part of my territory, and I do not believe in placing Indians on an equality with the white man as landholder.*

Some Native Americans resisted this policy, as was the case with the Sioux after the Battle of Little Bighorn (see page 118). The government reduced the size of the reservations without regard for earlier treaties. However, the battle also led to a change in approach from the government, with the introduction of the allotment policy.

The allotment policy

The defeat of Custer (see page 118) made some American politicians realise that the unrest was the result of the reservation policy. There was a growing recognition that the reservation policy had failed to bring about assimilation. Although Custer's defeat did not end the policy of assimilation, it led to the government changing the way in which it sought to bring it about.

Through the Dawes Act of 1887, the government introduced the allotment policy by which reservation lands were divided up into homesteads, or allotments. Although its supporters hoped that it would improve conditions for the Native Americans, it did nothing to help their civil rights. The Act continued to ignore the tribal nature of Native American life and continued the policy of trying to destroy it. As journalist Harold Evans wrote in *The American Century*, published in 1998:

> *The Dawes Act suffered from a defect basic to the democracy that spawned it. Nobody took much notice of what the Indians really wanted. The obverse of the glorious expansion west was that for the Indian, the American dream was a nightmare: oppression instead of democracy, poverty instead of prosperity, despair instead of hope, contraction instead of expansion, confinement instead of freedom.*

It could be argued that the Act improved the rights of the Native Americans and did therefore represent a change. Native Americans were given land, and, after 25 years, could own it and would have full citizenship and therefore rights. This was not what the Native Americans wanted, but what they wanted was scarcely appreciated by the government. Moreover, even if they had wanted the rights that land ownership gave them, it actually meant very little in practice as, like the African Americans (see Chapter 1), they were subject to discrimination. Not only did the allotment policy continue the determination of the government to assimilate these people, but it was a clear indication that the government either did not understand the wishes of the Native Americans or did not want to understand them.

The termination policy

There had been a change in government policy towards the Native Americans during Roosevelt's presidency and his introduction of the New Deal (see page 120). However, the change was short lived and in 1953 the policy of termination was implemented.

The policy was introduced because the government realised that previous policies had failed to bring about assimilation. The timing of its implementation can best be explained by economic factors. The lands on which many of the Native Americans lived were wanted by mining and forestry companies.

Therefore, in order to end the reservation system that had survived, the government gave the Native Americans the same rights as other American citizens. The policy ended the recognition of Native American tribes and saw proposals put forward to end the reservation system. Native Americans were to be encouraged to relocate by offering them accommodation and help in finding work. However, the policy also meant a loss of lands and the further disintegration of what remained of tribal life.

Government and the economy

The government's lack of support for Native Americans can also be seen at times of economic decline and when the government faced competing claims for revenue. During these periods the Native Americans suffered further decline in their position, a clear indication of how they were viewed by the government.

Even before 1865, when the government had established reservations as it attempted to secure land to the west of the Mississippi, it failed to provide aid to the Native Americans. Funding was stretched because of the cost of the Civil War. This problem was made worse as many of the officials responsible for ensuring the aid reached the reservations were corrupt. This was similar to the situation in the late 1880s, when meat subsidies to the Sioux were stopped because the government had other financial demands during a time of economic decline. In these instances it was their lives, not just their civil rights, that were not protected.

A similar situation was also seen during the Second World War, reversing many of the gains made during the New Deal (see page 120). The Native Americans who were still on the reservations found that financial resources were instead allocated to the war effort. This was made worse at the end of the war when Japanese Americans (many of whom were American citizens) were forcibly moved to live on the reservation lands alongside the Native Americans.

The lack of available funds and the attitude of Ronald Reagan in the 1980s also limited the gains that were made during the presidencies of Nixon and Ford in previous decades (see page 122). The programmes they introduced depended on federal funding, but economic decline meant that this was reduced. This was only reinforced by Reagan's attitude as he believed in **native capitalism**.

KEY TERM

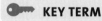

Native capitalism A belief in developing profitable businesses among Native Americans so that the spending of federal and state governments could be reduced.

However, there were periods when the government did appear to advance the progress of civil rights for Native Americans:

- the Roosevelt era of the New Deal
- the presidencies of Nixon and Ford.

The Roosevelt era and the New Deal

It has been suggested that poor economic conditions were a significant factor in the unwillingness of the government to support or advance the civil rights of Native Americans. However, the changes brought about by Roosevelt's New

John Collier

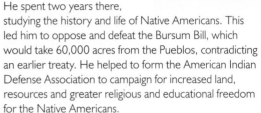

1884	Born in Atlanta, Georgia, where he grew up
1905	Entered social work
1909	Started work at the People's Institute
1915–19	Director of the National Training School for Community Workers
1919	Moved to California to run the state's adult education programme
1922	Led opposition to the Bursum Bill which authorised acquisition of Pueblo lands
1933	Appointed Commissioner of Indian Affairs
1934	Instrumental in the passing of the Indian Reorganization Act
1945	Resigned as commissioner
1947–63	Wrote a number of books on Native Americans
1968	Died

Early life and career

Both of Collier's parents died before he was sixteen. Educated at Columbia University and at the Collège de France in Paris, he took an interest in the impact of the industrial age on humankind. This led him into social work assisting migrants. He worked in the People's Institute, building a sense of community in immigrant areas in New York. In 1919, he moved to California to run the adult education programme, but because of the 'red scare' he was monitored by the Department of Justice, which suspected him of Communist beliefs.

Work with the Native Americans

Collier resigned and accepted an invitation to visit the Indian Pueblos at Taos, New Mexico. He spent two years there, studying the history and life of Native Americans. This led him to oppose and defeat the Bursum Bill, which would take 60,000 acres from the Pueblos, contradicting an earlier treaty. He helped to form the American Indian Defense Association to campaign for increased land, resources and greater religious and educational freedom for the Native Americans.

Appointed Commissioner of Indian Affairs, he implemented a number of reforms, including limiting the influence of Christian missionaries on reservations. His most notable success was the Indian Reorganization Act in 1934, as although it continued assimilation, it allowed cultural pluralism.

Collier resigned as commissioner in 1945, having served for longer than any other. His attitude encouraged young Native Americans to become more militant in order to secure their rights.

Later years

After resigning, Collier served as a director of the National Indian Institute, professor of sociology at the College of the City of New York and president of the Institute of Ethnic Affairs. He also wrote a number of books, including *Indians of the Americas* (1947).

Deal challenge that assumption and therefore suggest that the attitude of the president and other individuals was a more important factor.

The Depression of the 1930s was the worst time for the US economy in the period from 1865 to 1992, with record numbers unemployed. However, it was the first time that the civil rights of the Native Americans were advanced. In part, this was due to John Collier, but it was also due to the president, who appointed Collier as Commissioner for Indian Affairs.

The debate about the impact of the reforms is considered on pages 145–6. It did appear that there was a change in government policy as the Wheeler–Howard or Indian Reorganization Act of 1934 (see page 120) went some way towards helping to preserve Native American culture and gave the Native Americans the right to manage their land and mineral assets, as well as attempting to establish a more secure economic basis for the reservations. However, the original proposals were modified so that assimilation, rather than separation, for the Native Americans was pursued. The improvements that were made to the Native American way of life were therefore designed to convince them of the benefits of assimilation. Therefore, the overall government policy did not see a change, but the Act did bring to an end to the allotment policy, even if tribes were not allowed to become independent.

The presidencies of Nixon and Ford

There were already some signs of a change in attitude towards the Native Americans before Nixon became president in 1969. This change was encouraged by a realisation that their conditions and opportunities were the worst of any group in the USA. Although President Johnson, in March 1968, had spoken to Congress about the Native Americans as 'The Forgotten Americans' and set out a programme to promote self-help and respect, the greatest change came during the presidencies of Nixon and Ford. This was largely because of Nixon's view of how Native Americans had been treated, but also built on the ideas that Johnson had expressed. In July 1970, Nixon in his message to Congress criticised the treatment of Native Americans: 'American Indians have been oppressed and brutalized, deprived of their ancestral lands and denied the opportunity to control their own destiny.' In particular, he attacked the federal programmes designed to help them, but which had been dominated by white officials. He also attacked the policy of termination, which had failed to improve their lives and, as a result, ended many lives instead. Nixon introduced a programme of reform:

- Educational provision for Native Americans was improved through the 1972 Indian Education Act. This increased the amount of money available for Native American schools, even on reservations. This policy was continued by future presidents.
- Some Native American nations, which had lost their status, regained recognition and rights. This allowed them access to courts where they could seek redress for their lost rights.
- The pledge to restore lost lands was put into practice with the return of lands to the Makah, Taos Pueblo and Yakama Indians.
- A Native American, Louis R. Bruce Jr, was appointed Commissioner for Indian Affairs and a policy of affirmative action was pursued in appointments in the **Bureau of Indian Affairs**.

Although the progress in regaining tribal lands was slow because of the number of vested interest groups who opposed it, a start had been made.

The policy of support for the Native Americans continued after Nixon's resignation during Ford's presidency. Two important pieces of legislation were passed:

KEY TERM

Bureau of Indian Affairs
The name given to the Office of Indian Affairs after 1947. It controlled the money for the development of Native Americans, and was responsible for their education and the reservations.

- The Indian Self-Determination Act of 1975. This set out the process by which tribes could take responsibility for their own education, health and social service provision. Federal funding was provided for these programmes and this was therefore a further move towards self-sufficiency.
- The Indian Education Assistance Act of 1975. This allowed Native Americans to have much greater involvement in their children's educational process.

The advancement continued under Ford's successor, Jimmy Carter, with the passing of two more important Acts:

- The Native American Religious Freedom Act of 1978. This gave Native Americans the right to follow their traditional religion and use both their sacred objects and rituals.
- The Indian Child Welfare Act of 1978. This Act attempted to regulate the forced removal of Native American children from their families. Social workers throughout the twentieth century had often viewed Native American practices as neglect and therefore had still been taking children away.

Although there was some decline in the position of Native Americans as the economic situation worsened at the end of the period (see page 126), by 1992 the policy of assimilation had been abandoned and had been replaced by self-determination, supported by funding from the federal government. The changes in the period from 1970 to 1978 suggest that this was the time of the greatest support from US presidents for Native Americans, and therefore this period saw the greatest improvement in the position of Native Americans. This would suggest that the attitude of presidents to Native Americans was crucial in the development of their rights. The changes also prompted one historian to argue that Nixon had 'probably done more for them, in a short space of time, than any other president'.

The roles of the Supreme Court and State Supreme Courts

The role of the Supreme Court in upholding Native American rights changed considerably during the period. At the end of the nineteenth century, the Supreme Court had given some support to the rights of Native Americans, but this changed in the early twentieth century, particularly with the *Lone Wolf* v. *Hitchcock* case in 1903 (see page 119). During the period, the Supreme Court had been involved in numerous cases involving different concerns – the relationship between tribes, between the government and tribes, and tribal sovereignty and tribal rights (including issues such as fishing, hunting and religion). However, towards the end of the period, the Supreme Court was much more active in upholding the policies of the federal government which supported the Native Americans, and played a crucial role in the return of many of their former lands.

Court action during westward expansion

As settlers had moved west, the federal government had made numerous treaties with the Native Americans by which, each time, the Native Americans had given up some of their land. On some occasions, land was given up in return for other land, although the new land was usually smaller in size and less suited to the Native American way of life. However, on many occasions in the nineteenth century the federal government broke the treaties to satisfy the desires of settlers and the needs of railway companies. Moreover, the federal government was determined to impose its policy of assimilation on Native Americans.

The policies pursued by the federal government met some resistance as the Native Americans were determined not to be assimilated and abandon their customs or way of life. Although some of the resistance manifested itself in outbreaks of violence, particularly at the start of the period (see page 118), there were also challenges to government policy in the courts. In 1902, the Cherokees challenged Congress's right to deny them their rights to live according to their own laws. More importantly, in 1903, Lone Wolf, a Kiowa Chief, who along with the Commanches had signed a treaty with the government in 1867, challenged the government's right to ignore the treaty and hand over millions of acres of land. The court upheld Congress's right to revoke all treaties and therefore allowed the government to take away even more land from the Native Americans, overturning earlier court decisions that had been supportive of their rights. The judgment made the court's view of the Native American people very clear:

> *These Indian tribes are the wards of the nation. They are communities dependent upon the United States. Dependent largely for their daily food. Dependent for their political rights. They own no allegiance to the states, and receive from them no protection. Because of the local ill feeling, the people of the states where they are found are often their deadliest enemies. From their very weakness and helplessness, so largely due to the course of dealing of the Federal government with them and the treaties in which it has been promised, there arises the duty of protection, and with it the power. This has always been recognized by the executive and by Congress, and by this court, whenever the question has arisen.*

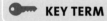

The court held that tribal consent to alter the treaties would hurt the Native Americans and they should assume that Congress would act to preserve their needs. It had a significant impact on the Native Americans: reports from the time clearly show that some 90 per cent of land allocated to them was lost. It also meant that the Native Americans could appeal only to Congress over land disputes. This tendency was seen to continue with a Supreme Court decision of 1913, which meant that in 1921 the Pueblo Indians lost much of their land as they were seen as incapable of managing it.

However, it was not just the Supreme Court that held back the rights of Native Americans in the first half of the period. The same was true of **State Supreme Courts**, particularly when Native Americans challenged the states in the West who refused to extend the franchise to them that had been guaranteed by the 1924 Act. The states were able to secure the upholding of their decisions in the State Supreme Courts and impose a range of voting qualifications to exclude them.

KEY TERM

State Supreme Courts
The federal nature of the USA means that each state has its own Supreme Court. The State Supreme Court is the final court for deciding on the legality of state legislation; only if the legislation has implications for the constitution of the USA will it go to the Supreme Court, and then only if the defeated party appeals.

Victories in the courts

The latter part of the period did, however, see a change in the attitude of both the federal and State Supreme Courts that reflected the gradual change in attitude taking place in US society. There were a number of victories for Native Americans at both state and federal level, although progress continued to be slow.

The first major victory was at state level when, in 1948, two Native Americans brought a case concerning voting rights before the Arizona Supreme Court. The two Native Americans, Frank Harrison and Harry Austin, belonged to the Mohawk–Apache tribe and lived on a reservation in Arizona. The county recorder, Laveen, refused to allow them to register to vote. This decision was successfully challenged as a result of the National Congress of American Indians (see the box) and the American Civil Liberties Union. Despite this victory, other states in the West still continued to restrict the voting rights of Native Americans.

National Congress of American Indians

Formed in 1944 by a group of educated Native Americans, the NCAI was one of a number of pressure groups that would play an important role in extending the rights of Native Americans. It saw its first task as to involve ordinary Native Americans in the struggle to stop the end of the reservations and integrate Native Americans into ordinary society so that they were no longer funded by the taxpayer. Much of its time was involved in legal battles over discrimination. The NCAI was the first sign of Native American peoples joining together and organising a protest movement.

The period from the 1960s witnessed the greatest change in the attitude of the Supreme Court towards Native Americans. The court was faced with more and more challenges from Native American activists, usually through the 'Red Power' movement (see page 136), as they sought to restore their '**native sovereignty**'. The cases usually involved claims for the restoration of their lands or simply fishing rights which had been taken away when dams had been built or hydroelectric power plants had been constructed.

In the previous section (see pages 128–9) the importance of Nixon's presidency was analysed. The progress and decisions that were made during his term in office were upheld by the Supreme Court in 1974. Moreover, the **Native American Rights Fund (NARF)** also put pressure on the Supreme Court to protect the Native American culture and way of life. A number of issues were raised, including:

- reinstating tribes that had been terminated
- restoring tribal sovereignty
- restoring lost tribal lands
- restoring hunting and fishing rights
- having the right to vote
- having the right to worship freely
- performing a proper burial of ancestral remains.

KEY TERMS

Native sovereignty
The power that the tribes had to live on their lands according to their laws, religion and customs. These rights existed until the settlers arrived and removed them.

Native American Rights Fund (NARF) Established in 1970 to defend the rights of Native Americans. NARF trained legal specialists with an interest in Native American issues and was responsible for most of the cases that went before the Supreme Court.

It was a combination of pressure from NARF and the willingness of the Supreme Court to uphold these rights that resulted in considerable progress for Native Americans.

The first meeting of the NCAI in Denver, 1944.

From 1974 to 1986, a number of crucial decisions by the Supreme Court were made (see Table 3.2).

Table 3.2 Supreme Court decisions

Year	Case	Decision
1974	*Oneida* v. *Oneida and Madison Counties, New York*	The Oneida tribe brought a case to the Supreme Court to sue for the return of their lands. This was an important ruling as the Court decided in favour of the tribe. The result was an increase in the number of actions taken by tribes to regain lands
1976	*Fisher* v. *Montana*	In the past, Native American children had often been forcibly removed from their families as part of the 'Americanisation' policy. The decision of the Supreme Court meant that in future tribal courts would decide on adoption. It was not just the significance of this that was important, it was also a further move towards the recognition of tribal courts
1980	*United States* v. *Sioux Nation*	The Supreme Court ruling that one of the major tribes was entitled to significant compensation for the loss of their lands encouraged others to pursue compensation for lost land in the Black Hills of Dakota. The Sioux were awarded $17.5 million compensation and five per cent interest a year since 1877, which gave them another $106 million. However, they rejected the compensation and preferred the return of their land
1982	*Seminole Tribe* v. *Butterworth*	The Supreme Court gave the Seminole the right to establish gambling enterprises on tribal land. This went against state law, but in doing so ruled that the Native Americans had their own rights on their own land
1986	*Charrier* v. *Bell*	The Supreme Court ruled that remains dug from burial grounds in Louisiana belonged to the Native Americans. As a result, states passed laws which protected Native American burial lands

The results of these five Supreme Court cases established important principles over land claims, the power of tribal courts and respect for Native American culture. These decisions began the process of the recovery of Native American lands, gave the tribes the right of self-determination, and showed a much greater respect for their traditions and culture than ever before.

Summary diagram: Federal government attitudes and actions

Factors affecting outlook	Policies	Presidents who helped Native Americans
• Belief in Manifest Destiny • Need to assimilate Native Americans • Imposition of US culture • Need to educate and Christianise • Economic situation • Native capitalism	• Reservations • Allotments • Termination • Urbanisation	Roosevelt Nixon Ford

Supreme Court decisions

Supportive	
Arizona Voting Rights	1948
Nixon's decisions upheld	1974
Oneida v. *Oneida and Madison Counties*	1974
Fisher v. *Montana*	1976
United States v. *Sioux*	1980
Seminole v. *Butterworth*	1982
Charrier v. *Bell*	1986

Not supportive	
Lone Wolf	1903
Pueblo Indians	1921

3 Native American responsibility

▶ *To what extent were Native Americans responsible for the improvements in their rights?*

For most of the period, Native Americans did little to directly help the advancement of their civil rights. Divisions between the different tribes made it much easier for both the state and federal governments to pursue their own policies (see page 130). It was only in the period after the Second World War that there was an increasing sense of unity between the different tribes and Native American organisations were founded. Progress was made most notably in the last decades of the period. Inspired by the civil rights movement, Native Americans took up their own cause through the 'Red Power' movement, although most progress can be attributed to the result of the action of other groups and individuals.

The lack of unity and its impact

Rivalries between the tribes meant that the Native Americans were unable to present a united front against the government. Not only did many of the tribes fight the government during the Plains Wars (see page 114), but they also fought against each other. Tribes were often willing to provide US forces with guides who knew the land and aid the government in their pursuit of other tribes. This rivalry continued on the reservations and added to their difficulty in stopping the theft of their lands. Moreover, many tribal leaders, aware that they could not resist the superior forces of the US government, made treaties with them (see page 114). There was some resistance to the amendment to the Dawes Act from the Five Civilised Tribes (see page 119). Although their action ended in failure, it was the first major attempt to resist assimilation.

The lack of unity continued to be a problem in the early decades of the twentieth century. Attempts at resistance did occur, as was seen in the *Lone Wolf* v. *Hitchcock* case (see page 119), but concerted action was rare. The Society of American Indians, founded in 1911, established the first Native American pressure group, but a lack of funds and mass support limited its impact, partly because Native Americans were spread out across the whole of the country but also because they had no agreed aim for the future.

The 1920s and 1930s witnessed some gains for the Native Americans (see pages 119–20), but these took place because of a change in attitude among some American people, rather than as a result of Native American actions. A group of reformers, social scientists and anthropologists who wanted to preserve Native American culture had emerged and it was their interest and work which resulted in the Meriam Report (1928). The report condemned the allotment policy and outlined the terrible conditions in which the Native Americans lived. It concluded that the government should be concerned with 'the social and economic advancement of the Indians so that they may be absorbed into the prevailing civilization at least in accordance with a minimum standard of health and decency'. The report encouraged change, leading to the **Rhoads reforms** of 1929 and the reforms of the 1930s during the New Deal.

KEY TERM

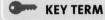

Rhoads reforms These reforms closed off-reservation boarding schools, to which Native American children had been sent. The schools were replaced by better schools on the reservations. There were also to be improvements in medical facilities.

A move towards unity?

The reforms of the New Deal period, like those of the 1920s, were also the result of pressure, not from Native Americans but from Americans, such as John Collier (see page 127). It would not be until the Second World War and the establishment of the National Congress of American Indians (NCAI, see page 131) that tribes joined together to improve their position and rights. The development of such organisations may have been encouraged by the events of the Second World War. A significant number of Native Americans fought in the war and during this time experienced both discrimination and racism, which encouraged them to join campaigns and pressure groups to end such treatment and improve their rights. The NCAI was able to exert pressure on the government, which responded by establishing the Indian Claims Commission. This initially appeared to be the means by which native lands would be returned. However, in practice it was a disappointment, as compensation – rather than the return of lands – was usually the outcome (see page 132).

The government policy of termination and the growing civil rights movement in the USA encouraged the growth of further Native American pressure groups, such as the **National Indian Youth Council (NIYC)**, established in 1961. This was a clear indication of a change in Native American attitudes and of a willingness to unite in protest, as seen most clearly in 1964 when hundreds of Native Americans assembled in Washington for recognition as part of Johnson's 'War on Poverty'.

KEY TERM

National Indian Youth Council (NIYC) Established in 1961 with the aim of protecting Native American fishing rights in the north-west of the country. However, its role developed and it took on lawsuits to protect treaty rights, voting rights and religious freedom.

A National Indian Youth Council demonstration at the Bureau of Indian Affairs office in Denver, 1970.

Despite the emergence of the NIYC and its successes in the courts, there were many Native Americans, particularly among the young, who believed that progress in obtaining rights was too slow. Inspired by movements such as Black Power (see Chapter 1), they adopted a more militant approach which culminated in the establishment of the American Indian Movement (AIM) in 1968 and the emergence of 'Red Power'. The term 'Red Power' was taken directly from 'Black Power', and many of the tactics and the desire to create a mass movement and pride in their race and culture followed from the inspiration of Malcolm X and Black Power (see Chapter 1).

It was the period from 1968 to the mid-1970s that witnessed the most concerted action by Native Americans themselves to improve their rights. How far this pressure influenced Nixon and Ford is a matter for debate, but certainly the coinciding of Red Power with two presidents who were sympathetic to the cause of Native Americans resulted in the greatest period of improvement in the position of Native Americans. The previous section considered the legislation that was introduced; this section will consider the actions of the Native Americans themselves in helping to bring about the changes.

Native American actions 1968–*c.*1975

Many of these actions were designed to draw attention to the condition of Native Americans, and put pressure on politicians to address injustices of the past.

Some of the most significant actions taken were:

- The establishment of AIM in 1968. Its main aim was to tackle the discrimination that many young Native Americans were facing. They established a group to patrol the streets and monitor police activities, which resulted in a decline in the number of arrests and imprisonment of young Native Americans.
- A fish-in (opposed to a sit-in, see page 131), staged in Washington state when the State Supreme Court failed to uphold the treaty rights stating that the Native Americans had the right to fish in the Columbia River.
- The publication of significant works of literature. These made many Americans, and others, aware of Native American history and culture, and the problems they were facing. These works included Vine Deloria Jr's *Custer Died for Your Sins* and, perhaps the most famous of all, Dee Brown's *Bury My Heart at Wounded Knee.*
- Pursuing cases through the Supreme Court (see pages 131–2) to gain the return of former tribal lands.

The siege of Alcatraz 1969

The island of Alcatraz had originally belonged to the Ohlone Indians before it had been taken and used as a jail. It now stood empty. A group of Native Americans from a range of tribes occupied it and demanded its return. Led by Richard Oakes, a member of the Mohawk tribe, in a symbolic gesture, the occupiers offered the government $24 in beads and cloth, the price that had been paid to Native Americans for the island of Manhattan. The government refused and the numbers involved in the siege increased to 80. Although the Native Americans were unsuccessful in regaining the land, the siege had some positive achievements. The worldwide media coverage that resulted from it made many aware of the conditions of Native Americans and may have forced the government to reconsider its policies. There is little doubt that it encouraged many other Native Americans to become involved in the movement, with some 10,000 visiting the island during the siege, while others occupied other government-owned land. It was therefore important in bringing Native Americans together and uniting them in their struggle. This was a significant change from the start of the period when the tribes had been divided. There was now an increased awareness of the need for solidarity if Native Americans were to achieve their goal of 'native sovereignty' (see page 111).

Richard Oakes

1942	Born in Akwesane, New York
1969	Led siege of Alcatraz Island
1970	Left Alcatraz following the death of his step-daughter
1971	End of siege of Alcatraz
1972	Shot and killed following an incident in northern California

Early life

A Mohawk, born in Akwesane, New York, Oakes' early life was spent fishing and planting beans, like his ancestors. Later, he worked in the local docks and then as a steelworker, moving to San Francisco in the early 1960s, where he enrolled at the state university. Little was taught about Native Americans, but he worked with an anthropology professor to change the curriculum, creating one of the first Native American studies departments.

Protest

In 1969, Oates met a Mohawk pressure group which was campaigning to protect the Mohawk religion. In protest at the treatment of Native Americans, he led a group of students and Native Americans in an occupation of Alcatraz Island, which lasted until 1971. The aims were to gain a deed to the island, and establish a Native American university, cultural centre and museum.

Collapse of the siege of Alcatraz

The death of his step-daughter in 1970 prompted Oakes to leave the island and the occupation collapsed. In June 1971, the US government removed the final protesters. The protesters had not succeeded but had drawn attention to the plight of Native Americans through media coverage.

After Alcatraz

Oakes continued fighting for Native American rights after Alcatraz, helping Pit River Indians in their fight to regain nearly 3 million acres of land taken by an energy firm. He was injured in a fight and spent 30 days in a coma. Soon after recovering he was shot and killed by Michael Morgan, a YMCA manager. What happened is disputed, but some argue that Oakes confronted Morgan after the latter had been rough towards some children. Morgan drew a handgun and shot Oakes. Morgan was charged with murder but charges were dropped on the grounds that Oakes had moved aggressively towards him. Oakes died in Sonoma, California, in 1972 at the age of 30.

Under an altered sign, Native Americans, who had taken over Alcatraz island in San Francisco, California, December 1969, unload supplies from a boat. For almost 19 months a group of Native Americans, under the name 'Indians of All Nations', occupied the island, which at the time was out of service as a federal prison. Their occupation was based on their interpretation of the 1868 Fort Laramie Treaty, which they believed granted them the right to reclaim any land originally theirs that had been sold to and subsequently abandoned by the US government.

The siege of Alcatraz encouraged further militant, and sometimes violent, action. The actions also gained AIM national attention and publicity. This was hugely important as Native Americans were unable to achieve anything through the ballot box as they made up only one per cent of the electorate.

However, there is some debate about the impact of the actions that were undertaken. Although it brought the Native Americans publicity, some have argued that the struggle, as militia and police ended the occupation, was counterproductive and went against Native American beliefs. The violence also split the movement, with some opposed to such methods, and this further limited their impact.

In the 1970s, further protests took place:

- *1971: occupation of Mount Rushmore, Black Hills, Dakota.* This was the sacred burial ground of the Sioux (see page 132) and protesters established a camp. They were evicted but Native Americans have continued to claim the Black Hills and have established further camps. The ownership of the land is still in dispute.

- *1972: AIM take over the Bureau of Indian Affairs, Washington DC.* This protest followed on from the journey made by some 1000 protesters who travelled across the USA in the 'Trail of Broken Treaties Caravan'. The protest aimed to draw attention to the treaties that previous US governments had broken with the Native Americans and, at a time of a presidential election, would gain further publicity. It was supposed to be a peaceful protest as the marchers handed in a list of some twenty issues to be resolved. However, without accommodation, they took over the Bureau and had to be evicted, which resulted in violence.
- *1973: the occupation of Wounded Knee.* The site of the Sioux massacre in 1890, Wounded Knee was a particularly important place for Native Americans. The occupation lasted for 71 days, and saw violence and resistance to government agents. A negotiated settlement was achieved, but two leaders were later arrested, although they were acquitted.
- *1975: Pine Ridge Reservation.* Near Wounded Knee further violence broke out and resulted in shootings which left two FBI agents and a protester dead. A member of AIM was found guilty of murder, but the Appeal Court blamed the killings on the overreaction of the authorities.

There is little doubt that the civil rights of the Native Americans had made progress in the last decades of the period. The ending of tribal rivalry and subsequent unity had undoubtedly helped in bringing this about. The 'Red Power' movement had exerted considerable pressure on the governments, who saw that the Native Americans were capable of being much more assertive. This, alongside a realisation from federal governments that Native Americans had previously been treated unfairly, was a crucial factor in the attainment of civil rights for the Native Americans.

Summary diagram: Native American responsibility

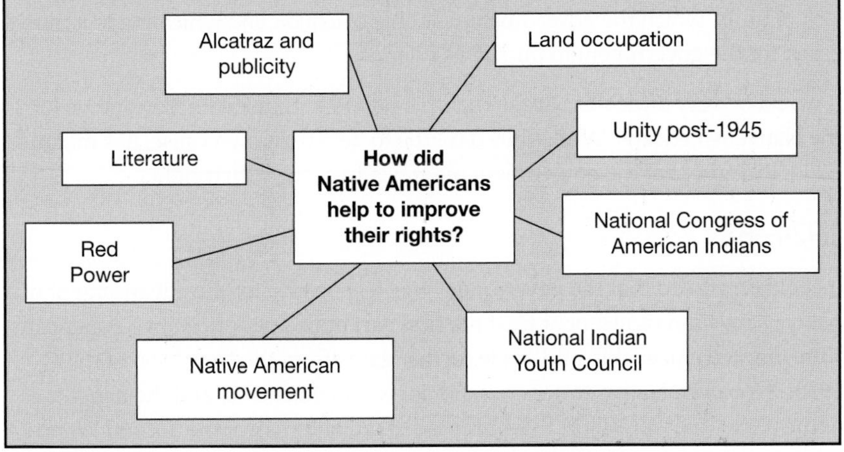

4 Conclusion: the improvement of Native American rights

▶ *Who was more responsible for the improvement in the rights of the Native Americans: the federal government or the Native Americans?*

The last two sections have considered the role of the governments, both federal and state, and the actions of the Native Americans in the gaining of rights for the Native Americans. This section will weigh up and compare their relative roles and show how they changed over the period from 1865 to 1992.

1865–1923

During this period, neither the government nor the Native Americans aided the progress of the rights of Native Americans. The government was more concerned with assimilating the Native Americans into US society and destroying their right to self-determination. Although the method of achieving this changed during the period – from a policy of reservation to one of allotment – the aim of destroying the rights of Native Americans remained. This outlook was reinforced by the views of most Americans who believed in the concept of Manifest Destiny and that the Native Americans were inferior. However, indirectly, the government helped to preserve Native American culture and tribal life by placing the people on reservations, which brought large numbers together.

The Native Americans did little to further their own cause during this period. They did attempt to resist assimilation, but divisions between the tribes and poor leadership meant that they were unable to achieve their aim of self-determination. In fighting to preserve their tribal structure, they perpetuated the lack of unity, which the government was able to exploit and which made it much easier for the government to pursue its policies.

It would be very difficult to argue that this period witnessed improvements for the Native Americans. While they did little to help their own cause, it is much easier to argue that the government did much to destroy their rights.

1924–68

It could be argued that the government was responsible for the advancement of Native American rights for at least the first part of this period. Native Americans were granted citizenship and made further gains from the New Deal of the 1930s. However, Native Americans did not want citizenship, and the benefits of the New Deal were short lived because of the outbreak of the Second World

War (see page 120). It should also be remembered that the government was still pursuing its policy of assimilation, designed to destroy the Native American way of life. Moreover, the government made the position of Native Americans worse by the policy of termination, which was pursued from 1953 to 1968. Even where some progress appeared to have been made, this was more due to changing attitudes among the US population and pressure from individuals for an improvement in the conditions of Native Americans.

Although Native Americans achieved little during this period, there was some evidence of increased unity, as seen in the emergence of pressure groups such as the NCAI. The experience of some Native Americans during the Second World War encouraged a greater determination to fight for their rights, which became more evident in the final period.

It is possible to argue that, despite the attitude towards the changes of the Native Americans, some gains were made in this period and that this was due to the government, albeit encouraged by the emergence of a group of reformers.

1969–92

This period witnessed the greatest advancement in civil rights for the Native Americans. The governments of Nixon, Ford and Carter brought about considerable improvements in the civil rights of the Native Americans. The presidency of Nixon has been described as a turning point. The US government abandoned the policy of assimilation and began to promote self-determination for the Native Americans. How far this was due to the attitudes of the government is a matter of debate, but there was certainly a gradual change in outlook of US governments from the 1960s onwards towards the Native Americans, with a realisation that they had not been treated fairly. As well as this gradual change, the decisions of the Supreme Court were crucial. The attitude of the president and the economic situation of the time were undoubtedly important influences on the advance of civil rights, as the limited progress under Reagan further illustrates (see page 126).

However, the actions of the Native Americans were also important. Their new-found unity meant that they were able to exert more pressure on the government. Pressure groups drew attention to their plight and exploited media attention. Groups such as AIM became adept at using the courts, and the recognition by successive presidents that previous treatment had been unjust, to further their cause and gain rights.

It would therefore be reasonable to conclude that the greatest advances took place when presidents supported the cause and accepted that past treatment had been unfair, the Supreme Court was sympathetic, and Native Americans were united and had powerful pressure groups to represent their views.

Summary diagram: Conclusion: the improvement of Native American rights

Government			Native Americans	
Help	**Hinder**	**Period**	**Help**	**Hinder**
	Manifest Destiny Assimilation	1865–1923		Disunited
Citizenship New Deal	Assimilation Termination	1924–68	NCAI/ pressure group	Disunited until 1945
Nixon and Ford Supreme Court		1969–92	AIM	

Chapter summary

In the first part of the period, Native Americans lost many of their rights as the government sought to assimilate them into US society and destroy their way of life. This policy was encouraged by the attitude of many Americans towards the Native Americans and by the divisions between the various tribes. The government continued this policy of assimilation until the latter part of the period. Therefore, any gains made by the Native Americans, as in the 1920s and 1930s, were only as a result of the government believing it would help their ultimate goal of absorbing them into US society. It was only when the Native Americans became more united and formed pressure groups, and US presidents and the Supreme Court became more sympathetic to their cause, that progress was made.

Refresher questions

Use these questions to remind yourself of the key material covered in this chapter.

1. How much progress had the Native Americans made in gaining their rights in the nineteenth century?
2. How important was the New Deal in the development of Native American rights?
3. In what ways did the position of Native Americans improve in the period after 1968?
4. Why did the US government pursue a policy of assimilation?
5. How successful was the Dawes Act in assimilating Native Americans?
6. In what ways was the Indian Reorganization Act a failure?
7. Why was the policy of termination abandoned?
8. Were the actions of the presidents or the Supreme Court more important in the advancement of the rights of Native Americans in the 1970s and 1980s?
9. Why were the Native Americans opposed to the policy of assimilation?
10. In what ways did Native Americans benefit from the allotment policy?
11. In what ways did the Second World War aid the cause of Native American civil rights?
12. How important were pressure groups in bringing about civil rights for the Native Americans?
13. What was the significance of the siege of Alcatraz in the development of Native American rights?
14. To what extent had Native Americans gained their rights by the end of the period?

In-depth studies and key debates

The examination requires you to study three depth studies. For this unit they are:

- Civil rights in the Gilded Age
- The New Deal and civil rights
- Malcolm X and Black Power.

This section will introduce you to some of the key debates about these depth studies, so that you will have enough depth of knowledge to be able to evaluate passages that are set on any of the three studies.

Key debate 1: to what extent did the Native Americans benefit from the Gilded Age?

The period from *c*.1875 to *c*.1890 saw a number of changes in the position of the Native Americans. Although it is possible to argue that the period offered the Native Americans opportunities to improve their conditions, particularly in the field of education, the large majority of Native Americans would view the period as a direct attack on their culture and rights as the government pursued a policy of assimilation.

It could be argued that the period did bring benefits to Native Americans:

- Victory against Custer at the Battle of Little Bighorn convinced some Americans that the conflict was in response to poor treatment of the Native Americans and that there needed to be a change in approach and policy, although they were a minority.
- Two off-reservation boarding schools were set up because the quality of education provided on the reservations was poor. These schools were in Virginia and Pennsylvania. They provided boys with vocational training and girls with the skills for domestic service.
- The education provided gave some Native Americans the opportunity to find better jobs, with some working in the Indian agency offices, others working as interpreters and others acting as scouts to army units.
- The establishment of reservations provided the opportunity for Native Americans to establish farming communities.
- The reservations gave the Native Americans the opportunity for better healthcare, which, given their rates of life expectancy, death and disease, needed addressing.
- The reservations, despite government intentions, allowed tribal life to continue, which perpetuated their culture and a sense of belonging.
- The Navajo tribe made considerable gains from reservation life. Its acreage of land increased from some 4 million acres to 10.5 million and the number of sheep and goats it possessed rose from 15,000 to 1.7 million. This success was reflected in a rise in population.

- The Dawes Act turned some Native Americans into landowners, which meant that they gained the full rights of American citizenship.

However, most would support the view that this was a period where the Native Americans lost much of their independence, as the American government pursued the policy of assimilation:

- In practice, the concept of reservation life was a failure. The Native Americans lost their freedom and were denied civil rights.
- Life on the reservations was harsh and the land they were given was often poor, which made it difficult to farm.
- Government subsidies were insufficient and were cut further when there were other demands on government resources.
- The massacre at Wounded Knee in 1890 was the final destruction of the Sioux, and as one commented, 'A people's dream died there'.
- The education on the reservations was of poor quality, while those taken away to off-reservation boarding schools often found no employment opportunities and simply returned to reservation life. Moreover, having been taken away from their culture they felt alienated when they returned and were regarded as 'untrustworthy' by those on the reservations.
- Most Native Americans were unable to adapt to the allotment policy and sold their land to white settlers. They often spent the money they had gained from the sale of their land and fell into poverty.
- The size of the reservations was significantly reduced so that the Native Americans had less and less land available to them.
- Women in tribes that had a matriarchal structure lost their status following the allotment policy. The land was given to the male head of the family.

Key debate 2: did the New Deal improve the position of Native Americans?

Native Americans were particularly badly hit by the Depression. However, they were already in poverty and were therefore in need of support. Some progress had been made in this direction during the 1920s. The debate centres around whether, as a result of the work of John Collier, there was a 'New Deal' for Native Americans. In assessing the impact of the reforms that were carried out it must always be remembered that Native Americans did not want to be US citizens. Their concern was to preserve their own culture and way of life, whereas the government's concern was to assimilate them into US society.

There is certainly some evidence to suggest that, for both the Native Americans and government attitudes, there were some achievements during this period:

- The Indian Reorganization Act (Wheeler–Howard Act) of 1934 gave Native Americans a greater role in the administration of their reservations. Corporations were established to ensure that resources on the reservations were better managed.

- The Act protected the Native Americans' right to practise their own religion and assert their cultural identity. This included the use of peyote, a hallucinatory substance used for religious visions which was seen as part of their culture.
- Their children were allowed to attend local schools and learn about Native American culture, rather than having Western culture forced on them.
- The Act stopped the sale of Native American lands and recovered large amounts of unallocated land, which was then used to expand or create reservations.
- Training in farming was provided and better medical services were established.
- The reforms helped to create a greater respect for Native American culture.
- The allotment policy, which had brought poverty and hardship, was abandoned and the further loss of land was prevented.
- Tribes that still lived on reservations were once again led by tribal councils and this helped to encourage tribal loyalties, which earlier governments had wanted to break up.

Despite these developments, it can also be argued that Native Americans did not benefit from the New Deal:

- The poverty of the Native Americans was so great that the measures did little to relieve their situation.
- Although tribes were organised into self-governing bodies, 75 out of 245 tribes rejected the measures.
- The use of the secret ballot among the tribes to see if they accepted the Act was unpopular as they saw the concept of democracy as alien and part of the 'white man's' culture. They preferred to continue their traditional tribal councils, which discussed matters openly and did not have a secret ballot.
- The improvements were not maintained in the period after the Second World War, so were, at best, of short-term benefit.
- The policy of assimilation continued, which was not what the Native Americans wanted. Moreover, the policy of termination was introduced after the war and this further limited the impact of the changes.
- The idea of a separate federal court for Native American issues was abandoned.
- There were insufficient federal funds to buy back former reservation lands.

Key debate 3: to what extent did the Black Power movement influence Native American protest?

The 1960s certainly witnessed a more assertive Native American protest movement. The extent to which this was inspired by the civil rights movement and particularly Black Power is an area of debate. It is unlikely that the influence of the civil rights movement would have completely by-passed the growing protests of the Native Americans, but it must be placed in the context of an already developing number of pressure groups.

It might be argued that Black Power had a significant influence on Native American protests:

- The more militant protests from groups such as AIM followed the period of greatest militant activity in the civil rights movement. The timing of the more militant Native American protests suggests that they were influenced by what they saw of the Black Power movement.
- The Native Americans may have been inspired to forget their tribal differences by the unity of the Black Power movement. This unity was certainly a factor in the success of the Native American protests.
- The Black Power movement's tactics encouraged many Native Americans, particularly the younger element, to abandon the more peaceful methods of legal cases, which they perceived as slow and failing to make much progress.
- Many Native Americans saw the popular appeal of the Black Power movement and its ability to create a mass movement, which could pressurise the government for change. This encouraged a similar response from Native Americans who saw the NCAI as limited in its appeal to those who had been assimilated and were doing well.
- The very term 'Red Power' was taken directly from 'Black Power' and similarly many of the tactics and the desire to create a mass movement followed from the inspiration of Malcolm X and the movement. They also took the idea of pride in their race and culture from the Black Power movement.

It can, however, be argued that Black Power was not as influential and that Native American protests were already underway before the Black Power movement:

- There were already clear indications from the Second World War and the policy of termination that the Native Americans were more united in their resistance to government policies and did not need the inspiration of Black Power.
- There were already Native American pressure groups that were achieving success in gaining civil rights, and the government had also established bodies such as the Indian Claims Commission.
- Militancy was already a feature of some Native American protest groups, such as the National Indian Youth Council, and therefore to suggest that militancy was simply inspired by the Black Power movement would deny the developments that were already taking place among Native Americans.
- The development of protest movements might be seen as simply a response to the wider developments in US society. Attitudes towards a range of groups within society were changing, as seen in the views of presidents such as Kennedy and Johnson. Johnson's 'Great Society' and his 'War on Poverty'

may have encouraged groups to take up their causes believing that they had a greater chance of success.

- The militancy was a direct response to the conditions that many Native Americans found themselves in when they moved into urban areas, and the ghettoisation simply made it easier for them to organise pressure groups to protest about living conditions and unemployment. The alien conditions they encountered in the cities made them more determined to preserve their culture and way of life.

Study skills: thematic essay question

How to answer turning-point questions

The mark scheme used by examiners is exactly the same for turning-point questions as it is for other thematic essays. This suggests that the approach should be exactly the same as it is for other themes essays and that the structure should be thematic and not chronological. It is much easier to compare the significance or importance of different turning points if a thematic approach, rather than a chronological one, is adopted.

Look at the following question:

> 'The Indian Reorganization Act in the New Deal was the most important turning point in the development of Native American civil rights in the USA in the period from 1865 to 1992.' How far do you agree with this view?

A range of events might be considered to be the most important turning point in the development of Native American civil rights, including:

- the Indian Reorganization Act
- the granting of US citizenship in 1924
- the (General Allotment) Dawes Act
- the reservation policy
- the development of Red Power
- the siege of Alcatraz.

A potential essay could analyse, evaluate and compare each of these events (in order to show synthesis), but it would make for a very cumbersome structure and would be difficult to undertake in 45 minutes.

It would be far easier to adopt a thematic approach which would allow you to compare the events. The following themes could be considered:

- political
- economic
- social
- cultural.

You would then select examples from the period and compare their relative importance and significance in terms of being a turning point for each theme.

Ultimately, you would reach a judgement on which event was politically, economically, socially and culturally the most important, before going on to reach an overall judgement as to which event was the most important turning point.

This means that the skills you have considered in the previous chapters are just as applicable to turning-point questions as to other essays.

Consider the following responses to the question above.

Response A

The Indian Reorganization or Wheeler–Howard Act of 1934 was not the most important turning point in the development of Native American civil rights. Although it was significant in that it ended the allotment policy, which had been implemented in 1887, it maintained the policy of assimilation that the Native Americans did not want and it prevented the tribes from becoming independent, which they did want. However, it was important in that it allowed the Native Americans to practise their own religion and overthrew the 1883 law that banned ceremonial dances and celebrations. The Act was also important with regard to measures to protect Native American land as it curtailed its sale to individual buyers and restored unallocated land lost between 1900 and 1930. There were also significant improvements to life on the reservations as more hospitals and schools were built. But, despite these improvements, it must be remembered that these attempts to assimilate the Native Americans were not what they wanted and therefore for them it was not a significant turning point.

Analysis of Response A

Strengths:

- The paragraph shows good knowledge of the Reorganization Act and its consequences.
- The knowledge is used to support an argument about the significance of the Act.
- The paragraph offers a clear view about the significance of the Act.

Weakness:

- There is no synthesis or comparison of the Act with other measures to establish whether it was the most significant turning point. It simply lists possible turning points and is more like a period study essay.

Response B

In terms of land, the most important turning point was the Dawes Act**[1]**. **This was more important than the Indian Reorganization Act as that simply confirmed the continuation of the allotment and assimilation policy, which had been established by the Dawes Act.** Moreover, there were limits to the Reorganization Act as financial considerations and vested interests limited the impact that the proposed return of allotted lands would have had. The Dawes

Act was a more important turning point because it established the principle of the ownership and division of land for Native Americans, which undermined the concept of tribal culture and was a clear indication that the government did not understand the wishes of Native Americans and that the policy of assimilation was to dominate government thinking**[2]**. **The Act was also significant as it ended the reservation policy, which had been introduced earlier in the nineteenth century. This was of greater importance than the Reorganization Act because the reservation policy, although it had seen the amount of land that Native Americans could live on dramatically reduced, had at least allowed some Native American customs and culture to continue[3]**. There was some indication by the end of the period that the Native Americans had made some progress in reclaiming their lost lands, with the peoples of Alaska and the Sioux making gains, but **as these successes were limited, the Dawes Act was still more important** than the Reorganization Act as its policy towards land was not completely reversed**[4]**.

Analysis of Response B

Strengths:

- The whole period is covered from 1865 to 1992.
- A clear view is offered: the Dawes Act was more important than the Indian Reorganization Act **[1]**.
- There is comparison between the Indian Reorganization Act and the Dawes Act, which is seen in the emboldened text.
- The view is explained and justified **[2]**.
- The change from the reservation policy to the allotment policy is examined and the significance of the Dawes Act further explained **[3]**.
- The significance of the changes brought about by the Dawes Act is then compared with the changes at the end of the period **[4]**.
- There is considerable comparison between periods and the significance of a range of events is evaluated.

Activity

Write thematic paragraphs that compare the importance of the Indian Reorganization Act with other events in terms of culture, economic progress, social change and political change.

Essay questions

1. To what extent was the acquisition of US citizenship in 1924 the most important turning point in the development of Native American civil rights in the period from 1865 to 1992?
2. To what extent do you agree that the Dawes Act (1887) was the most important turning point in the development of Native American civil rights in the period from 1865 to 1992?

Study skills: depth study interpretations question

How to evaluate

This chapter continues to look at how to evaluate, or apply own knowledge to one of the interpretations to judge its strengths and weaknesses. In the first paragraph in answer to this type of question, you will have explained the two interpretations and placed them in the context of the wider historical debate about the issue (see page 63), and in the second paragraph you will have evaluated the strengths and weaknesses of the first interpretation (see pages 106–9).

In the third paragraph you will evaluate the second passage and consider both its strengths and weaknesses by using your own knowledge. Read Passage A below, about the impact of the Dawes Act on Native Americans, and Response A which follows.

PASSAGE A

In so far as there was an intention within the [Dawes] Act to destroy the reservation system, it was largely successful. Although some reservations remained, most were significantly reduced in size or disappeared completely. They faced discrimination and prejudice when they attempted to assert their rights. The concept of the division and ownership of land was alien to their beliefs. Some settled to farming and were successful but much depended on the quality of land they were allocated. Many did not adapt and their enterprises failed. The extent to which the allotment of land authorized by the Dawes Act resulted in promoting the assimilation of Native Americans is doubtful. American Indians resisted assimilation. The loss of their tribal lands increased their determination to remain separate and to pursue the restoration of what had been, from their perspective, unlawfully taken away from them. Hence, the forecast of Thomas Jefferson Morgan, Commissioner of Indian Affairs, in 1900, that 'the great body of Indians will become merged in the indistinguishable mass of our population', may have been overly optimistic.

(Adapted from David Paterson, Doug Willoughby and Susan Willoughby, Civil Rights in the USA 1865–1992*, Heinemann, 2009, pp. 176–8.)*

Response A

The negative view offered of the Dawes Plan in Passage A is mostly valid. The passage is correct as the Dawes Plan largely destroyed the reservation system. The passage is also correct to note that some reservations, such as that for the Navajo Indians, did remain; however, the amount of land for Native Americans was reduced so that the 150 million acres recognised in the 1887 Act had been reduced to 78 million by 1900. The passage is also correct in arguing that the concept of land ownership was alien to Indians as it went against their concept of tribal culture and belief that land belonged to all living creatures and not individuals. The passage also rightly states that the success of the system often depended on the quality of land that they were given and in many instances it was barren, which made farming activity that much harder. Although the Act attempted to help the process of assimilation by granting those who paid land taxes the full rights of citizenship, it failed to recognise that the Native Americans did not want to be assimilated as the passage states, hence the resistance, and the refusal of the so-called 'Five Civilised Tribes' to accept the allotment policy.

Activities

1 What are the strengths of Response A?
2 Identify places where the passage is evaluated.
3 What other information could you use to either support or challenge the view offered?

Now read Passage B, on the impact of the New Deal on Native Americans, and consider the following question:

Evaluate the interpretation in Passage B and explain how convincing you think it is as an explanation of the impact of the New Deal on Native Americans.

Remember: in the examination you will have to evaluate two passages and reach a judgement as to which you think is more convincing, but this exercise will help to develop the required skills.

PASSAGE B

The Wheeler–Howard Act gave Native Americans a greater role in the administration of their reserves and protected their rights to practise their own religion and assert their cultural identity. Their children were allowed to attend local schools rather than being forced to assimilate into white western culture. Most importantly the Act stopped the sale of Native American lands. They also recovered large amounts of unallocated land. The Indian Reorganization Act succeeded in affirming and protecting Native American culture.

If Native Americans gained a 'New Deal', its implementation was slow and carried out reluctantly. Most were employed by the Bureau of Indian Affairs, but after years of persecution and deprivation of their rights, they were heavily dependent upon it. Therefore they did not take over the running of their own affairs because they were dependent upon federal aid. Furthermore, much of the land allocated to them was already leased to whites.

(Adapted from Nick Fellows and Mike Wells, The Great Depression and the Americas 1929–39, *Cambridge University Press, 2013, pp. 173 and 174.)*

Activities

Having looked at both the opening paragraph (see page 63) and two paragraphs that evaluated a passage (see pages 106–9 and above), you should now apply the skills to Passage B above. It might be helpful to consider the following questions before you write an evaluative paragraph:

1 What is the view of Passage B about the impact of the New Deal on the Native Americans?
2 What evidence is there in Passage B that supports this view?
3 What own knowledge do you have that agrees with the view?
4 What own knowledge do you have that challenges this view?
5 How convinced are you by the view offered in Passage B? Explain your answer.

Having answered these questions you are now in a position to evaluate the passage.

CHAPTER 4

Women and civil rights

The period between the end of the Civil War in 1865 and 1992 witnessed substantial political, social and economic change for women in the USA. This chapter will consider the ways in which women campaigned for the right to vote and hold office, and the consequences of a major political development, the Nineteenth Amendment, which guaranteed all American women the right to vote. Social and economic change did not always accompany political change. The chapter will consider the impact of economic development in the USA on the role of women in the national economy. It will also assess the main elements of social change, notably the family, reproductive and sexual issues, and attitudes in society towards women. The chapter explores these developments under the following headings:

★ The position of women in 1865
★ The campaign for political rights 1865–1960
★ The campaign for political rights 1960–92
★ The main developments of social and economic change 1865–1992

It also considers the debates surrounding the three in-depth topics:

★ What was the extent of the impact of the industrialisation of the Gilded Age on women?
★ How far did the New Deal improve the economic status and position of women?
★ What was the relationship between Black Power and women's rights?

Key dates

1869	NWSA and AWSA, rival suffrage organisations, founded
1874	Women's Christian Temperance Union
1890	Formation of the National American Woman Suffrage Association (NAWSA); rival suffrage organisations united
1917	Margaret Sanger set up first US birth-control clinic
1919	House of Representatives passed the women's suffrage (Nineteenth) Amendment
1933	Frances Perkins became the first woman in a presidential cabinet
1941	USA entered the Second World War. Seven million women supported the war effort
1957	Number of women and men voting was approximately equal for the first time
1963	Equal Pay Act
	Betty Friedan's *The Feminine Mystique*
1966	National Organization for Women founded
1972	Equal Rights Amendment passed by Congress but never ratified
1973	In *Roe* v. *Wade*, the Supreme Court established a woman's right to abortion
1984	Geraldine Ferraro was the first woman vice presidential candidate of a major political party (Democratic Party)

1 The position of women in 1865

▶ *What problems and opportunities did women face in 1865 in improving their status?*

Between the American Revolution (1776–83) and the 1860s, there had been considerable political changes in the USA that reflected the changes in society. America, socially and politically, became more democratic for the majority of the white male population. However, the right to vote was not extended to women, and women did not represent their states in Congress. They had begun to play a larger, more visible role in role in public affairs.

Women in public affairs before the Civil War

Women were increasingly active in several ways in the eighteenth century:

- First, as a result of a growth in religious enthusiasm, women were often active in church societies, Sunday schools and religious meetings.
- Second, women participated in the campaign against slavery and were often ardent abolitionists, supporting the end of slavery in the South.
- Some, like the former slave Harriet Tubman, played a heroic role in rescuing slaves and helping them to reach free territory in the North.
- The third element in which women took an active public role was in the promotion of **temperance**, that is, in discouraging the drinking of alcohol.
- Parallel to these activities was the development of a movement for women's **suffrage**.

There was a link between the social concerns that women took an interest in and organised themselves to promote and the wider political issue of suffrage. In order to promote change, women needed to have a political voice at national, state and local level. The sheer number of organisations for such causes shows that before the Civil War women were expanding their interests outside the home. They were involved in organisations for helping the poor, disseminating knowledge about childcare and good motherhood, Bible study and teaching, and campaigns for better working conditions and to improve property rights for women. They were also concerned with movements for moral reform and opposition to prostitution. However, the prevailing concept that a woman's place was in the home remained strong until well into the twentieth century, and politically active women remained in a minority.

KEY TERMS

Temperance The belief that alcohol was a major social evil and that a good family life was only possible if alcohol and its misuse was prohibited.

Suffrage The right to vote. In the USA this included not only voting for the president but also for senators and congressmen in the federal Congress as well as the state governors and congressmen. Local officials were also elected.

Political participation

It was the anti-slavery movement that led to women organising to promote a political cause. The first female Anti-Slavery Convention dates from 1837 and was a model for organisations set up to demand voting rights for women. The first convention held to discuss female suffrage was held in Seneca Falls, New York, in 1848. Significantly, it put the issue of suffrage into a wider context, discussing 'the social, civil and religious conditions and rights of women'. Abolition of slavery and temperance were often concerns of white, middle-class women, but there were also African American women who linked abolitionism with women's rights. If women had the vote they would bring compassion and social concern to bear on political decisions. A notable African American campaigner was **Sojourner Truth**, but the main instigators of the Seneca Falls convention, which led to regular meetings, were middle-class white women like **Lucretia Mott** and **Elizabeth Cady Stanton**. The cause of women's rights had able and eloquent leaders to act as role models for later campaigners.

KEY FIGURES

Sojourner Truth (1797–1883)

Real name Isabella Baumfree, was sold into slavery in 1808. She escaped in 1826 and rescued her son from slavery in Alabama in 1835. She campaigned for abolition and women's rights. Her speech at a women's rights convention in 1851, 'Ain't I a woman?', and her memoirs made her famous.

Lucretia Mott (1793–1880)

A Quaker teacher and tireless social reformer. She founded the American Anti-Slavery Society in 1833 and helped to organise the 1848 Seneca Falls Convention, writing a manifesto for women, the *Declaration of Sentiments*. She founded the American Equal Rights Association in 1866.

Elizabeth Cady Stanton (1815–1902)

Was influenced by leaders of the abolitionist movement in the 1840s and worked with Lucretia Mott against slavery. She was friendly with Susan B. Anthony, which led to the formation of the National Woman Suffrage Association in 1869, and helped to organise the Seneca Falls Convention of 1848. She campaigned for reform of divorce and property laws.

Economic and social developments

The interest of women in public causes was a reflection of the diversification in US society. There had been the development of urbanisation (villages becoming towns and then becoming cities), new technology bringing easier communication, greater literacy and better education for women before 1865. For those who prospered from the expansion of trade and industry, there was a new interest in domesticity – women not sharing the labours on the farm or in the workshop or pioneering expansion, but being responsible for the home. With greater prosperity, more middle-class women did not work outside the home and had more time to get involved with 'causes' by the mid-nineteenth century, although these were a minority. Most women struggled with day-to-day survival and these causes did not concern their daily reality. However, for some, expectations that they would look after and nurture the family became transferred to wider social concerns – looking after the interests of the wider community, and bringing 'womanly' values of care and love to those in need. To do this effectively, though, required a more public profile. This led to demands for women to have political representation.

The impact of the Civil War

Harriet Beecher Stowe's famous novel, *Uncle Tom's Cabin* (1852), had done much to publicise opposition to slavery. The following extract describes the escape of two female slaves from the clutches of a wicked overseer, Simon Legree, and the frenzied pursuit. By its vivid writing it established a view of a brutal and degraded system of slavery.

> *Emmeline did not faint, and succeeded in plunging, with Cassy, into a part of the swamp, so deep and dark that it was perfectly hopeless for Legree to think of following them, without assistance.*
>
> *'Well,' said he, chuckling brutally; 'at any rate, they've got themselves into a trap now—the baggage! They're safe enough. They shall sweat for it!'*
>
> *'Hulloa, there! Sambo! Quimbo! All hands!' called Legree, coming to the quarters, when the men and women were just returning from work. 'There's two runaways in the swamps. I'll give five dollars to any nigger as catches 'em. Turn out the dogs! Turn out Tiger, and Fury, and the rest!'*

The sensation produced by this news was immediate. Many of the men sprang forward, officiously, to offer their services, either from the hope of the reward, or from that cringing subserviency which is one of the most baleful effects of slavery. Some ran one way, and some another. Some were for getting flambeaux of pine-knots. Some were uncoupling the dogs, whose hoarse, savage bay added not a little to the animation of the scene.

'Mas'r, shall we shoot 'em, if can't cotch 'em?' said Sambo, to whom his master brought out a rifle.

'You may fire on Cass, if you like; it's time she was gone to the devil, where she belongs; but the gal, not,' said Legree.

'And now, boys, be spry and smart. Five dollars for him that gets 'em;

The whole band, with the glare of blazing torches, and whoop, and shout, and savage yell, of man and beast, proceeded down to the swamp, followed, at some distance, by every servant in the house.

Many women wanted to vote in order to protest about slavery. However, the men who led the abolitionist movement were not altogether comfortable when the cause of women's rights became associated with the cause of the abolition of slavery. Active abolition leaders did not want to lose support by making it appear that abolitionists were also **feminists**. After the Civil War (1861–5), the cause of African American rights and the cause of women's rights became separated.

KEY TERM

Feminism The belief in establishing equal political, economic, social and cultural rights for women. Feminist ideas had spread during the French Revolution and in the writings of the English campaigner Mary Wollstonecraft. In the USA, the turning point was the first convention to promote equality for women, held in Seneca Falls, New York, in 1848.

How did the Civil War affect women?

The Civil War led to more public participation by women. Women did not fight, but they supported the war effort on both sides, and organised a considerable array of charitable organisations and fund raising for the respective causes. The war also became something like a modern total war when Union forces marched through the South destroying crops and plantations in an effort to hit the economy of the Southern heartland. With men away, women had had to take on greater economic responsibility and were often left alone to take the brunt of this new type of warfare. Ideas of women being unfit for anything except genteel domestic activity were at odds with the reality of war in the South, while in the North the heavy demand for men to fight meant that women had to take on more work.

The war brought considerable economic and social change and disruption. The industries of the North expanded, and in the South with the eventual end of slavery and the granting of political rights to African Americans, old ways were challenged. If African Americans, a previously exploited and disenfranchised group, now could vote and sit in Congress and state legislatures (see page 11), as was the case during Reconstruction, why should not women who had played such an important part in the war and campaigned for abolition?

One historian, S.J. Kleinburg (1999), has summed up the impact of war as follows: 'The Civil War contributed to the redefinition of women's political roles … Women gained in moral authority as they raised funds for the relief of both Confederate and Union armies, sewed clothes and nursed the wounded.' Many women did not want to return to pre-war domesticity and built on their wartime experience of working in the public sphere.

The end of the war

By 1865, the opportunities for greater change for women seemed strong. However, there were also extensive inequalities to overcome. Few men supported political rights for women. With the growth of industry and greater prosperity came the view that the woman's place was inside the home, and men should work outside the home. By far the greatest female employments were in domestic service such as cleaning, or in low-paid manufacturing. Westward expansion (see page 113) did mean men and women working together but male attitudes were dominated by a view of women being responsible for the family. Limited birth control meant that family size remained relatively large. Creating and nurturing families took a great deal of women's energies.

Summary diagram: The position of women in 1865

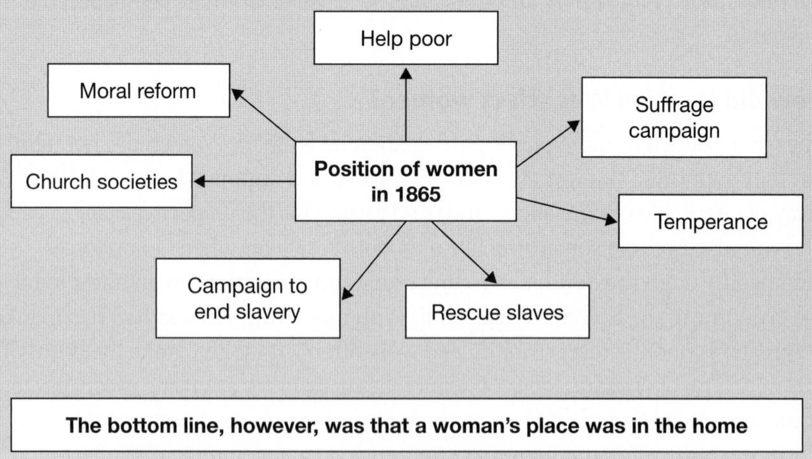

2 The campaign for political rights 1865–1960

▶ *How and why did women gain greater political rights from 1865 to 1960?*

In this period, women campaigned for political rights and in 1919 gained the key right to vote. They participated more in public life and were active in promoting a variety of causes which may have paved the way for greater equality in political rights. However, the vote by itself did not mean that men and women were equal participants in politics or enjoyed equal power and influence.

Prohibition

The development of the temperance movement for the **prohibition** of alcohol was for many women the introduction to greater participation in public life. It was also a major reason for the development of a suffrage movement. The degree of organisation required to achieve a change in law and society was essentially a political act. One of the first instances of this kind of major change was the foundation of the Women's Christian Temperance Union (WCTU) in 1874. Appealing to Protestant opinion in the Midwest (see the box below), initially the WCTU worked to ban alcoholic drinking to safeguard the family.

By 1880, the WCTU had grown to be a national organisation in 24 states with a membership of 27,000 women. By the 1880s, it had 168,000 members and membership reached 800,000 by 1920. Women organised its activities and set out its programme and strategy. This gained them valuable experience in publicity and mobilising support for a national cause. Under its leader, Frances Willard, the WCTU achieved its political aims when they persuaded local legislatures to ban alcohol. The campaign involved political pressure with **lobbying** and mass meetings. Much of the reforming energy of the pre-war women's groups was channelled into temperance.

KEY TERMS

Prohibition A ban on the creation, sale and consumption of alcohol was introduced in a constitutional amendment in 1919. It had already become law in many states. It was repealed in 1933 after problems with enforcement and increasing evidence that it was a cause of crime as gangsters traded in alcohol illegally.

Lobbying The practice of trying to influence the president and Congress to make changes by letters, petitions, appeals and meetings.

Protestant America

The British settlers in America in the seventeenth century had wanted to be free to practise their Nonconformist, Puritan religious beliefs. Quakers and Presbyterians did not believe in the theology or practices of the Church of England and were opposed to what they saw as 'Catholic' ideas. Protestant beliefs stressed the Bible as the main authority, local ministers rather than bishops, the importance of preaching and a stern code of morality. The so-called 'Bible Belt' and evangelist preachers show the continuing strength of the Protestant tradition. A strong element was the growth of Baptist churches that believed in the baptism of adults. An opposition to both alcohol and sexual promiscuity was a feature of these Protestant churches.

In the North, many members had supported abolitionism and women's suffrage. In the South, much of its appeal was due to a desire to restrict the sale of liquor to African Americans, as it was believed that drunkenness would make them uncontrollable and violent. However, African American women were also enthusiastic because of the moral aspect, their strong religious beliefs and membership of Baptist churches. This link between religion and political demands was to be an important aspect of the civil rights movement of the 1950s and 1960s and its leaders (see pages 36–8).

Rural and urban political involvement

Prohibition was not the only cause that women campaigned for. The greater food production of the 1870s meant falling prices and pressure on many farms in rural America. Small- and medium-sized farms came under competition and needed a political voice to represent their interests. Farmers were particularly concerned about the high costs and influence of the railway companies, and so they supported the **Populist Party**. Women were active in rural protests, especially in the so-called Grange movement and the Farmers' Alliance. Women spoke at public meetings against the influence of the spread of the railways (see page 115) and for the need to protect farmers' income. **Elizabeth Lease** was a well-known orator for the Populist Party, and she and female activists led protests despite bitter hostility from business interests. The reforming impulse which swept through rural America in the so-called Gilded Age (1875–95) also included Native American women, who, in 1883, formed the Women's National Indian Association for Native American rights.

In the cities, female public activity often centred around charities, continuing their work done during the Civil War to help the poor. The Charity Organization Society became a major outlet for many urban women's energies. The experience of charity work led many cities and states to appoint women to administer public charities, giving them experience of influencing local government. Women were effective in persuading many states to pass pension legislation in the 1900s, giving assistance to mothers, widows and wives whose husbands were unable to work through disability. Female graduates pioneered the settlement house movement in the late 1880s, establishing some 400 settlement houses in cities. These were where poorer people could find educational, recreational and cultural activities to relieve what were often bleak urban districts. In some areas, these took on a political aspect, providing meeting places for social reformers and offering rooms for trade union meetings.

The break with abolitionism

The struggle for legal and political rights has to be seen in the context of the continuing spread of public activities after 1865. Initially, a strong impetus came from abolitionism with the founding of the American Equal Rights Association (AERA), in 1866, to remove restrictions on rights on both racial and gender

KEY TERM

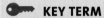

Populist Party The US People's Party was founded in 1891 and represented discontented Southern and Western farmers, hostile to big business and railway companies. It gained over eight per cent of the vote in the 1892 presidential election and ten per cent of the vote in subsequent congressional elections as part of a protest vote against the power and influence of big companies.

KEY FIGURE

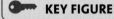

Elizabeth Lease (1850–1933)
Bitterly opposed to big business and helped to organise protests in Kansas against railways. A powerful and virulent orator, she was a leading member of the radical Populist Party but her outspoken views resulted in her splitting with it and withdrawing from active politics.

grounds. In the post-war period, the Republicans were able to secure rights for African Americans in the Fourteenth and Fifteenth Amendments (see page 19), but there were unintended consequences for women:

- The Fourteenth Amendment guaranteed equal rights but penalised states which denied rights to 'any of the male inhabitants of such state'.
- The Fifteenth Amendment specifically stated that voting rights could not be denied 'on account of race, color, or previous condition of servitude [slavery]' but did not mention sex.

Abolitionists felt that it was African Americans who commanded their first responsibility, not women. There was little support for the women's suffrage groups which continued to campaign, and the fact that abolitionism had distanced itself from women's rights to make sure that African Americans were prioritised weakened the cause of female suffrage.

Suffrage organisations

The leaders of the women's suffrage campaign were **Susan B. Anthony** and Elizabeth Cody Stanton. They found themselves without their former allies, the abolitionists, and in 1869 they formed an organisation specifically focused on women's suffrage, the National Woman Suffrage Association (NWSA), with membership restricted to women. The old link with abolitionism was maintained by a rival organisation led by **Lucy Stone** and **Julia Ward Howe**, which did include men, called the American Woman Suffrage Association (AWSA). The cause was weakened by the divide between them, as their strategies were different. The NWSA campaigned for national change, but the AWSA aimed to get women voting in individual states for the state legislatures. In addition, they were a one-issue organisation whereas the national organisation took a broader view and adopted a feminist line, opposing male domination in a number of spheres. Although the two organisations merged in 1890 to become the National American Woman Suffrage Association (NAWSA), the splits weakened the cause and many women put their energies into temperance and social reform as an alternative.

Throughout the period, divisions in aims and methods were a major factor in weakening the impact of movements for more rights for women.

Progress in some states

The federal political structure gave women more opportunities to make progress. Individual states granted the right to vote to some women, for example, Wyoming in 1869 and Utah in 1870. In Utah, the Mormons wished to show that polygamy (the practice of a man having more than one wife) did not mean that women were exploited or had no rights, and some Mormon women were enthusiastic workers for the franchise (right to vote).

KEY FIGURES

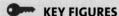

Susan B. Anthony (1820–1906)

A Quaker deeply opposed to slavery. With Elizabeth Cody Stanton she founded a temperance society in 1852. She was a joint founder of the NWSA in 1869 and led the united suffrage movement after 1890 as head of the new NAWSA. She gained notoriety for her arrest for attempting to vote in 1872.

Lucy Stone (1818–93)

An ardent abolitionist and campaigner for women's rights. She urged equal pay, refused to pay taxes as she was not represented in Congress and pioneered wearing trousers ('bloomers'). She founded the AERA and broke with Elizabeth Cady Stanton, leaving the women's movement disunited until 1890.

Julia Ward Howe (1819–1910)

The daughter of a New York banker. An unhappy marriage was revealed in an intimate book of poems which made her a famous literary figure. She wrote the 'Battle Hymn of the Republic'. She travelled the USA and the world lecturing on women's rights and other reforms including world peace, prison improvement and education.

The voting issue

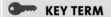

> **KEY TERM**
>
> **Malpractice** Professional negligence or incompetence.

To test the Fourteenth and Fifteenth Amendments, Susan B. Anthony and some 150 other women tried to vote in 1871 and 1872. Ignoring the ruling by polling officials, they registered, voted and then were arrested and tried for electoral **malpractice**. The judge refused them the right to speak, told the jury to find them guilty of violating voting rules and fined them. In a legal challenge in 1875, when Virginia Minor sued the state of Missouri for preventing her from voting, the Supreme Court ruled that women were not allowed national voting rights, but states could give women the right to vote. By 1890, the suffrage campaigners had managed to get eight states to hold a vote on the issue, but in all of these the reformers were defeated. In all, there were campaigns in 33 states to get votes on the issue, but only Colorado and Idaho voted in favour before 1912.

Throughout the late 1880s into the early 1900s, there was small but steady progress on voting on local issues but these were hedged with restrictions. Twenty states permitted only widows with school-age children to vote and, even then, hostile crowds often prevented women from casting their votes. Many men saw women voting as unnatural and a distraction from their domestic duties.

The basis of campaigning shifted from democratic arguments that women should have equal rights, to the practical advantages of women being used to looking after households and so being suitable for dealing with domestic and family issues such as temperance. Often arguments were based not on ideas of natural justice and inequality, but on arguments that women needed to influence laws to help them with working conditions, to ban alcohol, to help with social reforms, or to be involved with matters to do with raising children.

Opposition

There were also groups of women opposed to suffrage. The National Association Opposed to Woman Suffrage (established in 1911) was one of the largest and was supported by a special journal called *The Remonstrance*. The groups saw women's rights as eroding the special place and respect for women in their work in the home, in raising children and working for good causes. They feared that political equality would work against the interests of women who were happy with their existing status as 'angels of the hearth' and cherished by their menfolk. These ideas had a long life and surfaced again in the opposition to equality in the 1960s (see page 178).

Opposition built up in other ways, for example:

- Among some immigrants, Catholics, supported by their priests, saw suffrage reform as weakening the family.
- Southern Democrats disliked female suffrage, fearing that women in politics would introduce labour laws which might hurt the South, or work against the restrictions it had imposed on African Americans (such as the Jim Crow laws, see page 21).

A New York poster of 1912 opposes votes for women. Compare this with the poster on page 187 during the Second World War.

Suffrage reformers faced a re-emergence of ideas that women had a separate sphere and that their higher role was the home, not the world of politics.

How much progress had been made by 1900?

By 1900, the suffragists had made little impact:

- Old splits in the organisations for greater rights for women had not entirely healed.
- The Southern organisations were unwilling to give African American women the vote.
- There was not complete agreement about which types of women should be eligible to vote.
- While progress had been made and groups had organised, opposition had been built up and was quite vociferous.
- The movement was distracted by other causes, like temperance.
- The links with temperance were seen by some as 'too Protestant'.

In the 1900s, the US movement was influenced by the British suffragettes (see the box on page 164). Under Harriet Stanton Blatch there were public parades and more links with trade unions in the USA. In 1913, Alice Paul and Lucy Burns formed the more militant Congressional Union, which was renamed the National Women's Party in 1916.

Suffragettes

This was the name given to the militant organisation, the Women's Social and Political Union, formed in 1903 in Britain, which resorted to increasingly radical means to gain the parliamentary vote for women before 1914. Its campaigns included marches, interrupting meetings and breaking shop windows. There have been many depictions of them in literature and film, including a film made in 2015.

The impact of the First World War

The First World War (1914–19, but affecting the USA from 1917) offered opportunities for women to gain rights. The leader of the NAWSA, **Carrie Chapman Catt**, insisted that the promise of suffrage would induce women to support the war effort wholeheartedly, and President Wilson agreed.

KEY FIGURE

Carrie Chapman Catt (1859–1947)

Was a teacher from Iowa who had led the Woman Suffrage Association in the 1890s. She addressed Congress on women's rights and became Susan Anthony's successor as president of the NAWSA in 1900. She was effective in gaining support for women's suffrage at state level and her support for the war in 1917 helped to persuade Congress to pass the Nineteenth Amendment.

Was the First World War more important in the development of women's rights than the Civil War?

In both wars the cooperation and emotional commitment of women were needed. The Civil War was more protracted and for many in the South became a total war. The First World War did not involve women in a life-or-death struggle, but it did increase economic activity and mean that women's contribution to the workforce was important. Also, the Allied propaganda of a liberal alliance with progressive France and Britain, against an autocratic and militarist Germany, shifted opinion. How could one fight for democracy and then keep women disenfranchised?

The support given by some women to a Women's Peace Party, which called for an end to the war, showed the need to maintain support for the war. States were more receptive to NAWSA arguments. New York and Illinois enfranchised women in 1917; South Dakota, Michigan and Omaha in 1918. There had already been states which had enfranchised women before 1920 (see Figure 4.1, page 165). The NAWSA targeted anti-suffrage senators and some were defeated. By 1919, Congress was willing to pass the Nineteenth Amendment giving all American women the right to vote. This was effective from 1920.

Allied propaganda in the Second World War

The Allies in the Second World War were Britain, the USSR, the USA (from 1941), China and France (from 1944). There was a great deal of effort devoted to persuading their citizens of the rightness of the cause of fighting the Axis powers of Germany, Italy (until 1943) and Japan. It was portrayed as a war for freedom and democracy, even though Britain still ruled people in its empire, the USSR was a dictatorship and neither African Americans nor women enjoyed equal status in the USA.

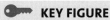

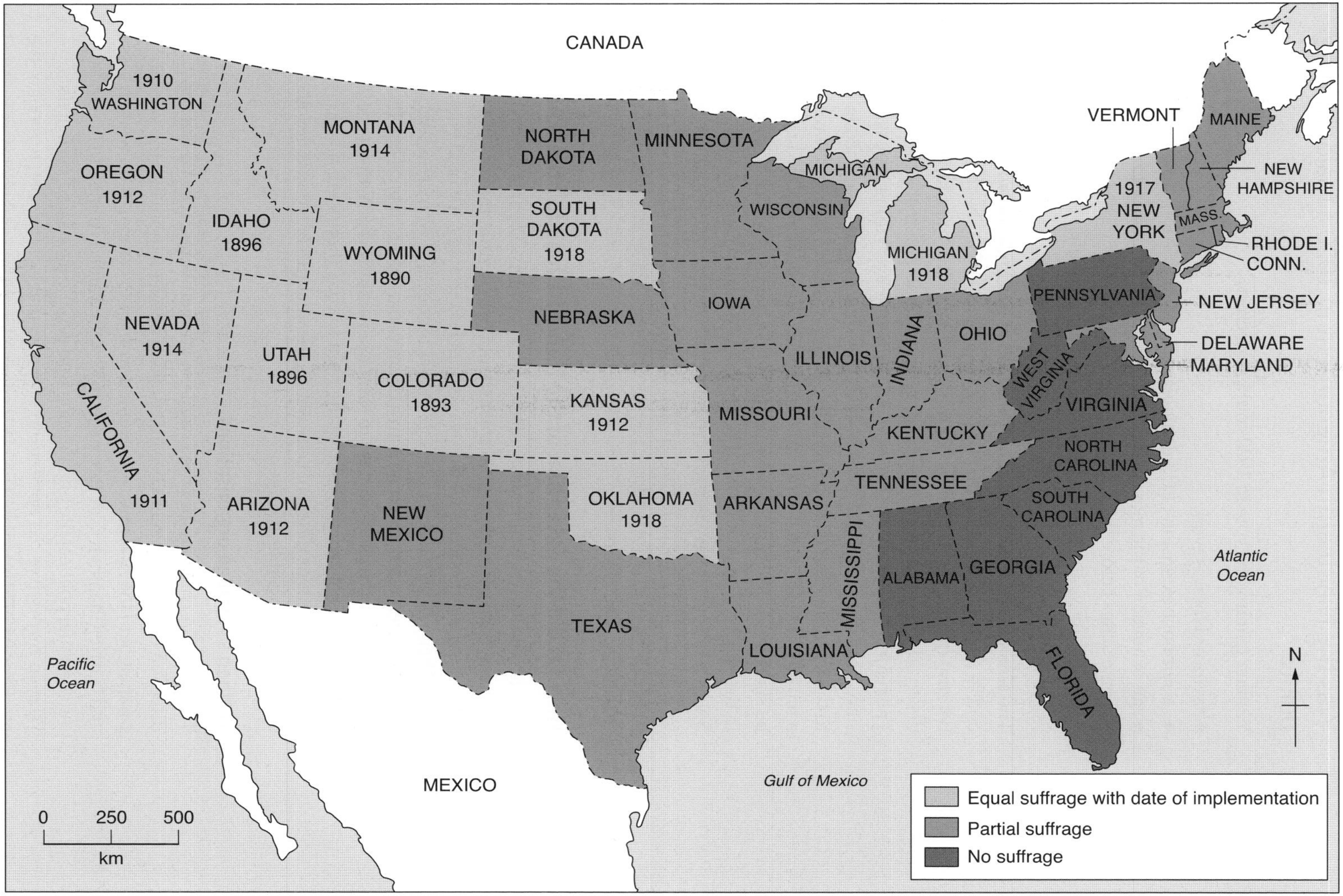

Figure 4.1 Female suffrage before the Nineteenth Amendment, 1920.

Was the Nineteenth Amendment in 1920 a major turning point?

Women gaining the vote in 1920 could be seen as:

- a reward for war work
- a symbolic extension of US democracy
- an extension of the movements towards giving women political rights, seen in some states before the war
- a major move towards using women's particular interests and abilities on a national scale.

The amendment emerged as an expression of gratitude for women's war work and as a result of an effective campaign by the NAWSA, but probably not because of any massive change of mind and heart by American men that women deserved the vote as a matter of natural justice and inherent democratic right. The reform did not mean that women could gain everything they wanted. It has since been suggested that once women were in Congress, they had to conform to the male-dominated society, voting in the way their husbands favoured. In a broader context, much economic and social change during the war proved to be short lived. The right to vote did not cure all evils. African American women in the North on the whole fared better than African American women in the South. However, after years of struggle, the Nineteenth Amendment seemed to some leaders like confirmation that women were free and equal citizens. Yet they still faced discrimination in terms of wages, social attitudes and the ability to exercise their rights.

How far did the extension of the franchise lead to other changes?

As with the suffrage campaign, splits within women's organisations impeded progress. Some thought that women should work within the existing two-party system; others thought that this was a hopeless strategy. It would be unlikely that either party would choose substantial numbers of women as candidates or that women would become active on an equal level to men. They thought the way forward was for women to form a separate party. Without the central unifying cause of actually gaining the right to vote, there were divisions and a loss of impetus as different causes took the energies of women devoted to contributing to public life.

Women's suffrage organisations

The NAWSA changed into the League of Women Voters (LWV). But the direction of this movement became divided between those like the veteran campaigner Jane Addams, who wanted women to campaign on women's issues, and Carrie Chapman Catt (see page 164), who wanted women to integrate into national political life and develop into equal citizens and participants. Women themselves did not flock to take advantage of the vote: turnout in the elections of 1920 was low. The LWV spent a lot of time and energy in persuading women to vote, and did not see many former suffragists join: only five to ten per cent of members of the NAWSA joined the new organisation. There was more continuity with the general tendency of the pre-war period for women to campaign for specific social and civic issues. There were many professional and business organisations; women were active in church organisations, in groups promoting educational improvement and better working conditions and also in the continuing campaigns for temperance and moral uplift. There was interest in non-party political issues like the Women's International League for Peace. Notable, too, was the work of the Association of Southern Women for the Prevention of Lynching, which urged federal action against increasing violence in the South against African Americans. Not all female political activity was radical, and conservative associations were also popular, most famously the **Daughters of the American Revolution**.

KEY TERM

Daughters of the American Revolution
An avowedly patriotic society open to women who can show that their ancestors played a role in achieving US independence. It was formed in 1890 by a descendant of George Washington and now has 180,000 members. It aimed to commemorate and celebrate key elements of US history.

Continuing opposition

Opposition to change was a feature throughout the period, with female suffragists being seen as 'unwomanly'; just as many women opposed the 'flappers' and more sexually emancipated women of the 1920s (see page 184), many thought that men should have first access to jobs during the Depression and many supported a return to the home after the Second World War. The National Association Opposed to Woman Suffrage had an outlook similar to the Daughters of the American Revolution and conservative women, who later opposed the new feminism of the later twentieth century and the Equal Rights Amendment (ERA, see page 177).

Despite opposition, the suffrage movement revived with the merging of the two main groups, the NWSA and the AWSA, in 1890, into the NAWSA. However, within the movement there remained different ideas of who would be eligible, with some wanting universal suffrage and others wanting to restrict it to a white elite. There was an attempt to recruit more support in the South with a Southern Committee. This linked suffrage to temperance and charity work. Fearing loss of support, the NAWSA did not encourage African American participation, although there was growing interest among this ethnic group.

Continuity or change in the period 1865–1920?

Thus, the pre-war pattern of women becoming more active in public life, but not entirely represented in legislatures, Congress, government or the judiciary, was not radically altered by the Nineteenth Amendment. Equality was far off by 1920. Political activity, too, tended to centre around issues specific to women rather than on national concerns. Inter-war campaigns included:

- a struggle for independent citizenship
- the right to own land
- the right to run for public office
- the right to register as voters in some states

- the right to have access to all posts in the civil service
- the right to serve on juries.

As there was considerable difference in practice between states on these issues, political activity became even more fragmented. The right to vote did, however, raise other issues. The vote depended on residence. This, in turn, depended on the power of the husband, who had the right to decide where his family lived and therefore voted. Some states, even by the 1960s, would not allow married women to sign contracts independently or run their own businesses without special permission. These inequalities remained in place even though the vote implied that women were equal citizens. Thus, while gaining the vote led to some citizenship issues being raised and campaigned over, these were often diffuse and state based, and progress towards full and equal legal and civic rights was intermittent. Men continued to dominate public life. US society did not accept women's social and economic equality to men, or that they should aspire to have the same political participation and opportunities for power as men.

The Equal Rights Amendment

The National Women's Party attempted to consolidate the reforms by appealing for an Equal Rights Amendment which would absolutely confirm the move towards the equality implied but not achieved in 1920. However, this divided opinion within women's groups. There was some fear that equal rights would remove some of the protection for women already gained, for example on working hours. The first state regulation of women's working hours was by Massachusetts in 1876, even though this was still ten hours. By 1900, 36 per cent of states had regulations about female working hours, ranging from eight to ten hours. A decision by the Supreme Court in 1912 declared that state regulation was legal and by 1920 over 75 per cent of states had passed regulations restricting women's hours of work. More radical activists argued that equal rights would mean that protection would have to be extended to both men and women. Some felt that if equal pay were introduced it would have a disastrous effect on women's employment prospects as employers would not be able to afford to employ women workers and unemployment among women would rise. Only Wisconsin passed equal rights legislation (in 1921). The issues over existing laws, which did discriminate but often in women's favour, were too complex an issue. Later attempts in the 1970s and after did not succeed either because of the deep divisions among women or opposition in Congress and state legislatures and from employers.

What problems did women face in actually voting?

Older attitudes remained strong. In terms of national politics, women often followed the lead of their husbands or families and traditional loyalties and interests remained strong. Voting gave rise to problems for many women. Registration was not always easy, as married women had to re-register as individuals (rather than having their husbands vote for them) and there were problems in meeting some local residency requirements. It was often difficult for women looking after children, with husbands away working, to even travel to the voting stations. Voting participation varied from area to area and was sometimes low where there were large numbers of immigrants. Political parties created women's committees and were keen to mobilise women voters, but women achieved substantial representation of party committees only in a minority of states by 1940. However, outside the political parties there could be problems in taking office. Some states were slow to amend legislation allowing women to be candidates for public office. Oklahoma prohibited this until 1942. By 1933 there were 146 women in state legislatures and by 1945 there were 234. In the twenty years after the Nineteenth Amendment there were only two female governors of states – both standing in for their husbands. Many African American women in the South could vote in theory but not in practice, because of restrictions such a literacy tests and the threat of verbal and physical abuse and harassment. It would only be a good 40 years later, in the 1960s, that these obstacles would be overcome. In some states, both Native American men and women were prohibited from voting.

Women and the New Deal

It remains controversial how far women benefited from the reforms that President Roosevelt put in place as part of his New Deal programme in the 1930s.

The New Deal made some political changes in bringing women into government, largely because social reform was thought an appropriate sphere for them. **Eleanor Roosevelt**, the first lady, pushed for more women in public office. The most significant appointment was Frances Perkins as Secretary for Labor and member of the cabinet. Women were significantly represented in the expanded government agencies of the New Deal. However, whether women achieved real positions of authority can be questioned:

- The federal agencies were largely run by men.
- Having political rights did not translate into being able to achieve social justice in the New Deal legislation, which discriminated against mothers and married women in an effort to boost employment for men.
- African American women also suffered from racial discrimination in social security in the South.
- There was built-in inequality in pensions, as much New Deal social legislation rested on the assumption that men worked and women looked after them and the home.
- There was no attempt in the labour legislation to secure equal wages.

These inequalities were accepted by the influential women on advisory boards in the New Deal. The desire for equal rights expressed by the more radical **National Women's Party** had limited influence. There remained a huge gap

KEY FIGURE

Eleanor Roosevelt (1884–1962)
From a wealthy New York family, she became a social worker. She married her cousin Franklin Roosevelt, becoming a leading supporter of the New Deal, women's rights and those of African and Asian Americans. She was the first chair of the United Nation Commission for Human Rights.

KEY TERM

National Women's Party
Founded in 1916 by two activists from the NAWSA, Alice Paul and Lucy Burns, who aimed at a suffragette-style campaign. They led protests, they held a silent protest outside the White House and there were minor acts of law breaking with arrests and hunger strikes. They demanded but failed to achieve an Equal Rights Amendment in the 1920s.

between the implications of equality in the Nineteenth Amendment and the actual degree of equality achieved.

How much progress had been made between 1865 and the 1940s?

Compared with the position in 1865, there had obviously been progress. Women did not vote in 1865 in either local or national elections, nor were they eligible to stand for office. By 1941, they were eligible to vote as a result of a constitutional amendment. They were members of Congress and local legislatures. They held office both locally and nationally, and there was a woman cabinet minister.

By 1945, there was more evidence of women being involved in national politics and they were active, if not on an equal basis with men, in both parties. Both parties campaigned for women's support, which of course they did not in 1865. The campaign for constitutional change in an Equal Rights Amendment was not a great deal more powerful or better supported than suffrage had been in the 1860s, and perhaps less so than when the suffrage organisations combined in 1890. There were more problems with this change to the constitution and more divisions within female opinion. Devotion to equality was not shown by women who achieved power and influence in New Deal organisations, and divisions were as apparent as during the period when the suffrage movement had been divided in the 1860s and 1870s (see page 161).

Attitudes had changed considerably, although not universally. The dismissal of women's attempt to register and vote in 1871–2 seemed part of a distant past when women did vote and were elected in 1941. However, in other respects the attitude to women working, to equal pay and in some states to legal rights had more resonance with 1870. Also, the ability of women from ethnic minorities to participate in voting and office holding in the South had not changed greatly from the 1860s because of the ability of the Southern states to maintain restrictions on African American registration and voting, which were only ended in the 1960s.

The impact of war in this period

The First World War had brought about political change and the constitutional amendment seemed a bigger and more significant change than the changes brought about by the Civil War. However, the Civil War might be seen as more important. This brought the increased participation in public affairs and the greater confidence and higher expectations of women to be seen as significant outside the home, together with the freeing of the slaves and the changes brought to African American women. This is especially true because the right to vote after the First World War was not accompanied by a comprehensive change in women's social, economic and legal status.

The Second World War and its impact on women

As the Second World War was, from the US point of view, closer to the total war of the Civil War than was the First World War, female cooperation and participation were essential. The main change was the greater number of women who went to work. The restrictions on women working that were made to protect men's jobs fell away as factories and workshops needed labour for government contracts, and men were taken in increasing numbers into the armed forces. The propaganda gave the impression of a considerable expansion of opportunity and responsibility for women, and there was a special Women's Advisory Committee to advise on the utilisation of women for the war effort. The war saw an increase in women in state legislatures from 144 to 228. There was some increase in women in Congress and women in public office, although it was not in any sense extensive. Women worked in more skilled jobs, rose to new challenges and may have increased in confidence and status. However, politically, there were limitations:

- Women were not involved in wartime decision-making on the home front or about the aims and methods of war.
- The New Deal practice of government agencies being dominated by men in top managerial positions continued.
- Women were unable to secure the type of support for working women in the form of childcare and cheap restaurants or canteens that British working women achieved during the war. They were still expected to combine domestic responsibilities with the most tiring and demanding work.
- Women had to accept unequal pay.
- Despite having an organisation called the National Council of Negro Women, there was little consultation with African American women and little opportunity for them to join the armed forces or take on managerial roles.
- Because of the harsh treatment of the Japanese community after Pearl Harbor, life for Japanese American women became hard and there was confinement and discrimination.
- Women remained with little real influence in the political parties.
- Women remained divided. Even in wartime, conservative women's groups did not support greater help for working mothers or equality of opportunity, believing that the war should not erode traditional family values.

The results of the war

The increased economic activity during the war led to a sustained period of prosperity. However, this, rather in the same way as early industrial and urban growth had before the Civil War, led to the greater domestication of women. The period of campaigning for rights seen in the progressive era from the 1870s to the 1900s seemed like another age when the growth of suburbs led to greater emphasis on women in the home, away from the public sphere and public issues. Great prosperity after the war led to a reduction of social issues which women campaigned for. The Cold War brought about a period of conservatism in which it was all too easy to see campaigning for equal rights as somehow subversive or supportive of communism. If women were rewarded for their war work in 1917–18 by the right to vote, the rewards for the huge efforts made in the war of 1941–5 were not political as such, but rather to offer prosperity, labour-saving technology, and to be entrusted with bringing up children to respect American values of prosperity and freedom. The post-war period can be seen as a period of stagnation, even regression.

Losses rather than gains?

By the end of 1946, 2 million women had been fired from heavy industry and 800,000 lost their jobs within two months of the end of the war against Japan in 1945. Whatever political gains had been made since 1920, the right to political participation could not prevent wholesale discrimination against women workers. Women workers did not all return home, but they did have to accept lower pay and lower status and exclusion from key jobs, which were now considered too heavy for them. The gap between men's pay and women's pay increased in the period from 1945 to 1960. Sexual exploitation increased as new consumerism tried to take advantage of women's sex appeal and coy flirtatiousness was often the only way to get some jobs. On the other hand, women were also expected to combine work with domestic responsibilities. There was still a concentration of women in the traditional caring roles of nursing, teaching and social work. Women's public political roles mirrored this in a way that was not very different from the post-Civil War period.

The situation for African American women in terms of wage differential was worse, but it was more expected that they would work, even if in low-paid work and domestic service. Economic discrimination was even more linked in the South with political discrimination, as states did their utmost to prevent African Americans qualifying to vote and made them the subject of discriminatory laws going back to the 1890s. However, there was significant African American female participation in civil rights movements. The most famous are Rosa Parks, who initiated the protest in Montgomery, Alabama, in 1955 (see page 46) and Elizabeth Eckford at Little Rock in 1957 (see page 27). African American women took a leading part in the grass-roots organisations that worked for civil rights, especially **Ella Baker**. Behind these were many determined and courageous campaigners. Other African American women had been arrested in Montgomery for riding in white seats in buses even before the NAACP chose to publicise the Rosa Parks case (one, Claudette Colvin, was a teenager who was pregnant by a married man at the time, whereas Rosa Parks was a 'respectable', older woman who was already active in the NAACP).

KEY FIGURE

Ella Baker (1903–86)

A highly influential campaigner for civil rights and a grass-roots organiser, part of the National Association for the Advancement of Colored People (NAACP), Southern Christian Leadership Conference (SCLC) and Student Nonviolent Coordinating Committee (SNCC) and one of the most important civil rights leaders.

Rosa Parks' 1955 police photograph. What impact would this photograph have had on public opinion? Why do you think that the local civil rights organisation chose a woman to deliberately challenge segregation on local transport?

Summary diagram: The campaign for political rights 1865–1960

Progress	Lack of progress
Gained vote	Many did not vote or voted as husband
Equal rights legislation	Passed in only one state
Working/job opportunities	Dismissed after war/during Depression Economic discrimination – lower pay
Women's cause	Disunited Opposition to help for working mothers/ equality of opportunity

3 The campaign for political rights 1960–92

▶ *How and why did women gain greater political rights from 1960 to 1992?*

Just as the issues of rights for African Americans and for women had been linked before the Civil War, and in the campaign against lynching in the 1920s, so they became linked with the increasing movement for civil rights in the 1960s.

In 1964, a Southern congressman, Howard Smith, wanted to sabotage the Civil Rights Act going through Congress, which outlawed employment discrimination on grounds of race, colour, religion or national origin. He jokingly suggested that 'sex' should be added, thinking to discredit the measure. In fact, his amendment was adopted. Women were quick to bring legal cases on the basis of the Act against discrimination and it led to the formation of the National Organization for Women (NOW) in 1966. This had a wider remit than many of the previous organisations and harked back to the 1920s' National Women's Party, or the more ambitious elements in the pre-1914 suffrage movement. Its aim was 'full participation in the mainstream of American society' and 'a truly equal relationship with men'.

These aims were more difficult than many of the previous aims of organised women's groups. The single constitutional aim of suffrage legislation provided a clear focus. Individual campaigns, for example, for temperance or citizenship, had a sharp focus. However, this was a wider mission, which threatened the suburban culture (see the box on page 176) and was more influenced by the civil rights movements for African Americans. It had emerged from a number of changes:

- A new kind of feminism, which challenged the basis of women's role in society and was influenced by writers such as Betty Friedan (1921–2006, see below). Demands for political and social change were underpinned by an ideology that had not been so apparent in previous women's movements since the early pioneers, who had been influenced by the ideas of the French Revolution after 1789.
- A study published in 1963 and commissioned by President Kennedy, called 'Report on American Women'. Several highly educated women had worked on this survey and it was read by the elite, who found the statistics of unequal pay, opportunities, political participation and status disturbing.
- By the 1960s, there was a movement for change. The Republican ascendancy of the Eisenhower years gave way to a reforming Democratic administration led by Kennedy. His 'New Frontier', while not very closely defined, gave the impression that change was needed after a long period of internal stagnation and that the USA needed modernisation.

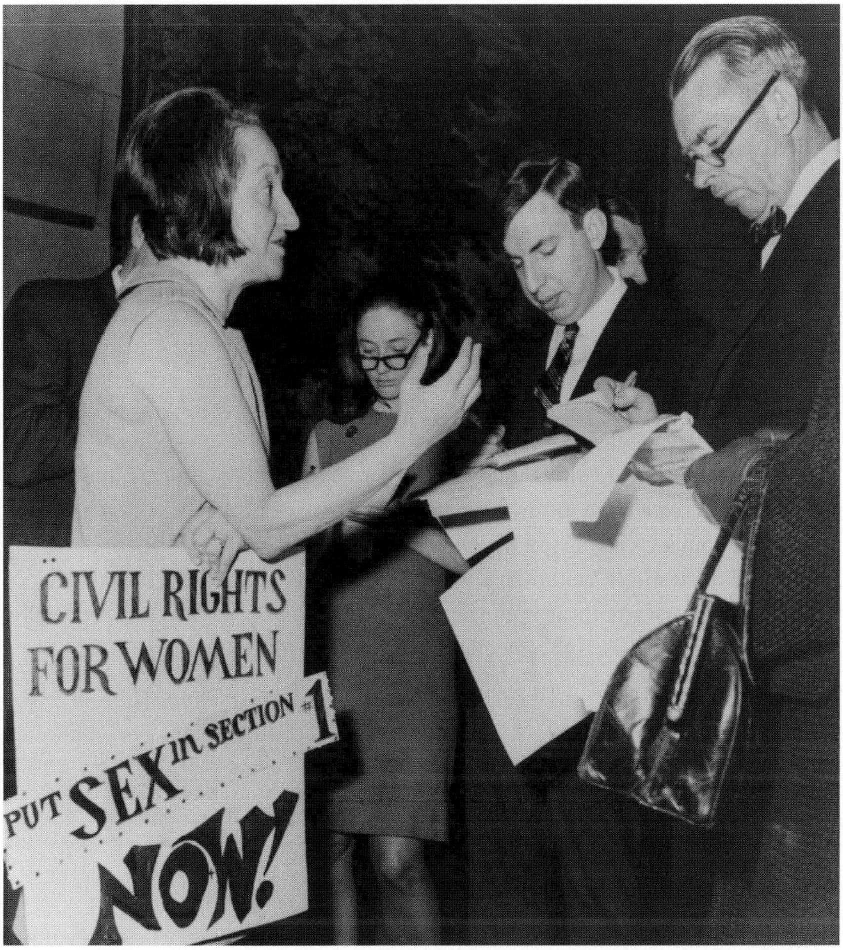

Betty Friedan (left) talks to reporters in the lobby of the New York State Assembly in 1967.

Betty Friedan's book *The Feminine Mystique* (1963) is a key text of feminism, expressing (mainly middle-class) women's discontent with the post-war period:

> *A woman is handicapped by her sex, and handicaps society, either by slavishly copying the pattern of man's advance in the professions, or by refusing to compete with man at all.*
>
> *The only way for a woman, as for a man, to find herself, to know herself as a person, is by creative work of her own. There is no other way.*
>
> *Man is not the enemy here, but the fellow victim.*
>
> *When she stopped conforming to the conventional picture of femininity she finally began to enjoy being a woman.*
>
> *The feminine mystique has succeeded in burying millions of American women alive.*
>
> *The only kind of work which permits an able woman to realize her abilities fully, to achieve identity in society in a life plan that can encompass marriage and motherhood, is the kind that was forbidden by the feminine mystique, the lifelong commitment to an art or science, to politics or profession.*

Suburban culture

At the core of women's lack of political advancement was a social change in which there was a major migration from urban centres to the suburbs. By the 1970s, some 80 million Americans or 40 per cent of the population were suburban dwellers. The suburbs developed a particular culture, which encouraged a divide in the roles and responsibilities of the sexes and acted against women taking an active political role. To be ambitious, to protest, to want power on an equal basis to men was widely seen as neurotic and unnatural – women were 'masculinising' themselves, going against a natural order.

After Kennedy's assassination in 1963, his Democrat successor Lyndon Johnson maintained the emphasis on reform with a rapid series of domestic measures. These dealt with a wide range of issues from civil rights to healthcare and education, to create what Johnson called the 'Great Society'. The re-emergence of political demands coincided with a period of change in US politics and society. Parallels might be drawn with the progressive era and the New Deal. This reappraisal of what was important to US society in the 1960s and especially after Kennedy's death led to a reconsideration of the role of women.

The new impetus for reform faced similar problems to other expressions of political concern by women:

- It was not united in its aims or strategy.
- It faced considerable conservative opposition, often from women.
- Neither of the political parties took up the causes directly.
- Radical supporters often alienated mainstream support.

Now, however, the subject matter of women's demands went way beyond what the suffrage organisations could have asked for, for example, the right to have abortions and 'the right of women to control their own reproductive lives' as expressed in the NOW conference of 1967. These new feminist campaigns and organisations worked within the existing system and wanted national laws. Although the women's groups, which were inspired or energised by this new feminism, were diverse, they did share an overall aim of equality which had been lacking in the 1930s and 1940s. There were specific female issues, such as paid maternity leave and tax concessions for housewives, but a unifying thrust was equality in key areas such as education, employment and political organisations. Even breakaway groups like the Women's Equity League Action (which rejected NOW's support for abortion-law reform) pressed hard for equality in education, bringing action against 300 schools and colleges that seemed to be discriminating against women. NOW brought legal actions against employers who broke the 1967 executive order against sex discrimination by companies with federal contracts.

The Equal Rights Amendment (ERA)

The major focus of the women's organisations from 1970 was the passing of the ERA. This was the late twentieth-century equivalent of the Nineteenth Amendment. It went back to 1923 and was a natural follow-on from the right to vote. The wording was simple:

> *Equality of rights under the law shall not be denied or abridged by the United States or by any State on account of sex.*

If the constitutional rights of men and women to vote were equal, why not their legal and social status? The supporters from 1970 used the same wording as those of 1923 who, in turn, harked back to the origins of the suffrage movement in the famous meeting at Seneca Falls in 1848 (see page 155). However, the same arguments that prevented the amendment being passed and which divided opinion re-emerged in the 1970s and 1980s. Every year from 1923 to 1970, a proposal to pass the amendment had been made but only in 1972, as a result of increased pressure from NOW and other women's groups, did it get to the stage of being debated by both houses of Congress. It had been passed previously in 1950 and 1953 by the Senate, but a condition had been attached. This added a new section to the ERA stating: 'The provisions of this article shall not be construed to impair any rights, benefits, or exemptions now or hereafter conferred by law upon persons of the female sex.' That is, women could keep their existing and future special protections that men did not have. Without full equality, the measure was not acceptable to its supporters. In 1961, Kennedy appointed a special commission on the status of women headed by the prestigious Eleanor Roosevelt, and this recommended an Equal Pay Act, which was passed in 1963, seemingly making a constitutional amendment unnecessary. That, and the continued opposition of some women's groups, prevented any more progress.

The evolution of the ERA

However, from 1967 an Equal Rights Amendment became the expressed policy of NOW, who regarded it as a vital symbol of equality. There were key speeches by supporters in Congress and a return to the type of suffrage agitation seen before 1917. In February 1970, supporters picketed Congress and disrupted a congressional committee considering lowering the voting age in order to raise the equality issue. In August 1972, there was a strike of 20,000 women calling for full equality. Betty Friedan's ardent advocacy, supported by Congresswoman Martha Griffiths, and plenty of direct action and demonstrations marked the most significant expansion of militancy since the period 1890–1917. It coincided with other movements for women's liberation and also with demonstrations on political issues, especially the Vietnam War.

In 1972, a resolution introduced by Martha Griffiths calling for an Equal Rights Amendment passed the House of Representatives. An edited version, exempting women from the **draft**, passed Congress.

KEY TERM

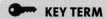

Draft The US term for conscription or calling up civilians for military service.

Martha Griffiths (1912–2003) was a lawyer who in 1954 became the first female Democrat to be elected to Congress by Michigan. She was a campaigner for women's rights who successfully got sex discrimination included in the Civil Rights Act of 1964. She went on to be assistant governor of Michigan.

President Nixon accepted the measure. It looked as if it would mirror the Nineteenth Amendment and be ratified by the states. Thirty states quickly accepted the amendment. However, the opposition to it becoming law was remarkably effective.

KEY FIGURE

Phyllis Schlafly (1924–)

Born in St Louis and financed her college education by testing machine guns in an arms factory during the war. She was a conservative journalist and wrote in support of family values and against feminism. She thought the real right of a woman was the right to stay at home.

Opposition to the ERA

This opposition was quite a remarkable and unexpected development. **Phyllis Schlafly**, a Republican from Illinois, organised women to oppose the measure as effectively as previous reformers had organised them in support of change. Schlafly's comments on feminism at various times since 1980 include the following:

> *Non-criminal sexual harassment on the job is not a problem for the virtuous woman except in the rarest of cases. [1981]*
>
> *And the first commandment of feminism is: I am woman; thou shalt not tolerate strange gods who assert that women have capabilities or often choose roles that are different from men's.*
>
> *Men should stop treating feminists like ladies, and instead treat them like the men they say they want to be.*
>
> *When will American men learn how to stand up to the nagging by the intolerant, uncivil feminists whose sport is to humiliate men?*

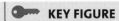

Opposition to the ERA was on two levels:

- The rational arguments were that women might find themselves liable for military service; that they would lose protection rights and, most significantly for older women, alimony would be threatened. It was said to be more a measure for younger single women, competing with men for jobs, rather than for older women or working-class women who needed special protection in the workplace.
- On another level, the appeal was for traditional values; for the type of lifestyle common in suburban America, for the need to be looked after by men and for 'mom and apple pie' values. There was also the danger that women would not gain custody so easily of children in divorce cases, undermining a widespread belief that children needed to be raised by their mother, and that this was a sort of sacred duty, which could not be done by men.

Nixon's '**silent majority**' asserted itself. These divisions among women had been one of the biggest barriers to change, and here were the Daughters of the American Revolution re-emerging, led by an articulate, trenchant and determined leader. The move towards conservatism, which led to a Republican victory by Ronald Reagan in 1980, was able to prevent the amendment being ratified. The Republicans withdrew their support in 1980, even though Eisenhower had backed the amendment much earlier. The new right, including religious conservatives, wanted to put the clock back. Like the whole issue of votes for women before 1919, the issue had drifted away from what was really being proposed into a symbol of opposition to, or support for, all sorts of social change. It was noticeable that opinion polls showed less support for the amendment by the 1980s than when it was introduced in the 1970s.

> **KEY TERM**
>
> **Silent majority** Used by Nixon in 1969 to describe the mass of middle-class Americans ('Middle America') who were conservative and opposed social change and did not join in anti-war demonstrations. The term was used in the nineteenth century to describe dead people.

Through the 1980s and 1990s, activists tried hard to revive the amendment, but by 1992 they had not been successful. A powerful woman had again had an effect on political developments, but unlike her predecessors to oppose rather than to promote change.

The significance of radical feminism

Parallel to these more traditional and broadly political activities were campaigns against social sexual discrimination. This was political agitation in a new sense – the demand that the whole way that men treated and regarded women needed to change. This was possibly implied by earlier women's political movements, but this was a new type of 'sexual politics'. It had its roots in political activism in favour of African American civil rights by radical student groups and also political protests about the war in Vietnam. However, once again, alliances between campaigns for women's issues and those supporting other civil rights proved problematic. The veteran civil rights campaigner Frederick Douglass rejected linking women's rights with rights for his fellow African Americans in 1868, and the black activists of the 1960s did not always see a role for women.

One African American leader made the outrageous comment that 'The only position for women in the SNCC is prone'.

Protests, writings and meetings against sexism did not take the form of an organised movement like many of the ones considered. It was more of a general attitude. One characteristic element was 'consciousness raising', which feminists saw as a political activity but not of a conventional kind. Small groups of women would meet to discuss the position of women, sexual relationships and so forth, which made women more aware of 'unequal power relationships'. This was manifested, as feminist writer and activist Kate Millett wrote in an influential book called *Sexual Politics* (1970), in inequality of opportunity. Her view was that 'every avenue of power is entirely in male hands'. Given that this was some 60 years after the 1920 amendment, there was some political disillusionment with conventional means of attempting to gain political influence.

The lack of political equality was mirrored in economic equality. Female wages were on average 63 per cent of men's in 1956 but by the time of the 1970s' agitation this had fallen to 57 per cent (1973). Day-care centres were not adequate for the number of working mothers, and there was no tax relief for children until 1977, although it was well established as a support for women in the UK.

The political movement of the 1970s and 1980s

The broader political movement of the 1970s saw 80,000–100,000 women as participants in some form of women's group, comparable to the wide support for temperance in the 1870s and 1880s. The social agenda was wider: health, abortion, marriage and divorce, sexuality, and rights for older women and working women. The direction that politics for women had taken had moved away from previous conventional forms and was more of an extension of the trend established after the Civil War for concerns over social and specifically women-centred issues. This has been described as 'second wave' feminism; 'first wave' feminism was more focused on the right to vote and to establish political rights in a narrower sense.

The situation by 1992

Despite the success of a conservative backlash against feminism and the ERA, the 1980s saw an expansion of education for women, with nearly half of undergraduate and master's degrees going to women. However, the old culture persisted. The proportion in science and engineering remained much lower. Fewer than eight per cent of engineers were women in 1990. Despite much greater political rights, the majority of women still studied 'female subjects' and worked in 'female occupations', much as they had done in the period before the First World War.

There were limited numbers of women in decision-making positions even 70 years after they had gained the right to make the political decision of voting. Also, despite the Equal Pay Act of 1963, women were paid on average 32 per cent less than men. It took until 1984 for a major party to select a woman as vice presidential candidate, and Geraldine Ferraro was on the losing side in 1984. It also took until 1981 for a woman to be appointed to the Supreme Court and to hold a major diplomatic post, when Jeanne Fitzpatrick was appointed ambassador to the United Nations. There had been a number of turning points, which had not led to the anticipated long-term political changes.

The major political development was the Nineteenth Amendment, but significant was the failure of the ERA, which might have made it more of a real milestone. The excitement of the 'second wave of feminism' did lead to major issues and a great deal of heightened awareness of gender issues. However, in political terms it did not lead to equal rights being guaranteed by the constitution, although they were incorporated into the laws of individual states. Wholesale changes in women holding major government posts, or having decision-making roles in local and national government or major national institutions, had still not occurred by 1992.

Summary diagram: The campaign for political rights 1960–92

Why gain?	What gain?	Limits?
Civil rights movement	Education	Top jobs
NOW formed 1966	Abortion	Equal pay
Reforming Democrats: Kennedy and Johnson		Roles in politics

4 The main developments of social and economic change 1865–1992

▶ *How great was social and economic change for women during this period?*

By the time of the Civil War, in 1865, the expansion of trade and industry had changed the nature of the USA. The expansion westwards had often led to women and men being partners in settlement, which needed enormous hard work and cooperation between family members. However, with economic change many women were separated from the world of work, and in the increasingly prosperous middle-class USA they dominated the home when their husbands went to work. Where women worked in the rural USA or in factories, they suffered from lower pay and, if they were married, had the double responsibility of looking after the home. African American women suffered considerably from these double standards, even when they were slaves.

Women and work after 1865: change and continuity

After 1865, there was a considerable expansion of the number of women in the labour market. Ten per cent of free women held jobs in 1840, fifteen per cent in 1870 and 24 per cent in 1924. The biggest increase was in white-collar work and the professions. In certain areas where there were textile factories, the proportion of working women was higher than the national average. In the South, among freed slaves, the problem of making smallholdings pay was so great that women were forced to contribute heavily to agricultural work.

The biggest change was the greater experience of paid work among both single and married women. There was a higher proportion of African American married women than white women, but, as the US economy grew, and as child labour declined, there was more demand for women workers. The range of female employment also changed. At the end of the Civil War, 60 per cent of female workers were domestic servants and one per cent worked in white-collar occupations. By 1920, these figures had changed to eighteen per cent servants and nearly 40 per cent in clerical or professional positions. However, this did not apply to African American women, who continued to be employed in factory work or domestic service. Within professional employment, teaching and nursing predominated, followed by charity and welfare. Thus, the stereotype that women's work was linked to their domestic, caring concerns predominated even when economic growth widened the female workforce.

One development from larger numbers of women workers was a growth in union organisation. There were more strikes and demands for better wages and conditions. But this has to be kept in proportion: only two per cent of trade unionists were women by 1914, even though 25 per cent of female employment was in factories.

Thus, between the Civil War and the First World War there was a mixture of change and continuity. The scale of women working and the nature of the employment changed. Work gave women more independence and was the background to greater involvement in public affairs and the beginnings of industrial organisation. However, most work was in traditional areas associated with women: in the caring professions, in producing garments, in domestic service, in education and nursing, and in meeting men's sexual needs. Also, there was little change in the attitude that the home was the woman's major responsibility.

Social change 1865–1914

Post-Civil War America was not a static society. There were changes within the family. The average of five children per couple before 1861 had declined to three by 1920. With prosperity, family size fell as middle-class Americans wanted to ensure their children could prosper. Women faced having fewer children and looking after them better, and they also expected more of their partners.

In many ways, women gained from social changes. In 1870, more boys than girls were in school, but by 1920 this had become more equal, with roughly two-thirds of white children of both sexes being educated. By 1890, there were more female high-school graduates than male and secondary education had expanded generally. African American girls did less well, but even here the percentage went from 10 to 30 per cent from 1870 to 1914. The proportion of women teachers increased from 60 to 86 per cent in the same period. However, the proportion of women in higher education remained lower. Although the number of women with degrees doubled, only 30 per cent of university degrees were awarded to women by 1920.

The growth in education and employment led to women being more confident in participating in public campaigns. It led to more cooperation and a considerable expansion of women's clubs. Women writers became more numerous. In terms of equality of economic opportunity; rewards; ability to gain access to managerial positions, to enter traditional male professions, such as medicine and law, to make decisions or to gain political equality, there was much less progress.

The social and economic impact of the First World War

The First World War did not bring women into factories for the first time, but it added to the numbers employed as demand grew for various products in engineering, food processing and textiles. Three million more women were working than in 1865. The diversity of female employment also increased, with more women working in heavy industry and transport. As the demand for food increased, the numbers in farming also grew. Newcomers to this work were nicknamed 'farmerettes', even though there was a well-established tradition of women in rural occupations. Around 30,000 women worked directly for the armed forces – here there was less change as the work centred on an extension of domestic service, such as laundry or nursing. The growth in government also extended opportunities already developed before 1917 for clerical work. The appearance of women as tram and train conductors, and women police made an impression on the public disproportionate to numbers and importance. Upwards of 20,000 women travelled overseas in support of the armed forces, as members of the YMCA, Red Cross and Salvation Army, but the army did not recruit women doctors in any number. There were 358 women who were killed serving overseas and many more suffered injuries or developed serious illnesses. Many African American women saw a change of lifestyle when they joined the considerable emigration from the Southern states, as Northern industries needed more labour.

The war accelerated higher levels of female employment, increased women's confidence in tackling more demanding work and associated women with the national cause. However, in many ways it did not mark radical change. Much of the work continued to be in traditional roles; and after the war, many women did not stay in their new roles in industry. They were under pressure to give up their jobs to men returning from the war. Also, although wages rose, there was not equality between male and female labour, and there was little attempt to provide childcare facilities or to help women who faced dual responsibilities at work and in the home. There was little suggestion that women were equal to men in the effort of fighting the war.

KEY TERM

Roaring Twenties
The popularity of elements of US culture, such as jazz, gives the impression of a freer society in search of pleasure, despite prohibition. The glamorisation of gangsters, short skirts, fast cars, jazz musicians and the cinema as a major source of entertainment points to a new, dangerous and exciting urban culture.

The 'flapper' era

The post-war social changes that were associated with the younger generation during the '**Roaring Twenties**' are often associated with the relaxation of traditional attitudes during the war. Women wore less restricting clothes; they had shorter hair; they smoked; they were more ostentatious about their sexuality, with shorter skirts and more 'daring' behaviour. This was symbolised by the 'flappers' – the seemingly more independent and emancipated younger women of the 1920s going against 'Victorian norms', wearing their skirts short (as high as just below the knee) and cutting their hair short. However, there are a number of objections to seeing this as a major turning point. In conservative, rural USA there was limited acceptance of this, and women would have found it difficult to behave in this way. In areas of the USA suffering from the fall in farm prices, there was little available money for make-up, fashion or nightclubs. In urban centres, the greater overt sexuality ended up with women becoming sex objects to attract men and increased double standards rather than achieving greater independence and emancipation. The pressure on women to be fashionable and alluring before marriage, and then adapt to become demure housewives, set the tone for the suburban culture of post-1945 America.

Also, there was a problem with sexualisation when birth control was limited and abortions were still the main means of preventing birth. It has been suggested that there were a million illegal abortions a year before 1973. There were alternatives such as the diaphragm, first made available in 1917 in a clinic in New York run by the birth-control pioneer **Margaret Sanger**. However, she was arrested for obscenity and there was limited acceptance of birth-control advice. Not until 1936 was import of birth-control devices made legal. Most doctors saw abstinence as the only sure means of preventing unwanted children. Men were often unwilling to use condoms; for poorer women diaphragms were difficult and unhygienic to use without running water. The birth-control pill was not available until the late 1950s, and not until 1973 was abortion legalised (see page 188).

KEY FIGURE

Margaret Sanger (1879–1966)

A nurse in New York who was shocked by hardships caused by unwanted pregnancies in poor areas. She invented the term 'birth control' and she opened a contraception clinic in 1916. She faced disapproval and prosecutions but persisted in her belief that every child should be wanted.

Thus, the sexual revolution of the flapper era encountered some problems and conflicts among women. They seemingly had the freedom to celebrate their own sexuality and independence, but faced massive social disapproval if they were promiscuous or gave birth to illegitimate children, while the men who fathered the children did not. Also, they had no really reliable and widespread control over their bodies until after 1945 and even then faced problems. Furthermore, they faced problems in adjusting once married to a different sexual role. This was compounded by a lot of rather tendentious sexual theory that women lacked the capacity for pleasure that men had and envied the penis.

Women and work

At work, women continued to face discrimination and attitudes were slow to change. Most of the twelve per cent of wives who worked in the 1920s did so because they needed to support their families, not as a means of independence. They made up 28 per cent of the female workforce, still worked mainly as domestics or in textiles and were predominantly African Americans or immigrants. The bulk of female labour was unmarried. Female occupations were more varied but in offices women often suffered from deep-seated sexual prejudice. They were very much less likely to make decisions than men. The single woman looking for work by 1930 was overwhelming likely to be a secretary, a clerk, a saleswoman, a waitress or a hairdresser. Better-educated women would be teachers or nurses. Thus, there was a considerable degree of continuity with the pre-war era despite some surface changes and despite the experience of the First World War. At root, the expectations that women would run the home, the difficulties in preventing unwanted pregnancy, entrenched male attitudes to inequality of pay, and divisions among women about what their role should be ensured that the past had something of a dead hand on women's rights and progress.

The Great Depression and New Deal

The onset of Depression made the position worse. The pressure was increased that women should not 'steal jobs' from men. However, as women worked for less they were often employed in preference to men by companies hard hit and anxious to reduce costs. The number of women workers increased in the 1930s from 11.7 per cent to 15.2 per cent of the total workforce. In other areas, married women found it more difficult and some states stopped married women from taking jobs in any publicly run institutions. The Depression put pressure on wages, and this hit African American women hard. The small amount of progress women had made in the professions in the 1920s was reversed by the Depression. Although progressive legislation made more equal pay levels mandatory, the problems in enforcing this were considerable. Unions put the interests of their male members first. As was seen above, the New Deal stimulated public activity, but the 1930s saw a regression in many ways. The idealised women seen in the movies were in sharp contrast to exploited and underused women in many economic sectors, to the hard-pressed women who moved from depressed areas to find new work and to the African American women suffering from low wages for menial work getting even lower.

The Second World War

The number of men taking part in the war was greater than between 1917 and 1918. The growth in the government machine and the expansion of industry were greater. There was less prejudice against direct participation, and 100,000 women served in the armed forces in the Women's Army Corps, the Navy and the Women's Air Force. Jobs included flying and testing planes, as well as the inevitable typing, sewing, cooking and nursing. Propaganda urged women to take over men's jobs, although it was clear that this was for the duration of the war, not permanently. Also, there was no parity in pay. In 1944, the average woman's salary was $31.21 a week for manufacturing work, even though the men that still remained made $54.65 a week. There were more women this time as taxi drivers, heavy industry workers, drivers, and workers in lumber and steel mills. Six million women entered the workforce, making them over a third of the labour force as the war absorbed 16 million men. Relatively small numbers of adventurous women made a considerable impact as new ventures, such as women training as pilots, were publicised.

How much social change did the war bring?

Women had shared challenges and dangers; 37,000 women were killed in accidents in ammunition factories. They had done new jobs and taken more responsibilities. They had travelled more inside and outside the USA and had been the subject of propaganda campaigns, which encouraged them to be adventurous and showed them in new roles. Arguably, the Second World War had taken social change much further than the First, even if there had been

A poster for female recruitment during the Second World War. What does this reveal about the attitudes to women during the Second World War?

no great symbolic change like gaining the vote. However, the reaction against change may have been greater than in the period after 1918. The Cold War encouraged a social conservatism; the extended period of prosperity and the growth of suburban America tended to reinforce traditional attitudes, and changes in rights tended to be focused on African Americans rather than on women.

The comments from a suburban woman below seem much closer to the stifling conformity of post-1865 America than an heir to the changes of the Second World War:

> *I get up at six. I get my son dressed and then give him breakfast. I wash the dishes and feed the baby. I get lunch and while the children sleep I sew or mend or iron. Then I cook supper for the family, and my husband watches TV while I do the dishes. After I get the children to bed I do my hair and then I go to bed.*

On the other hand, more women were going into higher education, more into the professions; more had taken a leading part in civil rights movements, more were using birth control. By the early 1960s, there was a reaction against the disappointments of the 1940s and 1950s and the stage was set for what has been called the 'New Feminism'. Once again, the issue of women's rights and other issues in US society, particularly over African American rights, were linked, just as in the 1850s and 1860s. There also emerged some dynamic female leaders on a par with the suffrage leaders and the women who led the temperance movement. The most significant victory was not a political one like the suffrage issue but a social one – the decision of *Roe* v. *Wade* (1973).

The abortion issue

The issue of abortion became a key element in women's rights when Norma McCorvey brought a case in 1970 under the name Jane Roe against the state of Texas in the person of Attorney General Wade. Texas, like most states, restricted or banned abortions. Abortion was only permitted in Texas when necessary for medical reasons to save the life of the mother. Roe and her female lawyers challenged this on constitutional grounds. Somewhat obscurely, they claimed that a woman's rights over her own body fell into 'a zone of privacy' and that privacy was protected under the Ninth Amendment of the constitution. To deny that privacy, Texas (and most other states) was acting unconstitutionally. The case reached the Supreme Court in 1973 and resulted in a historic decision. During the first three months of pregnancy, states could not prohibit abortions. In the second and third trimesters they could not enact any ban where a woman's health was concerned. After six months, states could protect the unborn foetus, but not if an abortion was considered necessary to protect the health of the mother. This put the rights of the mother above any rights of the foetus, which the court ruled was not a person whose rights needed to be protected in the earlier states of pregnancy.

Whatever the medical arguments, the decision was seen as supporting the rights of women over their own bodies and over attitudes which denied them freedom. As with the decisions taken over African American civil rights, it seemed to show that American official opinion had moved towards greater recognition of women's personal freedom. The decision challenged some traditional views about women. Many thought that women's first duties and responsibilities were as mothers and carers of others, rather than to themselves. This decision put the woman's right to choose whether to have children before other social responsibilities. However, there was a massive backlash of opposition which showed how strongly the counter-view was held, and that women's position in society was still a highly contentious issue.

The New Feminism

With the failure to pass a consolidated Equal Opportunities Amendment (see page 179) the feminist movement, or feminist opinion, in the 1980s focused on key social issues such as:

- domestic violence and providing shelters for women; issues of sexual abuse within and outside marriage
- protecting women from sexual harassment in the workplace
- education for women in their history and rights
- protecting women from conservative attempts to restrict abortion and access to contraception
- funding for education for young women and many social issues.

In a sense, the parallel was with the many and various concerns in the post-1865 period, but these issues were even more specific to women and often depended on looking at a male-dominated world with hostility. By 1990, there were still only two women senators and there was limited consensus about the aims and methods of what has been called 'second-wave feminism'. Some women felt that insufficient attention had been given to sexist language; others that feminine sexuality had been downplayed in a sort of puritanism; others that there had been too much association with the political left. However, once again women were divided. This had been a problem since 1865. The campaign for women's rights had suffered because women focused on all sorts of other reforms and the suffrage movement split. There were also divisions about the best way to use the vote after 1919. There had been no agreement about the ERA. Now there were further disagreements about abortion and also about the nature and direction of feminism.

The problems of divisions that had been so evident in the rather diffuse causes which women had campaigned for in the post-Civil War period; the divisions between the suffrage movement; the way best to use the newly won vote after 1919; the struggle over the ERA and the bitter controversies between those who supported relaxation of the abortion laws and those who opposed resurfaced over the nature and direction of feminism.

By now, women were becoming more represented in politics – there were seven female senators in Congress, for example, by 1993. Half of university graduates were women in 1986. Women in positions of authority were no longer unusual. The casual sexism of the 1950s and 1960s had come to seem as remote as Victorian concern over women wearing trousers. The much greater availability of contraception and the decline of illegal abortions had amounted to a revolution in women's lives. Technology and a much greater willingness by men to be part of the home and child-raising had meant a change in family life undreamed of in 1865. However, in many ways, the period between 1942 and 1945, when women were so important in the nation and where their achievements were so publicly praised, and their sense of adventure and enterprise so welcomed, may not have been entirely reconstructed even in the 1980s. The full social implications of the achievement of the franchise may be yet to be realised.

Summary diagram: The main developments of social and economic change 1865–1992

	1865–1914	1914–39	1939–69	1969 →
Gains	Job opportunities Nature of work Educational opportunities Family size fell	Factory work Clerical work Flapper – not rural	Armed forces More responsibility Travel More in higher education	Abortion New feminism
Limits	Little birth control	Lost jobs when men returned from war/ Depression Limited birth control Discrimination at work Divided organisations	Social conservatism during Cold War Divided	Failure of Equal Opportunities Divided

Chapter summary

Women campaigned for a variety of changes in this period and their most conspicuous political success was gaining the right to vote in 1920. However, the hopes of the campaigners of the previous century were not entirely realised as social and economic change did not follow automatically. The effects of two world wars on women were dramatic but many of the changes, both social and economic, did not last. There were two significant periods of activism among women in the period. The first was the suffrage movement and its allied campaigns from 1869 to 1919 and the second was the feminism movement in the 1960s and 1970s. Both had significant achievements, although the amendment to the constitution ratified in 1920 was not achieved by the feminists of the 1970s and 1980s, but by the *Roe* v. *Wade* decision, the result of a determined woman supported by female lawyers being symbolic of a change of attitude towards women and their rights.

Refresher questions

Use these questions to remind yourself of the key material covered in this chapter.

1. Did the opportunities facing women in 1865 outweigh the problems in changing their status?
2. How important was the campaign for prohibition in the history of women's rights?
3. How significant were individual leaders in developing more rights for women?
4. What motivated opposition to women's rights in this period?
5. How important were the two world wars in changing the status of women?
6. How important was the Nineteenth Amendment in changing women's status?
7. How far can the 1920s be seen as a key decade in the emancipation of women?
8. How far did women benefit from the New Deal?
9. How far did the Second World War lead to significant changes in the status of women?
10. Had women achieved more in terms of social and economic change by 1992 than political change?
11. Why was there so much disagreement among women over the Equal Rights Amendment?
12. What was the significance for women of *Roe* v. *Wade*?
13. How important were links between campaigns for women's rights and other political campaigns in this period?
14. How much progress in women's social, political and economic position had been made by 1992?

In-depth studies and key debates

The examination requires you to study three topics in depth, and for this unit they are:

- Civil Rights in the Gilded Age
- The New Deal and civil rights
- Malcolm X and Black Power.

This section will go into more detail about women in relation to these topics, and introduce you to some of the key debates so that you will have enough depth of knowledge to be able to evaluate passages that are set on any of the three studies.

Key debate 1: what was the extent of the impact of the industrialisation of the Gilded Age on women?

The economic expansion of industrial USA produced urbanisation and diversification. It offered more opportunities for women outside traditional domestic work. The number of domestic women servants fell by half between 1870 and 1900 while clerical occupations increased ten-fold and factory work from eighteen per cent of employed women in 1870 to 22 per cent in 1900. There was more evidence of women unionising to defend their rights. In 1881, the Knights of Labor, the national trade union organisation, offered support to women workers. Women became union organisers and by the mid-1880s there were 113 women's assemblies and a female membership of 50,000. This is not to say that progress was constant, but women did gain experience of standing up for their rights. Historians Carol Hymowitz and Michaela Weismann describe the work of Mary Harris Jones – 'Mother Jones' – who struggled for mine workers for 50 years, organising miners' wives to oppose strike breaking and a famous march of factory children from Pennsylvania to Washington. Other prominent organisers were Kate Richards O'Flynn, Rose Pastor Stokes and Elizabeth Gurney Flynn. Although industrialisation brought hardships it also brought opportunities, changing employment patterns and opportunities for women to organise and to assert themselves in a new industrial society.

The alternative view is that industrialisation, especially allied with the influx of cheap immigrant labour, accentuated inequality and led to harsh conditions and sexual exploitation. In industry, women were still concentrated in textiles and cotton mills. They were usually confined to unskilled labour and had few opportunities for advancement. An 1890 Bureau of Labor survey quoted by S.J. Kleinburg (1999) showed that where 800 men and women were surveyed doing the same work, the majority of men received higher wages. The gap was greater in the Southern factories. In sweatshops, another growth sector of the economy in the so-called Gilded Age, low wages and very hazardous and oppressive working conditions were common. Also, the expansion of cities brought the rapid growth of prostitution as some girls and women preferred the dangers of sex work to the poor wages and conditions which were the alternative in domestic service or factories and sweatshops. Male trade unionists offered limited support for female workers whom they saw as undercutting wages. In 1882, a strike in a textile mill in Lawrence, Massachusetts, over a twenty per cent pay cut failed after four months with no support from the male unions. Although the Knights of Labor did promote women membership, its successor as the largest union, the American Federation of Labor, was very much less sympathetic to women in the 1890s and represented skilled workers – something women could not become. By 1900, only two per cent of all trade unionists were women.

Much depends on what view is taken here. Women did strike repeatedly and despite the difficulties went on to form new organisations in the decade after the 1890s. For all the hard work and bad conditions, the cities offered opportunities that either rural America or the poverty-stricken areas of Europe, which immigrants had been forced to leave, did not. Women could run successful businesses even if many did not rise out of poverty. The decline in domestic service, which was notoriously poorly rewarded and oppressive, was probably a major benefit. However, contemporary accounts produced depressing stories of women being sexually harassed by foremen and employers, struggling to maintain themselves and their families, and enduring conditions that are similar to some of the worst contemporary developing world cities.

Key debate 2: how far did the New Deal improve the economic status and position of women?

Many historians think that the New Deal was disappointing for women. Women had been in the front line of job losses both in federal and state posts and also in private industry and commerce, where the pressure was to save the jobs of the men. Falling wages hit many, especially domestic workers who were largely unprotected by labour legislation and included many non-white and immigrant workers. Despite the women brought to Washington to advise and help to run New Deal agencies, historians like Louise Berkinow believed that gender discrimination was the norm.

The public works projects paid for by federal money were largely to provide jobs for men, who dominated the workforce in large-scale construction projects. Regulations of wages often confirmed the wage gap between men and women. While it was claimed that women's talents were being employed in the New Deal administration, major decisions were taken without much input from women and the high-powered women in New Deal agencies often accepted the priority of getting men back to work to ensure the stability of family life and to protect women and children.

The alternative view is that positions of power were held by what have been called 'social justice' feminists. They were anxious to use their power to achieve key aims such as child labour legislation. They were also anxious to show that women in power should take the wider view of national interests as opposed to merely acting as special pleaders for women's issues. Thus, it was important to support the overall aims of the Roosevelt administration in getting men back to work and to show objectivity in responding to the realities of the situation. One reformer, Florence Kelly, argued that it was their role to regulate industry as a whole, not merely to set up special regulations for women. The fact was that women had been taken into positions of authority. Frances Perkins was Secretary of Labor 1933–45, and Mary Dewson was director of the Women's Division of the Democratic National Party 1932–4, chair of the Women's Division Advisory Committee 1934–7 and member of the Social Security Board 1937–8. These, and other examples, show a major advance in the employment of women in government.

The practical aspects of relief were also of vital importance. Susan Ware in *Beyond Suffrage, Women in the New Deal* (1981) rejects the traditional view that the New Deal achieved little for women, and suggests that there was a considerable influx of high-powered women into politics and government who formed an important network for the future. If there was discrimination against married women, then it reflected the prevailing public mood, and she quotes a 1936 Gallup poll in which four-fifths of those asked agreed that married women with working husbands should not work and take jobs from men or single women. In any case, there were more married women working in 1940 than there had been in 1933. Her main argument is the importance of giving women experience in power. She refers to a special conference in 1940 for women, addressed by a line-up of women in senior posts in business and government. One of them expressed her admiration: 'My heart filled with pride at a long line of intelligent, competent, well balanced women leaders who repaid Roosevelt's confidence in our ability'. Their achievements in reform could be seen as important.

The 1933 passing of the Federal Emergency Relief Act finally allowed financial assistance, and homeless women could seek additional refuge in city shelters. As the legislation against employing married women passed in 1932 had created considerable hardship, this and similar relief measures were an indication of the vital support that the New Deal could offer even if, by modern standards, it continued to discriminate against women in terms of job creation and equal wages.

The limitations of New Deal legislation's ability to help women can be seen in the Farm Security Act of 1937. This improved the conditions of many poorer Southern farmers, but could do little about the traditional unfairness of rural life for women. The failure to help rural women was noted by a sociologist in 1939:

> *The pattern is for the woman to do everything inside the house, for the man to occupy himself on the farm ... So far this sounds fairly even balanced, but the wife does the field work also for about half the year in addition to her traditionally allocated sphere of labor.*

There were limits to how far the New Deal could change social attitudes.

Key debate 3: what was the relationship between Black Power and women's rights?

Even studies which generally recognise the importance of the role women played in the Black Power movement draw attention to the sexism inherent in it. The *macho* posturing of Black Power males and their talk of reclaiming male sexuality did not seem promising for women supporters. There was a tendency to see feminism as 'a white women's thing', and black activists called for black women to 'walk behind the men' in protesting and political activity. In 1965, the Nation of Islam organisation had condemned 'the sins of birth control' and referred to 'the deadly pill'. Women responded by forming their own organisations, instead of trying to influence and lead existing ones. Black women were conscious that they suffered a triple form of discrimination: racism, sexism and classism. The Black Power movement did not necessarily address their concerns, and, in some ways, was part of the problem rather than the solution.

In general terms, the radicalism of the Black Power groups was harmful to the cause of women's rights, as it suggested that both were part of a wider movement to destabilise US society and undermine the silent majority of middle-class conservative USA. However, some historians have argued that women took a key role in shaping Black Power, and women gained by participating in the movement. Farmer suggests that the pamphlets and posters produced portray women as revolutionary equals, and that women activists developed a wide range of aims involving day care, food aid and support for poorer neighbourhoods. Also, in the early 1970s, women made up two-thirds of the membership of the Black Panthers, and their activities, particularly at local level, helped to define the movement as much as the more dramatic image of male power.

The alternative view plays down the resistance and sexism faced by women, and stresses their role. Women had played an important role in the grass-roots element of the civil rights movement in the 1950s. They had taken a leading part in the Birmingham Bus Boycott, the freedom rides and sit-ins, and not only were women important organisers in the famous March on Washington (see page 36), but thousands joined in, although none was invited to speak.

There was a danger for women that they would simply provide support for the men by secretarial and catering roles, but this was rejected by younger activists like Elaine Brown and Kathleen Cleaver. Female members of Black Power were known as 'sisters'. Black Panther sisters wrote articles, designed posters, gave legal advice, and were organisers and speakers, often making links to local communities. Some of this fell into 'women's roles', but they did take leadership positions. Ericka Higgins was a high-ranking member of the organisation in Connecticut and Elaine Brown was second only in responsibility on the central committee to the founder, Huey Newton. Studies of the sisters showed that the experience of taking a major role in organised civil rights radicalism developed confidence and pride, which overrode the discrimination and suspicion of feminism in the movement. *Sisters in the Struggle*, edited by Bettye Collier-Thomas and published in 2001, shows both elements in the debate. The radical African American civil rights organiser Angela Davis had organised a rally in San Diego, California in 1967, but wrote: 'I ran headlong into a situation which was to be a constant problem. I was criticized by male members of the group for doing "a man's job." A woman had to "inspire her man" and educate his children'. On the other hand, Fannie Lou Hamer was such a powerful speaker about the wrongs done by women in Mississippi that Malcolm X, who was moved by hearing her, described her as 'the country's number one freedom fighter'.

Study skills: thematic essay question

How to write a conclusion to a thematic essay

You may have already considered the importance of a conclusion when studying units 1 and 2 of the OCR course. As with those units, a conclusion needs to reach a judgement based on what you have already written and should be briefly supported so that it is not an assertion. It should *not* introduce new ideas – if they were important they should have been in the main body of the essay. It is also important *not* to offer a contrary argument to the one you have pursued throughout the rest of your essay. This possibility will be avoided if you have planned and thought through your essay before you started writing (see page 61 for guidance on planning).

It might be that you are largely restating the view that you offered in the opening paragraph; or, in stronger answers, there might be a slight variation to that judgement so that you confirm your original view, but suggest, with a brief example, that there were occasions when this view was not always correct.

As with unit 1 and 2 answers, if the question has a named factor, then you should give a supported judgement about that factor's relative importance, explaining why it is or is not the most important and the role it played in the events you have discussed. If the question asks you to assess a range of issues, the conclusion should explain which you think was the most important and why, and give some brief support for your claim. Remember, a claim is simply an assertion unless there is some evidence to support it, and a simple assertion will not score highly.

Consider the question below and the sample conclusions in Responses A and B which follow. Response A is an example of a weak conclusion and Response B an example of a strong conclusion.

'The First World War was the major turning point in bringing about change in the status of women in the USA.' How far do you agree?

The focus of your answer should have been on the importance of the First World War and the subsequent granting of the right to vote by constitutional amendment. You should have assessed the degree of change and continuity. However, you will have needed to compare the war with other possible key turning points, such as the Second World War or the campaign for prohibition or the feminist movement which began in the 1960s. In the main body of the essay you should look to compare these elements and demonstrate any links between the developments so that your evaluation of the various factors is comparative.

You may have considered the following issues in your essay:

- The importance of the First World War in accelerating the franchise issue.
- The changes in female employment in the war.
- Social mobility in the war.
- The degree of continuity given changing patterns of employment during the industrialisation of the post-1865 period.
- The developed campaign for civil rights from the 1880s.
- The limitations of change given the failure to enact an equal opportunities amendment not only in the 1920s but also in the 1980s.
- The continuing social and economic inequality which meant more continuity between the pre-1917 situation and the post-1917 situation.
- The limited representation of women in politics which continued well into the post-1945 period.
- The possibility that changes in attitude, not franchise, were more important, so that the greater involvement of women in public life after 1865 or the new feminism after 1963 might be more important than the First World War.

Response A

The war was the most important turning point in the status of women. The war was the key factor which led to the constitutional amendment that gave the vote to women after a long period of campaigning. This symbolised a new appreciation of the status of women politically. Socially, the war gave women more confidence and freedom as they took on roles previously taken by men and become more important in the workplace, working in new roles such as munitions. After this, it would be easier for women to work in different occupations such as in the Second World War. There were other important turning points that also helped the status of women. The Second World War led to more women working and serving in the forces. There was also the emergence of the new feminism from the 1960s, and the industrial and urban growth of the USA after 1865 led to more women taking part in public life. Thus, various factors could be seen as turning points for women in this period.

Analysis of Response A

- A clear judgement is reached. It explains why the war was important, but does not explain why it was more important than other factors.
- There is some awareness of continuity and change or comparison over the period, which is a strong point.
- The relative importance of the factors is not discussed – there is simply a list with no relative judgement.

Response B

The war was the most important turning point in the status of women. The war was the key factor which led to the constitutional amendment that gave the vote to women after a long period of campaigning. This symbolised a new appreciation of the status of women politically. Socially, the war gave women more confidence and freedom as they took on roles hitherto taken by men and become more important in the workplace, working in new roles such as munitions. After this, it would be easier for women to work in different occupations such as in the Second World War. Without this experience the greater use of women and the expansion of opportunities in that war would not have been possible. Although more women worked and took on new responsibilities like flying in the Second World War, the First World War was the real turning point as it broke down conventions and assumptions. Neither the Second World War nor the subsequent growth of feminism achieved anything as important as the change in the constitution to allow women to vote. Without this important symbol, for which women had campaigned for so long before 1917, subsequent progress would have been impossible. The new feminism could not change the constitution to ensure equal rights but the war allowed this key change to be made and ratified by 1920. Although earlier groups which called for change were important, it took the First World War to bring their demands to fruition, so the war was the most important turning point.

Analysis of Response B

- A clear judgement is reached that the First World War was the most important factor and why it was more important than or linked to other factors.
- There is consideration of alternative turning points.
- Explanations are clear and there is supported comparative argument.

Activity

You should now try and write a conclusion to some of the questions below. Ensure that you reach a clear, supported judgement and that when you have to discuss more than one factor your evaluation of the importance of the factors is comparative.

Essay questions

1 How important a turning point in the development of women's rights from 1865 to 1992 was the Nineteenth Amendment?
2 'Divisions within women's movements were the biggest obstacle to the improvement of the rights and status of women in the period 1865–1992.' How far do you agree?
3 Assess the importance of individual women campaigners in the achievement of greater rights for women in the period 1865–1992.

Study skills: depth study interpretations question

How to reach a judgement

This section looks at how to reach a judgement about the two passages. In the first paragraph you will have explained the two interpretations and placed them in the context of the wider historical debate about the issue, and in the second and third paragraphs you will have evaluated the strengths and weaknesses of the two interpretations. However, in order to reach the higher mark bands you must reach a supported judgement as to which passage's view about the issue in the question you think is more convincing.

A good conclusion will:

- reach a clear judgement as to which passage's view about the issue in the question is more convincing
- explain why a particular passage is more convincing and why the other is less convincing
- suggest that there are some parts in both passages which are more or less convincing
- briefly support the judgement so that it is not simply an assertion.

Read the question and Passages A and B below about New Deal and then the example conclusions (Responses A and B) that follow:

Evaluate the interpretations in both of the passages and explain which you think is more convincing as a view of the impact of the New Deal on women.

PASSAGE A

President Franklin D. Roosevelt's New Deal promised to restore the good life by putting the nation back to work. Working class women benefited from protective labor legislation and union organizing drives. Middle class women carved a place for themselves in FDR's social-welfare administration. Several New Deal laws gave the federal government the unprecedented right to regulate wages and hours for both men and women. The formation of the Congress of Industrial Workers promised unions for women workers who had never before been organized. During the New Deal middle class professional women became involved in politics again. FDR's administration summoned to Washington scores of women reformers whose work had been eclipsed after the 1920 woman suffrage victory. None was more instrumental in helping women make a place for themselves than Eleanor Roosevelt.

(Adapted from Carol Hymowitz and Michaela Weissman, A History of Women in America, *Bantam, 1978, pp. 307–9.)*

PASSAGE B

New Deal programs concentrated primarily on men rather than women. Most programs were designed with men in mind: women received secondary consideration and less imaginative treatment. As a resolution sent to Frances Perkins commented, women were thrown out of jobs as married women; refused relief as single women; discriminated against by the National Recovery Administration and ignored by the Civil Works Administration. The New Deal program administrators assumed that the family wage was the natural state of family finances, that men should support their families, and that women and children should be dependent on them. The rise in women's labor force participation in the 1920s indicated that a growing number valued female employment outside the home. The New Deal harked back to an earlier era and negated that choice, and privileged men in the work place.

(Adapted from S.J. Kleinberg, Women in the United States 1830–1945, *Palgrave Macmillan, 1999, p. 220.)*

Response A

In conclusion, Passage A offers a more convincing view of the impact of the New Deal as it specifies what both working- and middle-class women gained. It does have some balance in that it makes the point that the legislation was aimed at both men and women. It correctly states that the administration did employ more women to advise and help to run new federal agencies. This was helped by having Frances Perkins in the cabinet as Secretary for Labor. Minimum wage laws helped those with low-paid work such as laundry workers and textile operatives and the NIRA set minimum standards for factories working on federal contracts. Passage B does not take account of the improvements and is more negative.

Response B

Both passages acknowledge that the New Deal was a time of change but have very different views of the impact of women. Passage A sees the positive improvements in terms of protective labour laws and increased unionisation as well as greater opportunities for political responsibility, especially given the influence of the president's wife, who was a lifelong campaigner for greater rights for women. Passage B is more negative and thinks that outdated attitudes were reinforced by the New Deal. Given the persistence of unequal pay and the attitudes described in Passage B this seems plausible, but the passage does not give enough weight to the help offered to low-paid workers such as laundry and textile workers, or the protective codes introduced by the NIRA, even if enforcement was not as widespread as Passage A might suggest. Neither passage has enough balance, but the total rejection that any improvement was made in Passage B is probably unfair and so Passage A, despite not considering the problems that the New Deal faced in enforcing legislation, is probably more convincing.

Analysis of Responses A and B

Both conclusions offer a judgement and both support their claims. However, Response B is the stronger conclusion:

- Response A focuses almost exclusively on Passage A, with mention of Passage B only in the final sentence.
- Response B compares the two interpretations in reaching its judgement and is more balanced.
- Response B, although it argues that Passage B is stronger, does not dismiss the valid points made in Passage A.

Activity

Revisit the questions on the passages in Chapters 1–3 (pages 62, 107 and 152) and write a conclusion for those questions.

Timeline

1865	Civil War ended. Black Codes passed by interim governments in the South
1866	Civil Rights Act
1862–7	Plains Wars
1867	Congressional Reconstruction
1869	Knights of Labor (KOL) founded
1869	NWSA and AWSA founded – rival suffrage organisations
1873	Molly Maguires
1874	Women's Christian Temperance Union
1876	Battle of Little Bighorn
1877	Hayes–Tilden Compromise
1886	Haymarket Affair
	American Federation of Labor founded
1887	Dawes Severalty Act
1890	Massacre at Wounded Knee
	Formation of the National American Woman Suffrage Association (NAWSA), the rival suffrage organisations united
1890	Sherman Anti-Trust Act
1890s	Increase in Jim Crow laws
1892	Homestead strike
1894	Pullman strike
1896	*Plessy* v. *Ferguson*: Supreme Court accepted 'separate but equal'
1898	Curtis Act
1905	*Lochner* v. *New York*
	Muskogee Convention
1909	National Association for the Advancement of Colored People (NAACP) founded
1911	Society of American Indians established
1914	Clayton Anti-Trust Act
1917	Margaret Sanger set up first US birth-control clinic
1919	House of Representatives passed the women's suffrage (Nineteenth) Amendment
1924	Indian Citizenship Act
1925	Brotherhood of Sleeping Car Porters and Maids established
1933	New Deal
	NIRA and NRA
	Frances Perkins became the first woman in a presidential cabinet
1934	Indian Reorganization (Wheeler–Howard) Act
1935	Wagner Act
1937	Congress of Industrial Organizations
1941	USA entered the Second World War; 7 million women supported the war effort
1942	Congress of Racial Equality (CORE) founded
1944	National Congress of American Indians
1947	Taft–Hartley Act
1948	Desegregation of armed forces
1953	Policy of termination introduced

1954	*Brown* v. *Topeka Board of Education*
1955	Merger of AFL and CIO
1957	Southern Christian Leadership Conference (SCLC) founded
	Montgomery Bus Boycott
	Number of women and men voting was approximately equal for the first time
1960	Student Nonviolent Coordinating Committee (SNCC) founded
1963	Equal Pay Act
	Betty Friedan's *The Feminine Mystique* published
1964	Civil Rights Act
1965	Malcolm X assassinated
1966	National Organization for Women founded
	Black Panthers formed
1968	American Indian Movement (AIM) established
	Martin Luther King Jr assassinated
1969	Siege of Alcatraz
1970	Occupational Safety and Health Act
1972	Equal Rights Amendment was passed by Congress but never ratified
1973	In *Roe* v. *Wade*, the Supreme Court established a woman's right to abortion
1974	*Oneida* v. *Oneida and Madison Counties, New York*
1975	Indian Self-Determination and Education Assistance Act
1981	PATCO strike
1984	Geraldine Ferraro was the first woman vice presidential candidate of a major political party (Democratic Party)
1984	Jesse Jackson stood as Democratic presidential candidate
1988	Jackson's second attempt as a Democratic presidential candidate

Glossary of terms

Abolitionist Member of the movement, largely in the Northern states, which saw slavery as a moral evil and socially and economically backward.

Affirmative action A change in the late 1960s was the policy of not merely trying to give African Americans equality of opportunity but of helping them by a form of positive action and quotas for education and employment. This proved controversial and was reduced under the Republican administration of Ronald Reagan in the 1980s.

Allotment process The reservation lands were divided into homesteads or allotted, hence the term, by the Dawes Act. This process attempted to turn the Native Americans into landholders, further destroying their tribal culture.

Amendment The USA has a fixed constitution, or set of rules, but Article 5 allows for some amendments for matters so important they cannot be dealt with by usual laws.

American Federation of Labor (AFL) This replaced the KOL and attempted to unite all unions, so that by 1914 it had some 2 million members.

Battle of Little Bighorn Probably the most famous battle in the history of the Native American struggles. It was the result of General Custer being sent to return a number of Sioux and Cheyenne who had left their reservation and refused to return. Custer attacked them without waiting for his full force to arrive, but his force of some 200 men were defeated and all were killed.

The Birth of a Nation The Southern film-maker D.W. Griffiths offered a notorious historical drama in 1915 showing a Confederate veteran meeting injustice and corruption when he returns home in 1865 and taking a heroic stand by joining the Ku Klux Klan. It was immensely controversial.

Black Codes Southern states' laws to control freed slaves.

Black Panthers A nationalist and socialist African American organisation formed in 1966 and lasting until 1982.

Black Power A movement or ideology determined by African Americans to gain power for themselves.

Blacklist A list of workers who are regarded as unacceptable.

Blue-collar workers Those who carry out manual work.

Boycotting Ignoring and isolating a person or an organisation with a view to exerting pressure. Here, African Americans refused to use the buses. As they were the majority of the customers this succeeded in putting pressure on the bus company as revenue fell.

Braves Native American warriors.

Bureau of Indian Affairs The name given to the Office of Indian Affairs after 1947. It controlled the money for the development of Native Americans, and was responsible for their education and the reservations.

Busing The policy of ensuring that children were in mixed-race schools to help socially disadvantaged African American children, who were thought to do better in mixed-race classrooms, and to promote racial integration. It proved unpopular and controversial among whites and there were disturbances in Kentucky in 1975–6.

Capitalism An economic system based on private enterprise, rather than state control, of the economy. Companies are privately owned and consumers therefore have a choice of which goods to buy.

Carpet bagging The South objected violently to Northern officials and businessmen after the Civil War interfering in their affairs and using corruption to gain the votes and support of the former slaves. Such intruders were often portrayed as carrying bags made out of carpet material, hence the name.

Closed shop A workplace where one union dominates and workers have to belong to that union.

Cold War After 1945, the USA clashed more and more with the Communist USSR and the countries it controlled in eastern Europe and its allies (the so-called 'Communist bloc'). There were two different world views. The USA supported parliamentary democracy and economic freedom, the so-called 'capitalist' free-market system. The Communists had a one-party state, dominated by a dictatorial leader, which controlled economic life through nationalised industry and agriculture. The Cold War lasted until the fall of the USSR after 1989.

Collective bargaining Workers' representatives join together and negotiate over issues such as pay and conditions.

Communists People who believe that the economy should be state controlled and planned.

Congress of Industrial Organizations (CIO) Originally the Committee for Industrial Organizations, it was established in 1935 and made up of eight unions from the American Federation of Labor (AFL). These unions remained within the AFL, but were expelled in 1936 because of suspected links with communism. The CIO broke away, but rejoined the AFL in 1955.

Daughters of the American Revolution An avowedly patriotic society open to women who can show that their ancestors played a role in achieving US independence. It was formed in 1890 by a descendant of George Washington and now has 180,000 members. It aimed to commemorate and celebrate key elements of US history.

Dawes Severalty Act Divided the reservations up into plots or allotments which were given to the Native Americans. As a result, they now owned the land.

Draft The US term for conscription or calling up civilians for military service.

Federal Bureau of Investigation (FBI) The US intelligence and security organisation founded in 1908. J. Edgar Hoover, its director from 1935 to 1972, called the Black Panthers 'the greatest threat to the internal security of the country'.

Feminism The belief in establishing equal political, economic, social and cultural rights for women. Feminist ideas had spread during the French Revolution and in the writings of the English campaigner Mary Wollstonecraft. In the USA, the turning point was the first convention to promote equality for women, held in Seneca Falls, New York, in 1848.

Five Civilised Tribes The Cherokee, Chickasaw, Choctaw, Creek and Seminole tribes that were forced to leave their lands and were settled on the Great Plains in 1838. Their journey from their traditional lands to the Plains has been called the 'Trail of Tears' as so many died on it.

Freedmen People released from enslavement.

Freedmen's Bureau Set up by Congress in March 1865 to care for former slaves. It provided food, shelter, hospitals and education. It set up two universities, but its 900 agents were subject to intimidation and violence by hostile white Southerners.

Great Society More changes were actually made during the presidency of Kennedy's successor, Lyndon Johnson, and the responsibilities of federal government in social reforms and civil rights expanded considerably to create a 'Great Society'. The feminist movement grew in the context of greater expectations in the Democrat era after 1960, of a fairer and more progressive society.

Great Spirit The Native Americans believed that there was a supreme being who had made them the guardians of the land, to look after it and pass it on to the next generation. As a result, they argued that the land could not be owned, but was to be shared, hence their tribal way of life.

Guerrilla warfare Warfare conducted by irregular forces rather than 'normal' armies, often behind enemy lines. It often involves raids on enemy troops and supply lines and usually little mercy is shown as the usual rules of war are not applied.

Habeas corpus The right only to be detained by lawful arrest.

Hajj The pilgrimage to the shrine of the Prophet Mohammed at Mecca. It is the duty of Muslims to make the journey at least once in their lifetime.

Heavy industry Industries such as coal, iron and steel, and textiles.

High-tech industries Industries such as computer-based enterprises that require a highly skilled and trained labour force.

Homesteads Act This gave farmers a 160-acre plot free on the condition that they farmed it for five years.

Industrial Workers of the World This union was set up in 1905 and had a reputation for violence and militancy, but did attempt to fight for the rights of poorer workers and immigrants. However, their violence meant that they were constantly under pressure from the authorities.

Industrialisation The development of large-scale industries, such as steel and textiles, across much of the country.

Injunction A legal order preventing an action from being carried out or, in some instances, forcing an action to be carried out.

Jim Crow An accepted term for an African American, coined in a music-hall song of the 1830s, used to name discriminatory laws. The laws affected the whole way of life in the South.

Knights of Labor (KOL) Founded in 1869 and developed in the period after 1879 under the leadership of Terence Powderly. It conducted a successful strike against the Wabash Railroad in 1885, which further encouraged workers to join. However, it lost influence following the Haymarket Affair of 1886.

Labour The workforce or workers as opposed to the employers or owners of the factories and other industrial enterprises. (Spelled as *labor* in the USA.)

Laissez-faire A belief that the government should not interfere in the economy and that businesses and owners should be allowed to manage their affairs free from regulation.

Lobbying The practice of trying to influence the president and Congress to make changes by letters, petitions, appeals and meetings.

Malpractice Professional negligence or incompetence.

Manifest Destiny A belief that it was Americans' God-given right to settle the rest of the continent. The term was first used in 1845 in the magazine *Democratic Review*: 'the fulfillment of our manifest destiny is to overspread the continent allocated by Providence for the free development of our yearly multiplying millions'.

Mediation Negotiations between employers and employees to resolve disputes and reach a settlement.

Nation of Islam A religious organisation founded in 1930.

National Guard US states, as well as having police forces, have volunteer part-time military forces which are used in emergencies. They are under the control of the governors of the individual states.

National Indian Youth Council (NIYC) Established in 1961 with the aim of protecting Native American fishing rights in the north-west of the country. However, its role developed and it took on lawsuits to protect treaty rights, voting rights and religious freedom.

National Mediation Board The US government established the agency to regulate labour relations in the railway industry. Its aim was to resolve disputes and prevent strikes through arbitration.

National War Labor Board (NWLB) First created by President Wilson in 1918 to settle disputes between workers and employers. This ensured that production would not be interrupted by strikes.

National Women's Party Founded in 1916 by two activists from the NAWSA, Alice Paul and Lucy Burns, who aimed at a suffragette-style campaign. They led protests, they held a silent protest outside the White House and there were minor acts of law breaking with arrests and hunger strikes. They demanded but failed to achieve an Equal Rights Amendment in the 1920s.

Native American Rights Fund (NARF) Established in 1970 to defend the rights of Native Americans. NARF trained legal specialists with an interest in Native American issues and was responsible for most of the cases that went before the Supreme Court.

Native capitalism A belief in developing profitable businesses among Native Americans so that the spending of federal and state governments could be reduced.

Native sovereignty The power that the tribes had to live on their lands according to their laws, religion and customs. These rights existed until the settlers arrived and removed them.

New Deal The early period of F.D. Roosevelt's presidency from 1933 to 1939, during which time a large number of reforms were passed to tackle the economic and social problems caused by a stock market crash and the resulting Great Depression.

New Frontier Kennedy promised that the pioneering tradition would be maintained in a new way, by space exploration, by changes in US society and by new attitudes of commitment to the American way of life.

Niagara Movement A black civil rights organisation formed in 1905. It opposed Booker T. Washington's ideas of working with the white system and wanted an end to desegregation. It was founded by a group of activists but its leading inspiration was W.E.B. Du Bois. Splits and disagreements led to its decline in 1909.

No-strike clauses Provisions in workers' contracts to forbid striking.

Nomadic The Plains Indians did not have permanent settlements as they followed the buffalo herds. They lived in tepees that could be taken down quickly in order to follow the buffalo, on which they depended for their existence.

Old South The Southern slave states of the period before the Civil War. It became a term of nostalgia, suggesting that there had been peace and harmony between owners who looked after their slaves and slaves who respected and loved their owners. That was not the reality of a system with considerable brutality and sexual exploitation.

Pan-Africanism A belief in the need for unity and solidarity among Africans all over the world. Its modern origins go back to the late nineteenth century. It recognises the distinct values and the common heritage of all Africans in terms of history, culture, values, achievements and rights. It was given expression by the Organisation of African Unity in 1963 but its supporters think that Africans in all countries should unite.

Party primary voting Voting for presidential candidates by registered members of the political parties. The 'primaries' precede the actual presidential elections.

Picketing During a strike, workers may stand outside a place of work to discourage other workers from entering the business.

Plains Wars These consisted of a number of clashes, most notable of which were: 1862 Little Crow's War against the Sioux, 1863 Cheyenne uprising, 1867 Red Cloud's War against the Sioux and 1868 Winter Campaign against the Cheyenne.

Polygamy The taking of more than one wife. It was the custom so that all women were cared for by a male, which helped to ensure the survival of the tribe. This went against Christian beliefs and was used as further evidence of the need to 'Americanise' Native Americans.

Populist Party The US People's Party was founded in 1891 and represented discontented Southern and Western farmers, hostile to big business and railway companies. It gained over eight per cent of the vote in the 1892 presidential election and ten per cent of the vote in subsequent congressional elections as part of a protest vote against the power and influence of big companies.

Porter Someone who looked after train passengers, particularly in sleeping cars, preparing the coaches and cleaning them after use.

Prohibition A ban on the creation, sale and consumption of alcohol was introduced in a constitutional amendment in 1919. It had already become law in many states. It was repealed in 1933 after problems with enforcement and increasing evidence that it was a cause of crime as gangsters traded in alcohol illegally.

Public sector Industries or businesses which are owned and managed by the state as opposed to being privately owned and managed.

Radical Republicans Republicans in Congress who had been active opponents of slavery. They saw the Southern slaveowners as evil exploiters and wanted radical changes to help the freed slaves. They were influential, but had limited support in the North as a whole.

Ratify Officially approve.

Real wages Used to describe what wages can actually buy. Wages might rise, but if prices rise faster then real wages are falling, and if wages rise faster than prices then real wages rise.

Republicans One of the two main political parties in the USA. The Republican Party is usually seen as being on the right of the political spectrum, believing in low taxes and little government intervention in the economy.

Rhoads reforms These reforms closed off-reservation boarding schools, to which Native American children had been sent. The schools were replaced by better schools on the reservations. There were also to be improvements in medical facilities.

Roaring Twenties The popularity of elements of US culture, such as jazz, gives the impression of a freer society in search of pleasure, despite prohibition. The glamorisation of gangsters, short skirts, fast cars, jazz musicians and the cinema as a major source of entertainment points to a new, dangerous and exciting urban culture.

Sand Creek Massacre An attack by US cavalry on an undefended Cheyenne camp. It resulted in the deaths of many elderly men, women and children.

'Scab' labour Similar to 'blackleg'; workers who are willing to work during strikes, often crossing picket lines.

Segregation The legal enforcement of division between races by laws passed by state legislatures. Hitherto, segregation had been a fact in some areas (although black and white people had often lived and worked together in the pre-war South), but it was not legalised.

Sherman Anti-Trust Act An attempt to restrict monopolies by which large companies were able to control a trade.

Silent majority Used by Nixon in 1969 to describe the mass of middle-class Americans ('Middle America') who were conservative and opposed social change and did not join in anti-war demonstrations. The term was used in the nineteenth century to describe dead people.

State Supreme Courts The federal nature of the USA means that each state has its own Supreme Court. The State Supreme Court is the final court for deciding on the legality of state legislation; only if the legislation has implications for the constitution of the USA will it go to the Supreme Court, and then only if the defeated party appeals.

Streetcars Trams.

Strike breakers Workers who are willing to work while others are on strike, thus making the strike ineffectual.

Suffrage The right to vote. In the USA this included not only voting for the president but also for senators and congressmen in the federal Congress as well as the state governors and congressmen. Local officials were also elected.

Taft–Hartley Act of 1947 Prevented unions from running a closed shop, where one union dominated and all workers had to belong to it, and regulated the relationship between unions and employers.

Temperance The belief that alcohol was a major social evil and that a good family life was only possible if alcohol and its misuse was prohibited.

Termination In order to speed up the policy of assimilation, which had always been the aim of the federal government, a more aggressive approach was adopted. Native Americans would now be treated as self-supporting Americans and lose any special protection they had been given as 'wards' of the government. It was planned to end the reservation system and encourage them to move to cities, where there was employment, in what can be described as a policy of 'urbanisation' of the Native Americans.

Tribal chief The head or leader of the tribe. They presided over the tribal courts and were therefore important in the running of the tribe, or 'nation' as the large tribes were called.

United Farm Workers (UFW) A major union for farm labourers that resulted from the merger of two workers' rights organisations, the AWOC and the NFWA. The alliance between the two groups resulted in a series of strikes in 1965 in the grape farming community and led to the creation of the UFW.

Wall Street Crash In October 1929, the prices of shares fell dramatically on Wall Street in New York, the USA's financial centre. This led to a loss of confidence and the prices of shares continued to fall, which sent the economy into recession. Workers were laid off and unemployment soared, not just in the USA; much of the world also went into recession.

Welfare capitalism A policy followed by employers during the boom of the 1920s to reduce industrial unrest. It entailed offering workers improved working conditions and other benefits such as pensions, in return for the establishment of unions under the control or direction of the employers.

White Citizens' Councils Formed in the South following the Brown decision of 1954. They had a more middle-class membership than the Klan but their aim was similar. They wanted to intimidate African Americans into not claiming their rights. Their members used not only violence but also their economic power, for example in pressuring insurance companies to cancel policies of African American church members. The councils were active into the 1960s.

White-collar workers Those who work in professional, technical or clerical work.

Yellow-dog contracts Contracts that workers signed whereby they agreed not to join a union.

Further reading

African Americans and civil rights

Jules Archer, *They Had A Dream* (Skyhorse Publishing, 2016)

Taylor Branch, *The King Years* (Simon & Schuster, 2013)

Clayborne Carson, *The Eyes on the Prize* (Prentice-Hall, 1992)

Ron Field, *Civil Rights in Americas, 1865–1980* (Cambridge University Press, 2002)

Eric Foner, *Reconstruction Updated Edition: America's Unfinished Revolution 1863–1877* (Harper Perennial, 2015)

Colin Grant, *Negro With a Hat: Marcus Garvey* (Vintage, 2009)

Louis R. Harlen, *Booker T. Washington: The Making of a Black Leader, 1856–1901* (Oxford University Press, 1975)

Troy Jackson, *Becoming King* (University Press of Kentucky, 2011)

Shane Mountjoy and Tim McNeese, *The Civil Rights Movement* (Chelsea House Publishers, 2008)

Mark Newman, *The Civil Rights Movement* (Edinburgh University Press, 2014)

Vivienne Sanders, *Access to History: Civil Rights in the USA 1945–68* (Hodder Education, 2008)

Kevern Verney, *The Debate on Black Civil Rights in America* (Manchester University Press, 2010)

Robert Weisbrot, *Freedom Bound: A History of America's Civil Rights Movement* (W.W. Norton, 1989)

Trade union and labour rights

Anthony Badger, *The New Deal: The Depression Years, 1933–40* (Palgrave Macmillan, 1989)

Harold Evans, *The American Century: People, Power and Politics* (Jonathan Cape, 1998)

Michael Harrington, *The Other America: Poverty in the USA* (Simon & Schuster, 1998)

David Kennedy, *Freedom from Fear: The American People in Depression and War, 1929–45* (Oxford University Press, 1999)

Richard Polenberg, *One Nation Divisible: Class, Race and Ethnicity in the United States Since 1938* (Penguin, 1981)

Howard Zinn, *A People's History of the United States* (HarperCollins, 1999)

Native Americans

Christine Bolt, *American Indian Policy and American Reform* (Routledge, 1989)

Dee Brown, *Bury My Heart at Wounded Knee* (Vintage, 1970)

Angie Debo, *A History of the Indians of the United States* (Pimlico, 1995)

Vine Deloria and C. Lytle, *The Nations Within* (University of Texas Press, 2006)

Peter Iverson, *'We are Still Here': American Indians in the Twentieth Century* (Harlan Davidson, 1998)

Jake Page, *In the Hands of the Great Spirit* (Free Press, 2003)

Women and civil rights

Dorothy Sue Cobble, Linda Gordon and Astrid Henry, *Feminism Unfinished: A Short, Surprising History of American Women's Movements* (Liveright, 2015)

Bettye Collier-Thomas and V.P. Franklin, *Sisters in the Struggle: African-American Women in the Civil Rights and Black Power Movements* (New York University Press, 2008)

Sara M. Evans, *Born for Liberty: A History of Women in America* (Prentice-Hall, 1997)

Betty Friedan, *The Female Mystique* (Norton Critical Edition, 2013)

Nancy Hewitt, *A Companion to American Women's History* (John Wiley, 2000)

Carol Hymowitz and Michaele Weissman, *A History of Women in America* (Bantam, 1984)

S.J. Kleinberg, *Women in the United States, 1830–1945* (Palgrave Macmillan, 1999)

Corrine M. McConnaughy, *The Woman Suffrage Movement in America* (Cambridge University Press, 2015)

Mary Beth Norton and Ruth M. Alexander, *Major Problems in American Women's History* (Wadsworth Publishing, 2006)

Susan Ware, *American Women's History: A Very Short Introduction* (Oxford University Press, 2015)

Index